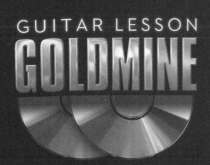

GUITAR LESSON
GOLDMINE

100

ROCK LESSONS

BY CHAD JOHNSON & MICHAEL MUELLER

MW00582748

ISBN 978-1-4234-9879-7

HAL•LEONARD®
CORPORATION

7777 W. BLUEMOUND RD. P.O. BOX 13819 MILWAUKEE, WI 53213

In Australia Contact:
Hal Leonard Australia Pty. Ltd.
4 Lentara Court
Cheltenham, Victoria, 3192 Australia
Email: ausadmin@halleonard.com.au

Visit Hal Leonard Online at
www.halleonard.com

CONTENTS

Lessons 1–50 by Chad Johnson

Lessons 51–100 by Michael Mueller

LESSON #1: FRET-HAND MUTING

Fret-hand muting is like a sound man: when he's doing a good job, no one notices him. When you're using proper fret-hand muting, you'll get only the notes you want. If not properly employed, however, you can end up with a sloppy mess. One listen to Jimi Hendrix, Angus Young, Eddie Van Halen, or Steve Vai, among countless others, will reveal the universal appeal of this technique.

How It Works

To understand fret-hand muting, we need to dispel the notion that there's only one proper fret-hand technique for guitar. Yes, classical guitar teachers cringe when they see the thumb creep over the top of the neck. But rock guitar is not classical guitar. For one, it's most often played with a pick, for Pete's sake! If the right-hand technique is so obviously different, why then can't the left-hand technique be different, too? Just as the classical technique (thumb behind the neck, fingers arched, etc.) suits that style, rock technique (thumb sometimes over the neck, fingers laid more flat at times, etc.) is designed for rock guitar. For example, let's say you're playing this G note on string 4:

A classical guitarist would fret the note with the finger arched and the thumb centered on the back of the neck.

However, a rock guitarist may fret the same note this way, with the first finger laying flatter and the thumb hanging over the top of the neck.

Why? Because a rock or blues guitarist may be using an extremely heavy pick attack and applying intense vibrato. He may be picking through *all six strings* to give the note added weight and punch. (This is exactly what Stevie Ray is doing in the boogie riff before the first verse in "Pride & Joy.") When this is done, you'd better be muting all but the string you want to sound, or you'll be in for a noisy surprise!

In the photo, the thumb is lightly touching the sixth string to keep it quiet. Along with fretting the G note, the tip of the index finger is lightly touching the fifth string to keep it quiet. And the third, second, and first strings are kept quiet by the underside of the first finger. Obviously, rock guitarists won't fret every note this way, but there are times when it's essential to producing only the notes you want. To demonstrate, let's now listen to that G note played both ways: first by picking only the fourth string, and then with fret-hand muting so that we can pick through every string for added punch (Track 1).

Examples

Let's check out some examples where fret-hand muting is absolutely essential for clarity.

EXAMPLE 1

This first one demonstrates one of the most common instances: *strumming an octave shape*. Use either (or both) fretting finger to quiet the string in between; use the curvature of the first finger to mute the treble strings, and use either the thumb or the second finger to mute the low strings.

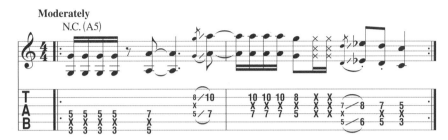

EXAMPLE 2

Here's a common use of strummed 6th intervals on non-adjacent strings, which is often affiliated with the Motown or Stax sound. Use your free left-hand fingers to make sure only the intended notes are sounding.

EXAMPLE 3

In this funkier example, strum freely through the strings while using fret-hand muting to only allow each chord, single note, or double stop to sound. This is easier than worrying about picking the exact number of strings each time, and it's also essential to the sound of this style. We're not only picking the strings with the notes on them; we're picking one or two muted strings on each side of them as well, and it adds weight to the sound.

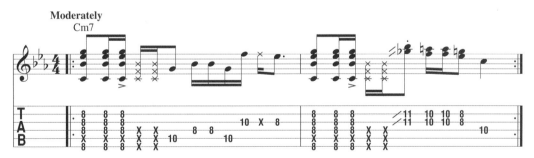

EXAMPLE 4

The final example touches upon two different concepts. Begin by rapidly picking triple stops in sextuplets, and climb up to different inversions of a G7 chord. With proper muting, you don't have to worry about picking only three strings. At the end, land on the high G note with an accented raked note. You're strumming through several strings, but thanks to the fret-hand muting, you're only hearing the high G.

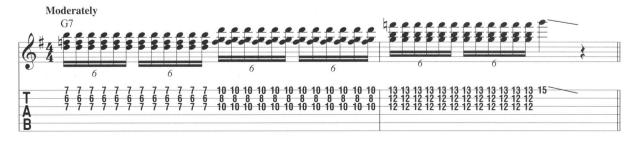

LESSON #2: SCRATCH RHYTHMS

Scratch rhythm is a ubiquitous sound in rock guitar that appears on many more recordings than it does in transcriptions. The technique includes any time you pick one or more strings with your hands lightly resting on them to produce a dead, muted sound. It can be unconscious or deliberate, but it's one of the most important "non-tone" sounds we can create on the guitar. Certain riffs played without it (using silence instead) can sound downright unnatural.

The Basic Idea

To hear what this sounds like, simply lay your fingers lightly across the strings (don't push them down to the fretboard) and strum. It'll sound thicker or thinner depending on how much gain you're using. Here's an example of the basic sound. Measure 1 is played with a clean tone, measure 2 is half dirty, and measure 3 is fully distorted.

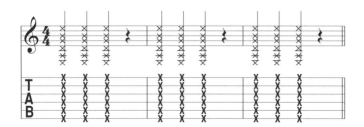

Exercises

Let's play a few exercises to get used to moving back and forth between normal chords or notes and scratch rhythms. Most of the work here falls on the fret hand. Even when you do fret chords or notes, you'll be employing a bit of fret-hand muting to make sure that only those notes are sounding. This way, the pick hand can strum freely without worrying about accidentally sounding other strings.

EXERCISE 1

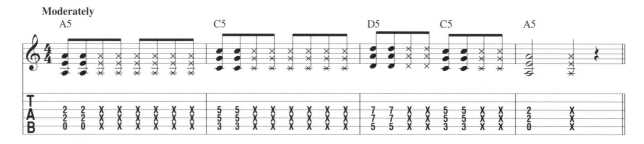

EXERCISE 2

In this one, we're accenting syncopated (off the beat) chords amidst the scratch rhythm strums.

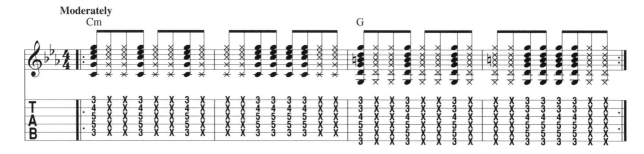

Riffs

Now let's check out the technique with a few riffs. Usually, the scratch rhythms are used more as a percussive, time-keeping factor that helps a riff groove. But other times, as in Examples 3 and 4, they're featured more deliberately as a sound of their own.

RIFF 1

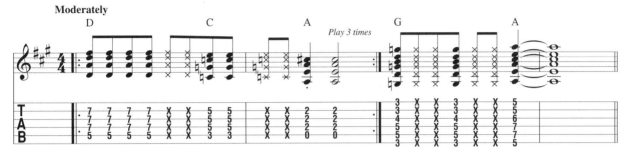

RIFF 2

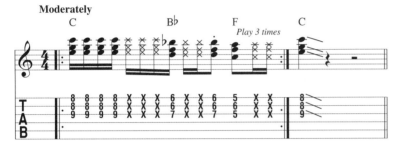

RIFF 3

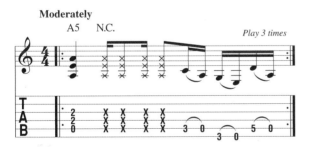

RIFF 4

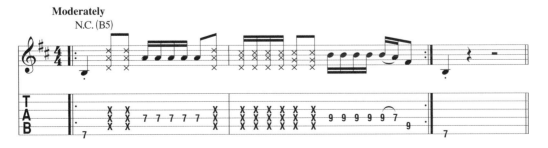

The scratch rhythm technique can add depth and groove to your playing and help your rhythmic feel. It can even act as a well-placed hook in certain riffs. It's a huge part of the rock guitar sound, and many classic riffs would sound much less ballsy if it were absent. Try to imagine Hendrix's "Machine Gun" or Eddie's famous intro to "You Really Got Me" without it, and you'll see what I mean.

LESSON #3: PHRASING "ACROSS THE BAR"

As rock guitarists, we have a tendency to be a bit narrow in terms of musical influences. Many rock guitarists listen to mainly… other rock guitarists. While this certainly encompasses a huge amount of material, we can further broaden our repertoire of phrasing tools if we step outside the box occasionally and listen to other styles and/or other instruments. Take jazz, for example. Although the harmonic palette may be a bit rich for the common rocker, there are many rhythmic concepts that can be applied with ease. One of these is phrasing "across the bar."

How It Works

In order to prevent your licks from sounding too rhythmically predictable, it's a good idea to vary where you begin and end your phrases. If you make it a habit of always starting a lick on beat 1 (or always ending there), for example, it's going to get old quickly. Playing "across the bar line" is a great way to mix it up. This means that, instead of beginning a phrase on beat 1, you begin on beat 4 or beat 4 1/2 of the previous measure. This can really make your phrases stand out and keep things interesting.

For example, here's a typical C major pentatonic phrase. Notice that it begins and ends on beat 1.

Now, there's nothing wrong with this phrase, but it's just a little square in terms of rhythm. Listen to what happens when we alter it so that we're phrasing across the bar line. In this example, we haven't changed any notes; we've just moved both the first and last notes back by an 8th note. Check out how it comes to life.

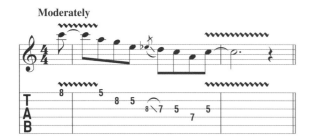

And here's how it sounds with the first and last notes moved back a full beat. Notice that we omitted one C note toward the end in order to accomplish this.

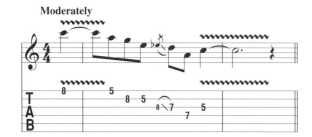

Licks

Let's check out how this sounds in a few licks. We'll first check out how a lick might normally be played, and then we'll alter it to include across-the-bar phrasing.

LICK 1
Normal Lick

TRACK 3
0:22
CD 1

Across the Bar

TRACK 3
0:32
CD 1

LICK 2
Normal Lick

TRACK 3
0:42
CD 1

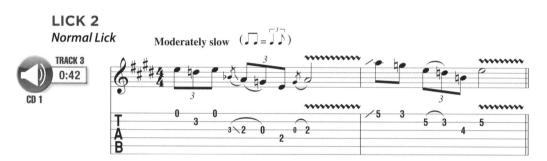

Across the Bar

TRACK 3
0:53
CD 1

LICK 3

The across-the-bar concept can also apply to phrase endings, as demonstrated in this final lick.

Normal Lick

TRACK 3
1:04
CD 1

Across the Bar

TRACK 3
1:14
CD 1

LESSON #4: VOLUME SWELLS

If you haven't messed around with this fun little technique, you don't know what you're missing. They can produce some very non-guitar-like sounds, and depending on your approach, you can emulate strings, flutes, synths, and more. Or in the hands of a seasoned veteran, such as Roy Buchanan or Mark Knopfler, they can simply make the guitar weep uncontrollably.

Technical Considerations

We can accomplish swells one of two ways: with the volume knob on your guitar or with a volume pedal. The basic idea involves picking a note while the volume is off and then raising the volume so the note "swells" into being. The use of ambient effects such as reverb and/or delay is common with the technique, as it adds length to the notes and provides an ethereal vibe.

Strats are most common with the knob swell, as the pinky can reach the knob while picking the string. Alternatively, on a Gibson-style guitar, you can twist the knob with your right hand while sounding notes by hammering with your left hand (while employing careful fret-hand muting to keep things clean). Volume pedals offer the most flexibility, but some players don't like having to involve their feet in the coordination equation (or having to lug the pedal around in the first place). Keep in mind though that all pedals are not created equally, and you'll get what you pay for in terms of smoothness of envelope.

Licks

Let's hear what this technique can do…

LICK 1

This first lick is simply the notes of a C minor pentatonic scale. If you were to play this line in a standard fashion, it would sound pretty unremarkable. There's a good bit of reverb and delay added on the audio to enhance the effect.

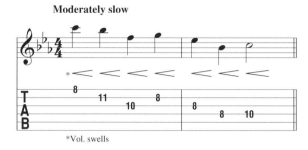

LICK 2

This technique also sounds great with chords—particularly if they're a bit more colorful than your standard triad. Again, use liberal amounts of delay, compression, and reverb for best effect. It creates a sound closer to a synth pad patch than a guitar.

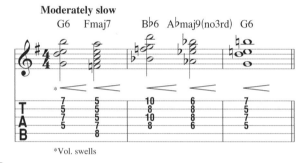

LICK 3

This lick is in the vein of Mark Knopfler or Roy Buchanan. The pre-bends begin to release just as the notes swell in, creating a weeping effect. Again, some delay will enhance things.

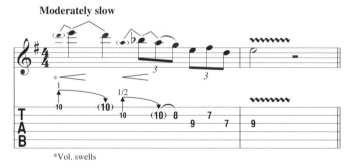

LICK 4

And let's close out with the famous timed delay trick. This has been used by Eddie Van Halen ("Cathedral") and Yngwie Malmsteen (intro to "Black Star"), among others. It works by setting a delay for one strong repeat at a dotted 8th note. When you swell notes in straight 8th notes, the repeated notes fall in between the notes you play, creating a seamless 16th-note line. Add a bit of reverb to smooth things over.

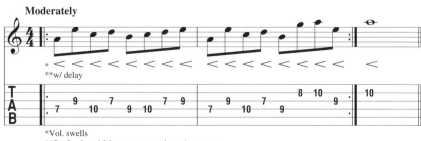

Use your imagination with this technique; it can really open up a whole new world of sounds when you bring effects into the equation. Have fun experimenting!

LESSON #5: TOGGLE SWITCH TRICKS

This classic rock trick, which goes by several other names, including "machine gun trick" and "kill switch effect," is an ultra-cool effect that can create an otherworldly sound without any additional equipment (though it can benefit from some other pieces of gear as well). The only prerequisite is that you have a guitar with Gibson-style wiring. This includes (typically) a three-way pickup selector switch and independent volume controls for both pickups. Many guitarists, such as Tom Morello, include a custom-wired "kill switch" on their Strats specifically for this sound.

How It Works

To set up this move, you need to turn one volume knob all the way up and one all the way down. Typically, the bridge is turned up, and the neck is turned down, but this is by no means a rule. Crank up the gain, strike a chord (or a note), and then flick the toggle switch back and forth between the middle and bridge positions. The chord will stutter in the rhythm of your toggle switch manipulation. It's common to use a good amount of reverb or some ambient delay when performing this move as well.

Licks

Let's check out the technique in action now to see what we can do with it.

LICK 1

This first one shows how we can apply the technique to an A5 chord and create a rhythmic hook in the process.

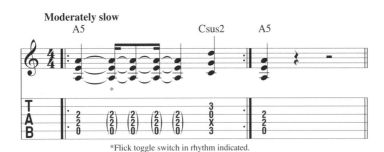

*Flick toggle switch in rhythm indicated.

LICK 2

Here's another great effect: the falling bend. After plucking the bent note, gradually release it while toggling the switch back and forth.

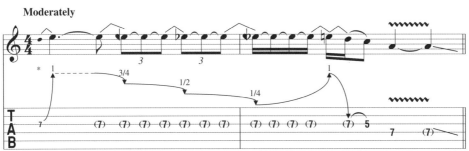

*Gradually release bend while flicking toggle switch in rhythm indicated.

LICK 3

This next lick uses the "hammer-on from nowhere" technique to sound every note. If you use a good amount of gain, you can simply hammer on to the string forcefully and still sound a good, solid note—no pick needed. This frees up your pick hand to operate the toggle switch. You can begin with it in the off position and flick it on each time you hammer a new note for a robotic, synthesized effect. You'll need to employ a generous amount of fret-hand muting as well to keep the notes clear.

*Flick toggle switch in rhythm indicated.

LICK 4

Now we'll expand on the last lick by using the timed delay trick. Set the delay for a strong, single repeat at a dotted 8th note and use a bit of reverb. When you play 8th notes using the "hammer from nowhere" technique described in Example 3, the delayed notes will fall in between, creating a 16th-note line.

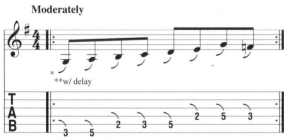

*Hammer on w/ fret hand and flick toggle switch to sound notes.
**Set for dotted 8th note regeneration w/ one repeat.

Be sure to check out Tom Morello's playing, both in Rage Against the Machine and Audioslave, to hear mastery of this effect, but you can also hear it famously used by Eddie Van Halen in "You Really Got Me" and Randy Rhoads in "Crazy Train" (live version). It's a ton of fun and sounds awesome, so enjoy messing around with it.

LESSON #6: VIBRATO

It's hard to imagine the licks of Hendrix, Clapton, Stevie Ray, Steve Vai, or Zakk Wylde without their trademark vibratos. Clearly one of the most expressive guitar techniques of all, it's a shame that more players don't spend time cultivating this technique. There are some players for which it comes naturally, while others have to work at it. It can be learned though, just like any other technique, and it's well worth the effort.

How It Works

Vibrato is a fluctuation of pitch. It can be fast, slow, controlled, frenetic, subtle, over-the-top, or any combination thereof. On the electric guitar, vibrato is usually created by slightly bending a string and releasing it to its unbent state over and over. The more drastic the bend, the "wider" the vibrato sounds. This is why Zakk Wylde's vibrato sounds different than Eric Clapton's.

There are numerous ways to produce vibrato, but there's no single "correct" method, and many players actually master several different types. The motion Eric Clapton uses is completely different than what Hendrix used, yet both are equally beautiful in sound. We'll look at the two main types of vibrato used in rock here (epitomized by those two mentioned), but feel free to experiment in this regard.

Hendrix Style – Wrist Motion

Many consider the Hendrix style of vibrato *the* classic rock vibrato. It's most commonly played with the first finger, though it can be played by any finger. The motion comes from rotating the wrist back and forth, similar to the act of turning a door knob. It may take a while to get the fluidity down, but once you do, it's a very musical vibrato. Practice slowly at first and build up the speed gradually. Practice with every finger, because it's nice to be able to add vibrato on any note.

On strings 2–6, most players pull down (toward the floor) for the slight bends during the vibrato. But on string 1, you'll need to push up (toward the ceiling), or you'll fall off the edge of the frets!

Clapton Style – Forearm Motion

The other popular school of vibrato is the Clapton variety, where the motion comes from the forearm. With this vibrato, the wrist remains in place, but the entire hand is pushed up and down with the forearm. Many players tend to bend and release up toward the ceiling when using this style, which is opposite from the wrist type. This means that you'll need to make an adjustment on string 6 so you don't push the string off the edge.

Adding Vibrato to Bent Notes

It's quite common in rock to add vibrato to bent notes. The basic idea is to bend to pitch and slightly release over and over again. Vibrato on a fretted note will always produce an average note that's slightly sharp (because you're bending it sharp and releasing it back to pitch), but with vibrato on a bent note, you have the ability to generate an average note that's in tune, because you can control exactly where the pitch peaks in each direction. This technique is most commonly applied with the third finger while pushing the string up toward the ceiling, but it can be applied to any finger with a bend in either direction.

Licks

LICK 1

This first lick in B minor uses the wrist type vibrato on string 3. You've heard this in thousands of solos. Finish off by applying vibrato with the third finger on string 4.

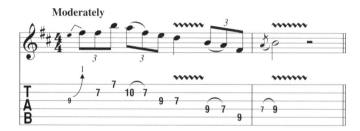

LICK 2

This lick in G takes place in the B.B. King box and is reminiscent of Clapton. We're using forearm vibrato here with the first and third fingers.

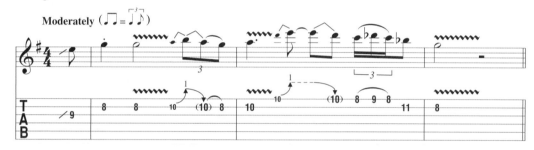

LICK 3

In this Hendrix/Stevie Ray-type D minor pentatonic example, we're applying wrist vibrato to two strings simultaneously, which can be difficult. The motion is the same, but you may need to shift the pressure of your fretting finger slightly so that both notes sound clearly.

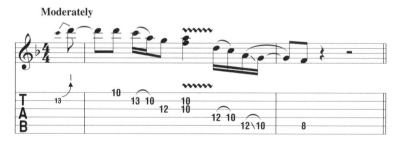

LICK 4

Here's an E minor Clapton-style lick where we're applying vibrato to a note on string 2 that's bent up a whole step to the tonic and a note on string 3 that's bent a whole step to the 5th. These are both common applications.

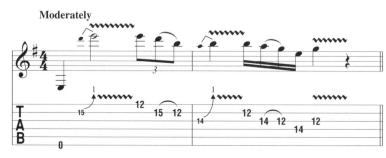

Although there was a movement in the late eighties geared toward recognizing rock music (and rock guitar) as serious endeavors worthy of classroom study, let's face it: sometimes rock guitar is just all about attitude and flash. With that sentiment, let's examine the pick scrape (also called the pick slide)—one of many unique noises possible on the guitar.

How It Works

One might think the technique is pretty self-explanatory. I mean… you're *scraping* your *pick* along the strings to make a cool sound. How tough can it be, right? But there are several pointers that will help achieve maximum "scrape-age."

▶ **Bass strings work best:** For the classic rock pick scrape, you'll want to scrape along the lowest strings—the sixth and fifth will produce awesome results every time.

▶ **Press *into* the strings while scraping:** This will provide some tension that will cause the pick to slightly catch on the grooves in the wound strings, which will help to enhance the effect.

▶ **Don't go too fast:** You don't need to traverse the entire length of the string. In fact, the sound produced will be most effective while you're over the pickups. You can finish off quickly with a flashy move down the length of the string, but if you want a nice, thick scrape to be audible, you'll want to spend most of the time in front of the neck.

▶ **Experiment with wrist up and wrist down methods:** Some people scrape with their wrist aimed up (as if zipping a zipper laterally across your belly), and some scrape with their wrist aimed down (as if holding a bucket close into your body). One method will probably feel more natural to you, so experiment with both.

WRIST UP

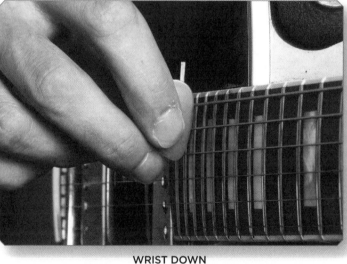
WRIST DOWN

The following example demonstrates the classic pick scrape. In the audio example, the entire length of the string is traveled for demonstration purposes. Notice how the effect is strongest in the beginning, when the pick is out in front of the neck.

TRACK 7
0:00
CD 1

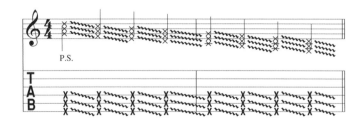

Riffs

RIFF 1

Let's get our scrape on with some classic riffs. Our first is a typical use for the pick scrape: a dynamic intro with big, sustained power chords.

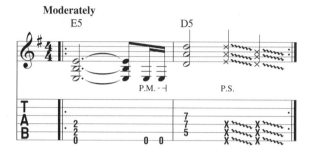

RIFF 2

In this example, we're scraping back and forth in rhythm to create another type of scrape effect.

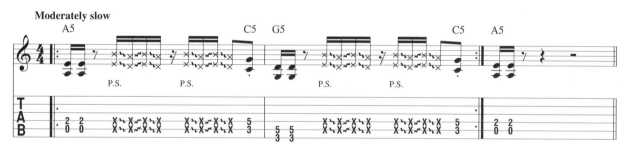

RIFF 3

And Example 3 presents another option: the bouncing scrape. To produce this effect, quickly jab the strings with your pick in scrape position for a stuttering effect.

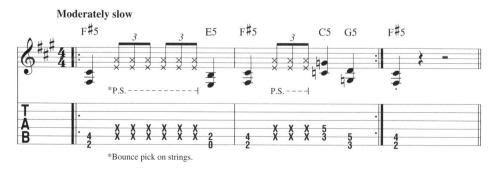

*Bounce pick on strings.

There really are no rules when it comes to this kind of thing. You're just trying to make some cool noises. So unleash your child-like curiosity and experiment!

LESSON #8: RAKES

The rake is an expressive device you can use for extra intensity and added sonic weight. Many players use rakes without even realizing it, but it can be more deliberate as well. It's one of those subtle sounds that may be hard to detect, but would certainly be missed if it weren't there. One listen to any solo by Stevie Ray Vaughan, Steve Vai, Joe Satriani, or Zakk Wylde, and you're bound to hear some well-placed rakes.

How It Works

Like grace notes, rakes don't really take up any real time. They usually appear at the very last second before a note to give it some extra punch. Ascending rakes are by far the most common, but descending rakes are used as well. However, the technique used to produce each is quite different.

THE ASCENDING RAKE

With an ascending rake, we're basically strumming up through several muted strings on the way to our target note—usually on one of the top three strings. The strings below the target note are muted by the palm, a fret-hand finger, or a combination of both to keep them quiet. The pick is raked across them quite deliberately to produce a clicking sound. As mentioned, this happens very quickly, so the individual clicks of the muted strings blur together into one "bpttttt" sound.

The following example demonstrates the sound of a normal note followed by the same note with an ascending rake.

THE DESCENDING RAKE

In a descending rake, you'll be strumming up through muted strings on your way to a target note on a lower string. With this technique, though, the strings are muted with the underside of the first, second, or third finger on your fretting hand. Because of this, it produces a slightly different sound than the ascending rake, but the effect is similar.

Here's an example of a normal note on the D string followed by the same with a descending rake.

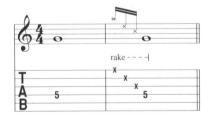

UP IS DOWN?

The terms "up" and "down" or "ascending" and "descending" may be slightly confusing if you're thinking solely of physical direction. In this instance, the terms refer to the orientation of the guitar's pitches, where the thinner strings are called the high strings, and the thicker strings are called the low strings. So, an ascending rake, while going from low to high *in pitch*, actually involves moving the pick *down* toward the floor—vice versa for a descending rake.

Licks

Now let's put some rakes to use in a few licks…

LICK 1

One of the most dramatic uses for the descending rake is the open E string—a favorite move of Jimi Hendrix and Stevie Ray, among others. Check it out in this E minor pentatonic lick.

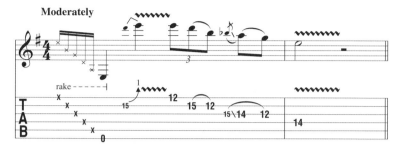

LICK 2

Here's a classic ascending rake: a B-string note bent up a whole step to the tonic of a minor pentatonic scale. This one's been used by just about everyone who's ever played a blues scale.

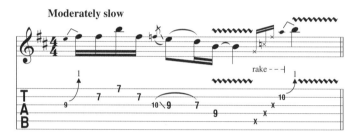

LICK 3

In this bluesy lick in C, we're finishing off a slippery phrase with a descending rake into the tonic C note on string 4.

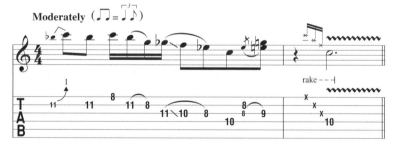

LICK 4

Let's finish off with a B.B. King trademark: the octave "yelp." Use your pinky for the final high A note so that you can lay your other fingers across the strings to make sure they're quiet. That's the way B.B. does it!

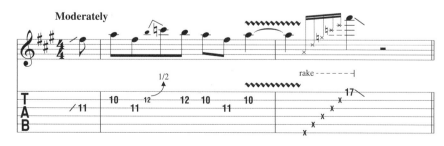

Be sure to play around with this technique. It's a subtle sound, but it really does make a difference.

LESSON #9: TREMOLO PICKING

Although tremolo picking is often used to generate mounds of intensity, it can also be used to provide feathery mandolin-style flourishes or the melodic backbone to a surf tune. Of course, in the hands of Stevie Ray Vaughan, it could be used to grind the audience into a pulp of submission! In this lesson, we'll take a look at its many uses.

What Is Tremolo Picking?

The concept is pretty simple: you pick a note (or notes) as fast as you possibly can. There's not one set standard motion that all players use for tremolo picking, and many players even venture from their standard picking technique when they tremolo pick. Eddie Van Halen is a good example of this, as he arches his wrist away from the guitar and flutters his wrist rapidly to produce the effect. You'll need to experiment to see which motion feels natural to you. You may even use different motions depending on the effect you're going for. If you're tremolo picking a triple stop with reckless abandon, for example, you may find that you'll put your whole forearm into it. If you're picking a soft melody mandolin-style, you may find that the motion will all come from the wrist. Or maybe exactly the opposite will work best for you.

Technical Concerns

Whichever motion you choose, you'll need to be precise and controlled about it if you want to tremolo pick a melody on any of the inner strings. Try to remain relaxed, and don't hold your breath. There may be times when you'll need to continue the technique for an extended period of time, and tensing up and/or holding your breath will make that difficult. Try to visualize an even, steady flow of motion and allow your hands to do what's needed to make that happen.

Fret-Hand Muting

If you're "mowing the lawn"—i.e., tremolo picking double- or triple-stops with reckless abandon—during a high-energy solo, you're going to need to employ some fret-hand muting to make sure only the notes you want to sound are sounding. When you're playing that intensely, you shouldn't have to worry about picking only two or three strings at a time. It will actually sound beefier if you can include a few muted strings in your strumming, anyway.

Exercises

Let's quickly look at a few exercises to get you acclimated to the technique. The first exercise ascends through the strings with single notes, and the second uses double stops. You'll find there are different challenges with each approach.

EXERCISE 1

EXERCISE 2

Licks

Now let's hear how the technique sounds in some various applications.

LICK 1

This first lick is a melody played entirely on the G string with one finger sliding to every note—a common application of the tremolo technique.

LICK 2

Here's a softer example where we're tremolo picking chords in a mandolin-like fashion. Try to imagine a calm, even bed of sound.

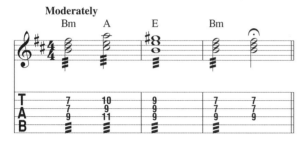

LICK 3

In this lick, we're playing a single-note melody, but we're moving through several strings. This will take a bit of getting used to, but it's not as troublesome as it might first appear.

LICK 4

Here's a more raucous example using double stops. Notice also that we're re-attacking each quarter note with slides for added effect. Be sure to use fret-hand muting here!

LICK 5

Let's close with a classic use: the final chord of the night. This happens when the drummer's going crazy with his super extended drum fill and you're all looking around for the cue to bash the chord one last time.

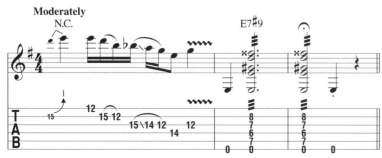

LESSON #10: BARRE CHORDS

If you want to play major, minor, or seventh chords in any key, you need to learn barre chords; it's as simple as that. They allow you to slide the same chord form anywhere on the neck to play a chord from any root. The tradeoff is that they're not easy for a beginner to do, as it requires a specific strength in order to clamp so many strings down. However, even if barre chords are completely new to you, a few weeks of consistent practice should be all that's required.

What Is a Barre Chord?

In a barre chord, one or more fingers on the frethand holds down several strings at the same fret—anywhere from two strings to all six. The important thing to remember is that *all* barre chords are generated from an open chord shape. Remember those E and A chords you learned when you first started playing? Well, those shapes are responsible for two of the most commonly used barre chord forms of all.

E-Form Barre Chords

Let's take a look at an open E chord to start.

TRACK 10
0:00
CD 1

To transform this into an "E-form" G major barre chord, do the following:

1. Re-finger this open E chord *without* using your first finger; instead, fret with fingers 3, 4, and 2, low to high.

2. Lay your first finger across all six strings just behind the nut. This is the E-form barre chord shape. In this instance, the nut is acting as your barre, which is why you don't need a finger barring all the strings.

3. Keep this same shape and slide your hand up the neck so that your first finger is "barring" across all six strings on the 3rd fret. Presto! You have an E-form G major barre chord!

Now, if you remove your second finger, this becomes a G minor chord. Notice how it resembles an open E minor chord.

You can move these shapes anywhere on the neck to play major or minor chords from any root.

A-Form Barre Chords

The other common barre chord shape is the A-form, which is derived from the open A chord. To play it, re-finger an open A chord by using your third finger to barre across the 2nd fret on strings 4, 3, and 2.

Keep this same shape and slide your hand up the neck so that your first finger is at fret 3 of string 5. You have an A-form C major barre chord!

Some people prefer to use a first-finger barre to fret strings 1 and 5, but your third finger must be flexible enough to bend away from the first string so that it doesn't dampen it. If you want to include the high E string, but your third finger isn't that flexible (most of ours aren't!), then try using fingers 2, 3, and 4 on strings 4–2, like this:

For the minor variation, we mimic the shape of the open A minor chord, using the first-finger barre. Here's an A-form Cm barre chord.

Other Forms

Other less common and more difficult barre forms include the C-form and the G-form. In these diagrams, the dots in white are optional and show the full forms; the commonly used partial forms are shown in black.

C-FORM E MAJOR BARRE CHORD

G-FORM D MAJOR BARRE CHORD

Riffs

RIFF 1

Let's check these forms out in action! Here's a punk style riff using E- and A-forms.

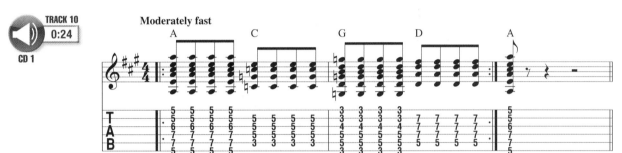

RIFF 2

Here we use a partial G-form to create a Stones-like groove in C. Notice that we're using a partial C-form for embellishments, but we're not including the high E string, so there's no barre up there. For the final chord, we add the pinky on the top string for the high C note—another common version of the partial G-form shape.

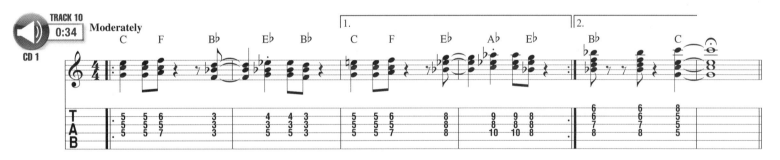

RIFF 3

Here's a mellow riff in G that mixes major and minor A- and E-forms.

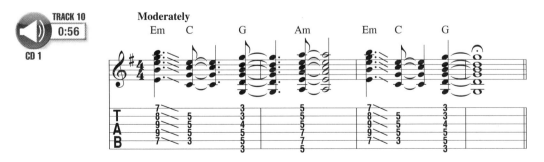

Though they don't come easily at first, barre chords will soon become an indispensable part of your chord repertoire, so learn them well!

LESSON #11: SLIDE GUITAR BASICS

Though many players never mess with it, some of the most memorable riffs in rock history were played on slide. It's a specific skill and takes years to master; developing Derek Trucks' kind of facility is not an easy task. However, you don't have to become a virtuoso in order to appreciate the slide and exploit its unique tonal qualities. They're great for simple riffs as well, as we'll soon see.

The Basic Technique

Some players wear the slide on the pinky, some wear it on their third finger, and others wear it on their middle finger. There's no set rule on this (although, the index finger is rarely used), so experiment to see what feels best. To play a note with the slide, make contact with the string, but don't push it down to the fretboard. For proper tuning, align the slide *directly over* the fret wire. If you're out in front of the wire, you'll be sharp; if you're behind, you'll be flat.

After plucking the string, move the slide up or down to raise the pitch in a steady gliss.

TRACK 11
0:00
CD 1

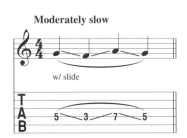

CORRECT SLIDE POSITION FOR A NOTE ON
STRING 4, FRET 5

KEEPING IT CLEAN: THE IMPORTANCE OF MUTING

Muting is a very important part of clean slide playing. This is accomplished by both hands working in conjunction with each other. On the fret hand, the fingers behind the slide should lightly touch all the strings to keep them quiet. This will prevent the other strings from making noise. Regarding the pick hand, some players play slide with a pick, and others use fingerstyle or hybrid picking (pick and fingers). Regardless of your preference, use your palm to mute all the bass strings below the string you're playing. That's the easy part. The tricky part is when you want to play single notes with the slide *on different strings* without allowing them to ring together. To do this, you'll need to mute a string with the pick hand once you're not playing on it anymore.

For example, if I'm not concerned about keeping the notes separate, these two notes will ring together.

However, if I want the notes to be distinct from one another, I'll mute the B string with a fret-hand finger as soon as I pluck the G string. This will take some work at first, but it will eventually become second nature.

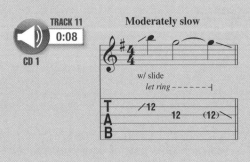
TRACK 11
0:08
CD 1

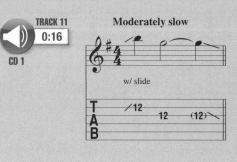
TRACK 11
0:16
CD 1

Exercises

Let's start with a few exercises to get the fundamentals down.

EXERCISE 1

This first exercise concentrates on playing in tune on all six strings.

EXERCISE 2

This exercise focuses on sliding double stops. Keep the slide perpendicular to the neck so that both notes stay in tune.

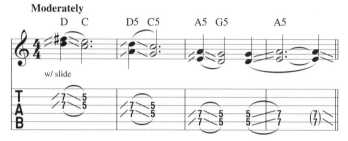

Licks

LICK 1

Our first standard tuned lick uses the G minor pentatonic scale and requires good pick-hand muting technique.

LICK 2

Here's one in E major that's reminiscent of George Harrison's slide work, which is not as bluesy. To add vibrato on the last note, simply volley the slide back and forth, surrounding the target pitch to create an average "in tune" note.

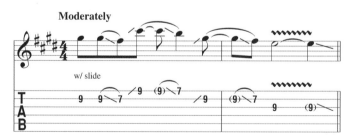

LICK 3

This last lick exploits the fact that strings 4, 3, and 2 form a major triad on the same fret. We're sliding chords around in a Black Crowes fashion here.

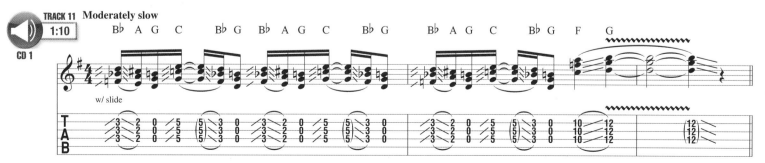

If you spend a good deal of time with slide, you're bound to get into open tunings. That's a whole other world of fun. But now you're armed with the basic technique, which will translate to any tuning. Have fun!

LESSON #12: WHAMMY BAR TRICKS

Though the first tremolo systems appeared in the forties, they don't much resemble the ones that flooded the market in the eighties. Designs by Floyd Rose and Kahler came with locking nuts and also allowed the bar to be pulled back to raise the pitch as well as dip it. By the middle of the decade, virtually every hard rock guitar was outfitted with one of these units. In this lesson, we'll take a look at some of the sounds we can conjure up with the wiggle stick.

Vibrato

To produce vibrato with the bar, simply sustain a note or chord and gently depress and release the bar repeatedly. The farther you push the bar down, the wider the vibrato will be. It can be anywhere from a subtle ripple to a treacherous avalanche. Try it on chords as well.

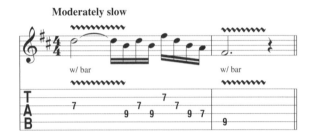

Scoop

To execute a scoop, dip the bar before you pick the note, and, as you pick, release the bar back up to pitch. This results in a flat note that quickly rises to pitch. The depth of the scoop is left up to the discretion of the scooper.

Dive Bomb

The dive bomb is simple, but it's just plain fun! This is one of the first things players do when they get a guitar with a whammy on it. Play a note, usually the open low E string, and slowly depress the bar until the strings go slack and stick to the pickups.

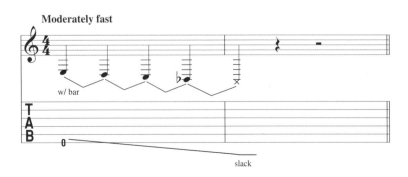

Siren

There are a few different ways to create the siren, which is most commonly played on the G string. The first method is to pick a natural harmonic on the 4th fret or closer to the nut—basically the highest one that you can get to sound clearly. When you get a good scream, pull and push the bar back and forth to imitate a police car siren. Joe Satriani has mastered the other method, in which you play a pinch harmonic on the open G string—you'll have to experiment to find the best place along the string—and then use your fret hand to maneuver the bar.

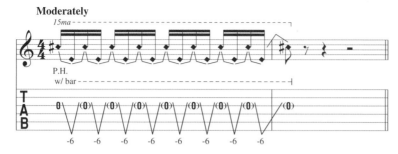

Reverse Scoop (Hiccup)

This next technique goes by various names, and Steve Vai calls it "little grace notes from India." Turn the bar around so that it's pointing away from the neck and play the notes with your fret hand using all legato techniques. At the beginning of every note, quickly dip the bar. Since it's turned around, this will actually cause the pitch to go sharp, which creates an interesting effect.

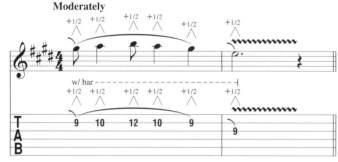

Flutter

The flutter is one of Vai's signature moves. To execute it, pick a note and then swat at the end of the bar quickly, as if you were trying to swat a fly. What's happening is that we're depressing the bar very quickly and then allowing it to snap back into place. You can also use hammer-ons from nowhere in the fret hand and flutter each note from the very beginning.

The Elephant

With your volume rolled off, play the natural harmonics notated in the music; whack them really hard and let them all ring together. Then, lower the bar with the pick hand. As you begin to raise the bar, start to swell the volume knob up with your fret hand. Bring the bar up (past normal pitch if possible) and smoothly dive it down once again, rolling off the volume before you bottom out. You're on safari!

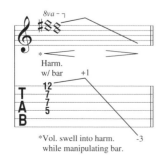

LESSON #13: TRILLS

Used often in classical Baroque melodies, the trill—the rapid fluctuation of two pitches—has since been adopted by blues and rock guitarists and put to good use. It can be flashy or understated, and it's not easy, though Hendrix, Stevie Ray, and many others make it look that way. You'll need a solid command of legato technique and a good bit of endurance too. You'll feel the burn in your forearm for sure!

How It Works

We perform trills on the guitar by continuously stringing hammer-ons and pull-offs together. Usually, the lower note is picked once, which is almost always fretted by the first finger (unless it's an open string). Then a higher note is hammered on, pulled off, hammered on, pulled off, ad infinitum as quickly as possible. Whole- or half-step trills are most common, although larger intervals are sometimes used. Here's the basic idea on the D string.

And here's the idea with an open string.

Trills do not come easily. If you've never worked on them before, don't expect to be blurring through them the way Stevie Ray or Hendrix did. Your arm is going to get tired, so be sure to rest if you feel any pain.

Tapped Trills

A variation on the technique is the tapped trill. Here, you use your tapping finger to hammer and pull. This is a nice option because it can save your left hand from turning to jelly if you need to trill for an extended period of time. Many players, such as Joe Satriani, use their pick to tap with when performing a tapped trill. This provides a different tone, and it can produce a faster trill because less motion is required.

You can also combine the tapped trill with a normal trill, alternating your tapping finger with a fret-hand finger.

Licks

Now let's check out this technique in some licks.

LICK 1

This first one is a classic blues rock move and involves playing a C7 triple stop and trilling on the middle string.

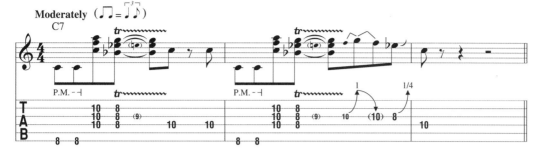

LICK 2

Here's another staple: the open-string trill in the key of E. We're using a slight palm mute here, so it's a bit more subdued. This one's been used by everyone from Hendrix to Satriani.

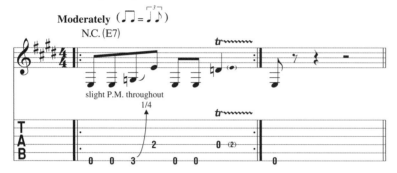

LICK 3

Here's something else that Hendrix would do occasionally: a continuous trill on the G string while moving to different areas of the neck. Notice that the trill size varies in order to conform to the notes of the key—E Dorian in this case.

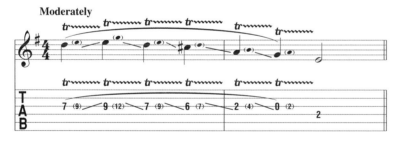

LICK 4

Here's a common application of the tapped trill. We're tapping the same fret while moving the fret hand further down the neck. As a result, the trill intervals get wider and wider.

As I said earlier, trills are not as easy as they look, so take your time. It'll take a while to build up the strength to do them for extended periods of time. Once you have them, though, they can provide the perfect embellishment at the right moment.

LESSON #14: COMMON ROCK PROGRESSIONS

Have you ever heard a song that sounded really similar to another one? Even though they may be in a *different key*, many rock songs use similar chord progressions. In this lesson, we're going to look at some of the most common rock progressions of all.

A Bit of Theory Background

To understand chord progressions and how they're notated, we need to know a little bit of chord theory—starting with the major scale. Let's look at the key of C major:

C MAJOR SCALE

You can see that the notes are numbered 1–7. To build chords, we stack two other notes on top of each of these scale degrees. For instance, on top of the C note, we stack E and G. This creates a C major chord.

C MAJOR CHORD

Notice the pattern: C, skip a note (D), E, skip a note (F), and G. When we apply this same process to each one of the notes in the C major scale, we end up with the harmonized major scale.

HARMONIZED C MAJOR SCALE

As you can see, we have three different types of chords: major (no suffix), minor ("m" suffix), and diminished (with the "°" symbol). The chords have been identified with Roman numerals, which we use when discussing chords and chord progressions. (The reason will become clear soon enough.) Upper case numerals are used for major chords, lower case for minor chords, and lower case with the "°" symbol for diminished. Since we're dealing with three-note chords, these are called triads. This pattern of triad qualities is the same in any major key:

major	minor	minor	major	major	minor	diminished
I	ii	iii	IV	V	vi	vii°

So, if I asked, "What's the IV chord in the key of C?" You would say F major. The vi chord? That's Am, etc.

HARMONIZED C MINOR SCALE

When we harmonize the minor scale the same way, we end up with another pattern of triad qualities: i–ii°–♭III–iv–v–♭VI–♭VII.

This pattern of qualities—for a major key or minor key—isn't impenetrable. Sometimes the qualities or root notes are altered, as we'll soon see. But these are the default chords and are the ones said to be diatonic to the key.

TRANSPOSITION

Let's say we had a chord progression in C that went C–F–G–C. We could write the chord names (C–F–G–C), or we could write I–IV–V–I. With the Roman numeral method, we don't have to rewrite the chord chart if we want to change keys! Once you know the pattern of chord qualities (shown above), and you know your twelve major scales (which every good musician should learn!), you can instantly transpose any chord progression using Roman numerals.

For example, let's say we want the I–IV–V–I progression in D major. If you know the D major scale, D–E–F#–G–A–B–C#, it's easy: **D** (I)–**G** (IV)–**A** (V)–**D** (I).

Progressions

Now let's get to the progressions. Only the Roman numerals are shown, so you can play these in any key. For simplicity, they're all demonstrated in the key of C on the audio.

1. I–IV–V

Probably the most common of all, the I–IV–V has been used in literally hundreds of thousands of songs. Check out "Louie, Louie" for a classic example.

2. I–V–vi–IV

This one is extremely ubiquitous as well. You can hear it in U2's "With or Without You" and the Beatles' "Let It Be," among countless others.

3. I–♭VII–IV

Notice the ♭VII. What does this mean? Well, the ♭ tells us to lower the seventh degree by one half step, and the upper case Roman numeral tells us it's a major chord. So, in the key of C, this progression would read C–B♭–F. In the key of A, it would be A–G–D, and so on.

4. I–IV

Many songs have been built with only these two chords—back and forth, over and over.

5. ♭VI–♭VII–i

This is Iron Maiden's favorite progression by far (although they'd most likely play it with power chords).

6. i–IV

This is a minor key progression with a major IV chord—a common substitution.

Believe it or not, these progressions (or some variation of them using a different pattern of the same chords) make up probably half or more of the well-known rock songs out there. Learn them, and you'll be well-prepared to tackle a good portion of the rock repertoire!

LESSON #15: RECORDING TIPS

With the digital revolution, more and more players are able to produce stellar sounding guitar tracks right from the privacy of their own bedroom. A modest computer, some affordable software, and a decent interface will get you well on your way in the recording world. Here we'll discuss some tips that'll help you make the most of that digital audio workstation (DAW).

Studio Layout

Although most bedrooms aren't designed with recording in mind, there are several things you can do to help the acoustic situation. Obviously, you're limited by a slew of factors, but the more of these suggestions you can employ, the better.

MONITOR (SPEAKER) PLACEMENT

It's best to set up the speakers with their backs to the short wall (assuming a rectangular room); try to place them equidistant from each other in the middle of the width of the room. Bring them out from the back wall as far as possible to avoid the buildup of bass frequencies. Your head should form an equidistant triangle with the other two monitors.

ABSORBENT MATERIAL

If you have heavy curtains/drapes, a soft chair/sofa, or some other similar object, it will help to place them anywhere along the walls at reflective points. See the image below for the placement of these items. Ideally, you could hang something above your head to block reflections from the ceiling as well. The goal is to hear only the sound coming from the speakers and not bouncing off any walls.

The other part of the equation is the "bass traps" in the corner. The more soft, dense material you can place in the corners, the better, as this will help cut down on the bass frequencies that tend to build up there. If a bed or a plush chair is already sitting in the corner, that's a good start.

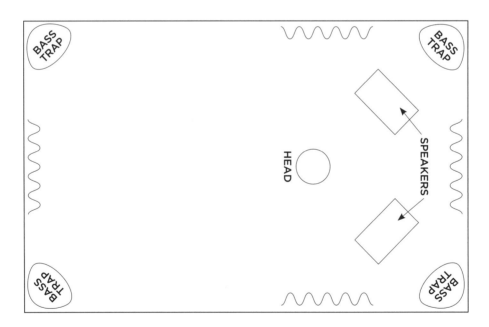

SOUND PANELS

Many companies make mountable absorptive sound panels for the purpose of cutting down on reflections, but they can get pricey. If you're the DIY type, you can make a comparable panel on your own using rigid fiberglass (such as Owens Corning 703) or mineral wool covered with a breathable fabric. There are lots of websites that show how.

These suggestions will all help you hear a more accurate representation of the music you're recording. This, in turn, will help you mix your tracks in a way that will translate better to everyone else's stereo system.

Electric Guitars

Let's look at some specific pointers for recording electric guitars.

DIAL BACK THE DISTORTION A BIT!

If you spend any amount of time critically listening to your favorite songs, you'll most likely discover that the sounds aren't quite as distorted as you remember. Distortion compresses the sound (levels out the dynamics), and many riffs sound better with a tone that can breathe a bit more. Check out the audio to hear the difference.

TRY CONTRASTING TONES WHEN DOUBLING A PART

Doubling guitars is a very common practice, but many players use the same exact sound for both. Check it out on the audio, where you'll hear two different tones on their own and then combined. This often results in a bigger-sounding composite tone.

MINUTE CHANGES IN MIC PLACEMENT MAKE BIG DIFFERENCES!

When miking an amp, the slightest change in position (even an inch) can make a noticeable difference, so experiment. Listen to the audio to hear how moving the mic a few inches can change the tone considerably.

Acoustic Guitars

Acoustic guitars are different animals than electrics, so let's talk about them as well.

CONDENSER MICS ARE THE WAY TO GO

Though dynamic mics, such as the Shure SM57, are often used when miking electric guitar amps, a condenser mic is usually better suited to capture the wide frequency spectrum of an acoustic guitar. They're a bit more delicate than a dynamic mic, so handle them carefully. Listen to the audio to hear the same thing recorded first with a dynamic and then a condenser mic.

ALWAYS USE A MIC IF POSSIBLE!

Although many acoustics have onboard pickups these days, they should really only be used for live playing. A condenser mic will always sound more natural than a pickup. Listen to the audio to hear a similar riff to the previous one recorded with an onboard pickup; the difference is night and day.

TRY MIXING TWO MICS

You can place one mic about a foot away from the neck pointing toward the neck/body joint, and the other can be placed a foot out from the bridge. Then you can blend the levels (and EQ if necessary) to get a full-bodied tone. Check it out on the audio.

LESSON #16: OPEN G TUNING

From the Rolling Stones to the Black Crowes, Open G tuning has seen a lot of action over the years. Besides allowing you to play a chord (G major) with absolutely no fretting required, it facilitates easy, one-finger barre chords anywhere on the neck. In this lesson, we'll talk about benefits of Open G tuning and learn some cool riffs in the meantime.

Open Wide and Say Ahhh

To access Open G tuning from standard tuning, we need to tune our sixth, fifth, and first strings down a whole step. This is pretty easy to do, even without a tuner, as we have other open strings on the guitar that match these pitches:

▶ Tune your sixth string down a whole step so that it's an octave lower than your open fourth string.

▶ Tune your first string down a whole step so that it's an octave higher than your open fourth string.

▶ Tune your fifth string down a whole step so that it's an octave lower than your third string.

Remember that, in each instance, you want to overshoot the mark by tuning first below the pitch and then back up to match it for the best stability.

Open G Tuning: D–G–D–G–B–D

This tuning is identical to Open A tuning in its intervallic structure. The only difference is that Open A will sound a whole step higher. Any lick you know in Open G, however, will also work in Open A and vice versa.

Common Chord Forms

Just as standard tuning has its cowboy chords, Open G has some common chord forms as well.
Let's look at some of them now.

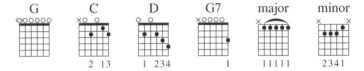

And here are a few that aren't quite as common, but they illustrate the colorful possibilities that exist.

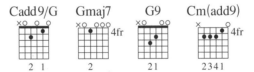

Riffs

Now that you've got the basics down, let's hear what this tuning can do.

RIFF 1

Here's a classic rock riff in the Stones or John Mellencamp vein.

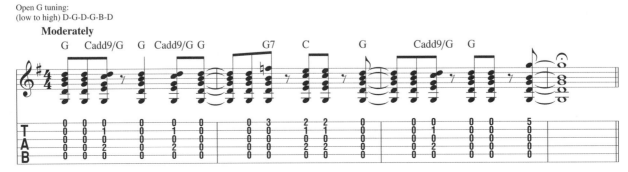

34

RIFF 2

And here's another one in the Stones style that makes use of the famous add9 chord embellishment in barre chord form.

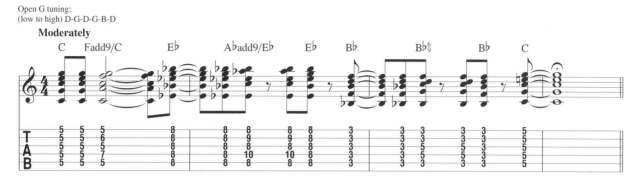

RIFF 3

This acoustic riff uses an arpeggio pattern with a changing note on the D string and sounds similar to what Zeppelin or the Black Crowes might do.

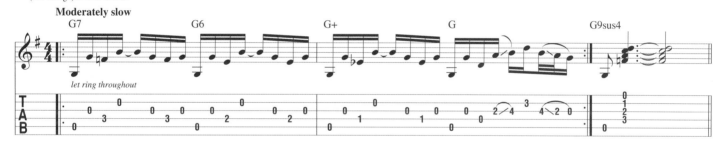

RIFF 4

It's really fun to use open drone strings with this tuning as well. Here's an example of that approach.

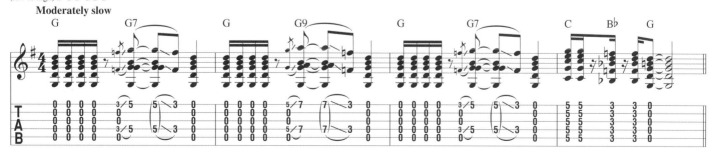

Take some time to really explore this tuning when you get a chance; you'll be glad you did. Besides leading to many fresh sounds, it's also the only way to authentically play some of the greatest rock riffs ever. Not to mention it's very often used in slide playing, but that's a whole other can of worms!

Besides writing some of the most immortal songs in pop history, the Beatles also wrote their share of killer guitar parts. Countless classics, from "Day Tripper" to "Helter Skelter," instantly bring to mind timeless riffs. Though the band rarely repeated itself, we'll do our best to find some common threads in their music. If you've got a Vox, crank it up!

Rhythm Styles

The Fab Four created some of the most enduring riffs in rock history. Let's check out a few examples that touch upon their favorite sounds.

BLUESY OR PENTATONIC-FLAVORED RIFFS

Many of the band's classic riffs made use of bluesy pentatonic ideas. Here's a typical example in the key of E. Notice the mixture of the minor and major 3rds, G and G♯, respectively—a common practice in bluesier riffs of this type. The inclusion of the 9th, F♯—not nearly as common—is also characteristic of the Beatles' exploratory spirit.

Here's an example of a swampier riff that uses a bit more space—perhaps to allow for one of Ringo's catchy drum fills.

RINGING ARPEGGIO PARTS

Another classic Beatles sound is the ringing, chimey parts, usually played by George on electric 12-string. These often used suspended voicings for an open, expansive sound. You'd hear things like this.

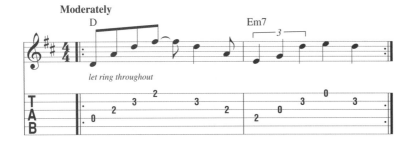

Lead Styles

Though George was technically the lead guitarist, John and Paul played their share of lead. Let's take a brief glimpse at each one's style.

GEORGE HARRISON

On the early recordings, many of George's lead breaks sounded very rockabilly with hybrid picking and chordal embellishments. Here's a typical example.

TRACK 17
0:37
CD 1

As time went on, George developed a very melodic style, blending largely pentatonic sounds with intelligent note choices to create some memorable statements.

TRACK 17
0:49
CD 1

PAUL McCARTNEY

Paul usually had a more frenetic, aggressive energy, as illustrated in this slippery D Dorian phrase.

TRACK 17
1:03
CD 1

JOHN LENNON

John was perhaps the bluesiest soloist of the bunch, often mixing major and minor pentatonic scales to great effect. This phrase in A demonstrates.

TRACK 17
1:13
CD 1

Be sure to listen to the masters themselves to hear other brilliant guitar moments. They didn't get to be the greatest band in history for nothing!

LESSON #18: THE BEATLES STYLE - ACOUSTIC GUITAR

Though you can't help thinking about the jangly electric Vox tones when talking about the Beatles, the acoustic guitar actually drove many of their songs—especially in the early days. In this lesson, we'll explore the unplugged side of the Beatles' guitar style and see how they used the acoustic guitar to add depth to their sound.

Strumming

Many times, a simple strummed acoustic part provided the backbone of a song, so let's look at the different ways they approached this technique.

BALLAD STYLE

In many tender ballads (and some not-so-tender ones), the acoustic laid down a bed of harmony consisting of an even pattern that mixed quarter and 8th notes—something like this. You're going for a smooth sound here, so strive for an even volume throughout.

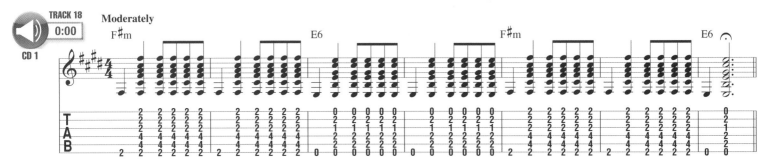

SKIFFLE FEEL

Another common sound in their early catalog was the skiffle feel—a fast, bluegrass-like style. In this style, the backbeat is heavily accented during the strumming pattern. This basically entails strumming harder on beats 2 and 4. Here's a typical example.

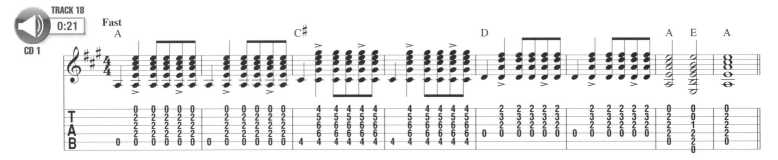

DESCENDING BASS LINE PATTERNS

A device that appeared time and again throughout the Beatles career was a chord progression with a descending bass line. On the acoustic guitar, this was articulated with strumming or fingerstyle techniques. A typical strumming example might sound like this.

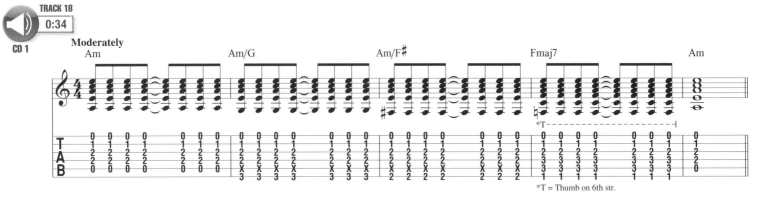

*T = Thumb on 6th str.

They also used this idea in higher register parts, where they often played fingerstyle—maybe something like this.

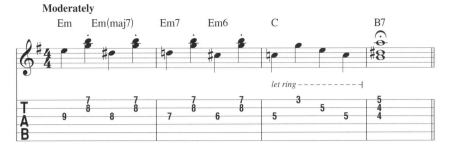

Fingerstyle Techniques

The fingerstyle technique adorned many songs of Lennon and McCartney, and both had distinctly different approaches. Let's look at each closely.

PAUL McCARTNEY

Paul's approach was non-traditional, but he made it sound very natural and fluid. He used a combination of plucking with the thumb and one or two fingers and strumming with the index finger or thumb to get things like this.

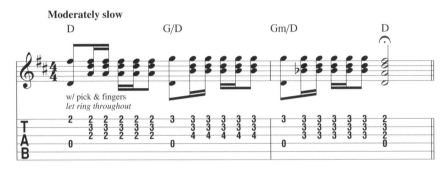

He would also often add bass runs or move 10th intervals around to create melodic parts.

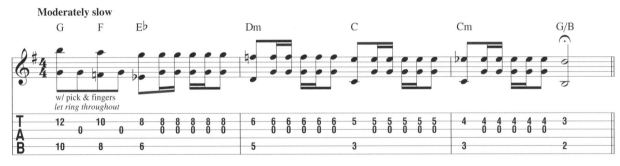

JOHN LENNON

Lennon played in the more traditional Travis picking style, using alternating bass notes and filling in the gaps on the treble strings with his fingers.

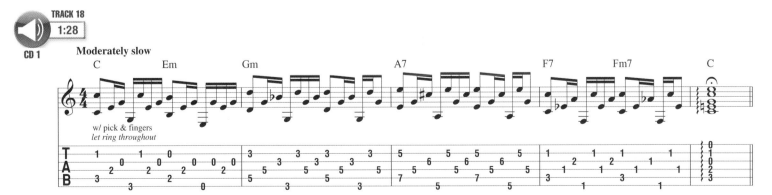

Well, that does it for this lesson. Be sure to listen to plenty of Beatles tunes to hear these concepts in action; *Rubber Soul* is especially acoustic-laden, as is the *White Album*, so those are good places to start.

LESSON #19: DOUBLE- AND TRIPLE-PICKING

Many guitarists have specific skills in their bag of tricks that serve a variety of purposes. It may be hybrid picking, which allows you to play a riff faster than you would with the pick alone. Or maybe you've got a few tapping licks under your belt that you can unleash on an unsuspecting audience. Well, if you haven't worked much on double picking or triple picking, now's the time. This is an interesting sound that some players use when building to a climax of a solo. But it requires a specific skill set, and if you've never worked at it, it'll take some practice.

The Basic Idea

So what do we mean by double- or triple-picking? Well, it's fairly self-explanatory. Basically, instead of picking each note in a line only once, we pick each one twice or three times. You may think, "If I can play a lick picking each note only once, surely I can play it picking each note twice!" As I mentioned earlier, however, the coordination involved with this is specific, and you need to work on it in order to achieve a perfectly synchronized sound.

TECHNICAL CONCERNS

When we double pick, we can either pick at the same speed as in the normal lick (straight 16th notes, for instance), in which case the lick would take up twice the amount of musical space. Or we can pick twice as fast, in which case the lick would take up the same amount of musical space, but our picking hand would be doing twice the work (picking 32nd notes). Both ideas are demonstrated here.

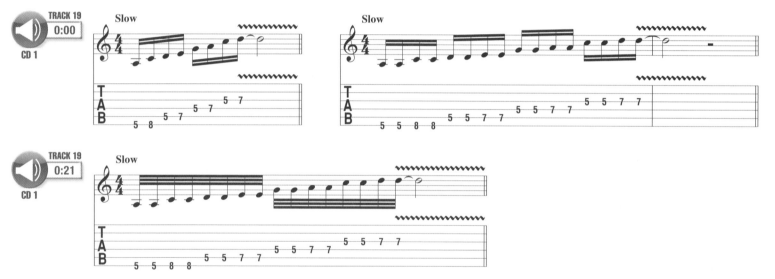

When we triple pick, things get a little more interesting. If we pick at the same speed as in the normal lick, we'll get a three-against-four effect, because we'll be picking, say, groups of three notes in a 16th-note rhythm. The other, probably more common approach is to pick three notes in the space of one. That is to say, if the normal lick was played as 16th notes, we'd be picking 32nd-note triplets. Needless to say, this gets pretty fast even at moderate tempos. Here's an example of these two approaches.

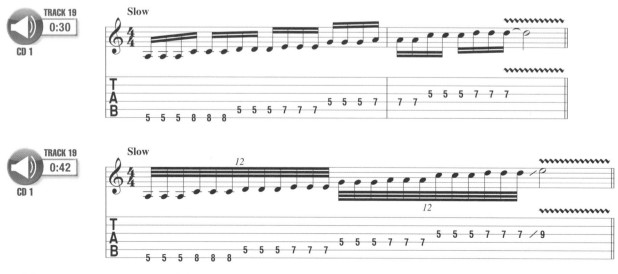

With triple picking, we can also kind of divide the two and pick the line in sextuplets. This is much easier than 32nd-note triplets, but our left hand will be moving at a different speed—faster than when picking 16th notes, but slower than when picking 32nd-note triplets. Here's how that would sound.

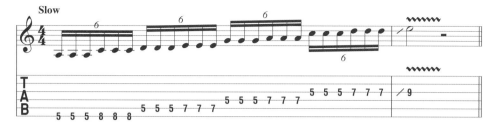

In order to pull these lines off as cleanly as someone like Steve Vai or John Petrucci does, you'll need to concentrate on efficient picking and absolute synchronization between the hands. Remember, we're not tremolo picking here. We're picking a very specific amount of times for each note. If your hands fall out of sync, slow it down and work back up to tempo.

Licks

Ok, now that we have the idea, let's check out some licks using the technique.

LICK 1

This first one makes use of a common idea with this technique—kind of a staggering, intervallic, ascending melody.

LICK 2

Here's another intervallic idea, but with a rhythmic twist. Instead of starting with the double pick on a downbeat, I'm starting on the last 16th note. This creates an entirely different effect, which is quite striking.

LICK 3

This next example is a Guns N' Roses-style riff that includes mostly triple picking, but uses double picking to turn the pattern back around at the end.

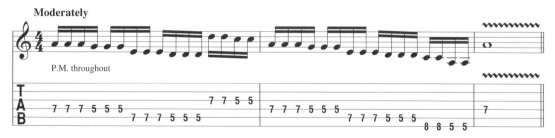

LICK 4

Here's a flashy one. After a bluesy open-position lick, we triple pick down an E blues scale in straight sextuplets.

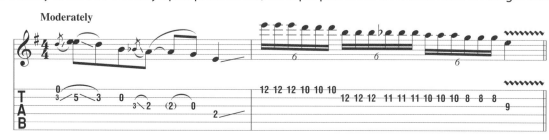

LESSON #20: USING RESTS

As rock guitar players, we have a knack for being "note-y," filling up every second of musical space in the process. Even when we're not burning through some scale pattern, we're likely grinding some note into submission with vibrato. When you listen to horn players though, for instance, you'll notice that there are many periods of silence (rests) in their phrases. This is necessary for them; they have to breathe. We can take a tip from them and start employing rests ourselves. The result is almost always a more memorable solo with more clearly delineated phrases.

Exercises

Let's try a few exercises to get used to this idea.

EXERCISE 1

This first one works on a simple concept. Pick a beat in the measure, and leave it blank every time. In this example, we've done this with beat 1. Notice that every time beat 1 comes around, there's a rest.

EXERCISE 2

In this exercise, we're doing the same thing, except we're moving the rest one beat forward each time. It's on beat 1 in measure 1, beat 2 in measure 2, beat 3 in measure 3, and so on. This will really get you thinking about your phrasing. We've altered the phrase in Exercise 1 to suit this idea.

The idea here is to realize that you don't need to fill every beat. I'm sure you've heard the expression, "What you *don't* play is just as important as what you *do* play." Many people let this breeze past them without giving it a second thought, but it really is true. The space in between your notes can do some great work for you if you just let it. It can bookend a phrase, or it can create a sense of anticipation that really makes that note count when it arrives.

EXERCISE 3

This final exercise is more visceral. You're literally going to breathe your phrases. Take a breath in and exhale as you play a phrase. When you inhale to take another breath, stop playing and rest. Here's what I came up with when I tried this method.

If you're anything like me, you probably ended up playing some very different things than what you're used to when you tried this. Just having to think about the coordination puts you in a different space mentally, and it no doubt caught you off guard. You may even be breathing a little heavier or out of breath. I'm not suggesting that this is how you should always play. On the contrary, I think you should be breathing normally without any thought given to it. But, as an exercise, it's great for getting you in a new mindset. The hope is that eventually you'll start to get in the habit of using rests without having to think about it.

Licks

Now that you've got the idea, let's put it to use with some spacious, roomy licks. The idea is to take your time and let phrases end so that others have a place to begin.

LICK 1

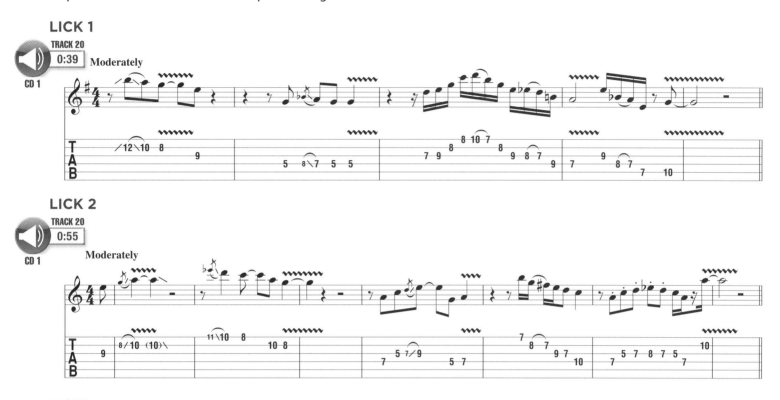

LICK 2

Riffs

Did I neglect to mention that rests have a place in riffs too? You can create a lot of drama this way.

RIFF 1

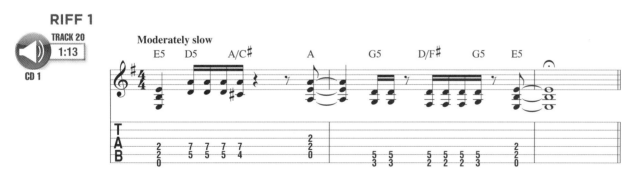

RIFF 2

This last one is in Drop D tuning, so be sure to lower your sixth string down to D.

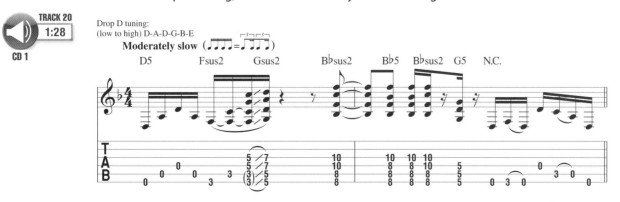

ERIC JOHNSON STYLE

Eric Johnson's style is not easy to describe, but if you took Jimi Hendrix, Jeff Beck, Chet Atkins, Wes Montgomery, and John McLaughlin and put them in a blender, you might get close. He's a unique virtuoso, to say the least. In this lesson, we'll take a look at a few of his trademark techniques and favorite devices.

Rhythm Style

When it comes to guitar, Eric never takes the easy way out. Tone is his main concern, and he'll do whatever it takes to get the sound he wants. This results in specifically voiced chords and techniques that aren't always a walk in the park.

HYBRID PICKING

Eric is famous for his use of hybrid picking, which means using the pick and fingers to pluck the strings. For instance, he doesn't just strum chords like these with the pick:

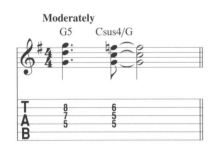

Instead, he's more likely to used hybrid picking, plucking string 4 with the pick and using the second and third pick-hand fingers on strings 3 and 2, respectively.

Here's an example of a bluesy shuffle-type riff that Eric might play hybrid-style.

OPEN VOICED TRIADS AND INVERSIONS

Another Eric trademark is his use of open voiced triads and inversions. An open voiced triad is one in which the notes span more than one octave. For example, here's a typical C major triad:

Instead of this shape, Eric would more likely play it in an open voicing. To do this, we can shift the 3rd (E) up an octave and move the 5th (G) down one string.

An inversion is a chord in which a note other than the root is on the bottom. For example, Eric may re-voice the previous open-voiced C triad in first inversion, which has the 3rd (E) on the bottom, or in second inversion, which has the 5th (G) on the bottom.

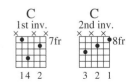

When you pair the open-voiced and inversion ideas with hybrid picking, you start getting some of those famous Eric chord phrases—maybe something like this.

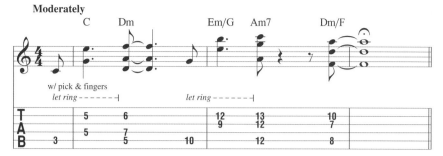

Lead Style

Eric's is one of the most immediately recognizable lead styles in rock history. His tone is legendary, as is his cleanliness and attention to detail.

MINOR PENTATONIC SCALE

Almost every guitar player knows it, but few can make it sound like Eric. He can burn through it at blazing speed and traverse the entire neck in one quick run if the mood strikes him. Here's a typical Eric pentatonic lick in F minor.

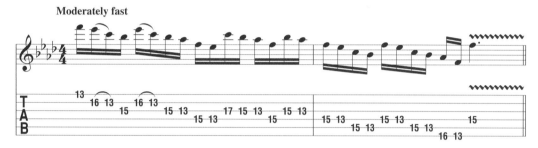

And here's how he may move down through various positions of the scale to span the length of the neck.

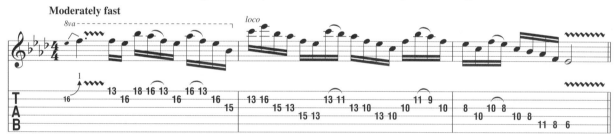

WIDE INTERVALS AND STRING SKIPPING

One of the most attention-grabbing features of Eric's lead style is his use of wide intervals and string skipping. For instance, he'll use the same open-voiced triad concept and apply it to arpeggios to get things like this. Be sure to keep it clean!

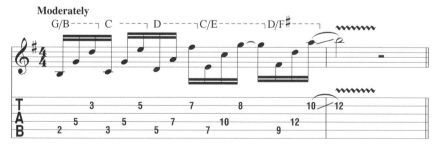

Here's an example using another of his favorite melodic devices—the minor hexatonic scale—which is a minor pentatonic scale with an added 2nd (or 9th). This B minor lick takes place in the standard box position, but sounds anything but standard.

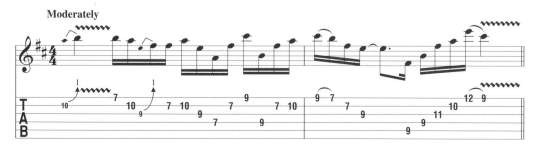

LESSON #22: JOE SATRIANI STYLE

With his breakthrough album in 1987, *Surfing with the Alien*, Joe Satriani just about single-handedly launched the concept of the modern guitar instrumental album. In this lesson, we're going to dissect the Satch style and examine what's made him the guitar god he is today.

Riffs and Rhythm Parts

Although he normally turns heads with his dizzying lead work, Satch is quite the accomplished rhythm player as well. Let's take a look at some concepts he employs in his rhythm work.

BOOGIE RIFFS

Satriani has a bit more of a bluesy side to him than many shredders, and he loves a good boogie. Here's a typical boogie riff in A he might play, mixing elements of old and new to create something all his own.

INTERESTING HARMONIC TURNS

Other times, he'll throw a monkey wrench into an otherwise fairly standard riff, which can really turn heads. Here's that kind of idea in E.

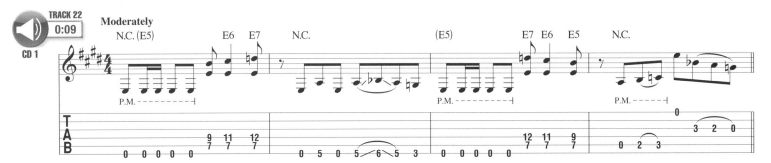

PEDAL TONE CLEAN RIFFS

Joe also crafts catchy, interesting clean-tone riffs that put different intervals, such as octaves, 5ths, and 6ths, above a low pedal tone. Here's an example of this style in E minor. You'll need to employ some fret-hand muting for the dyads that aren't on adjacent strings.

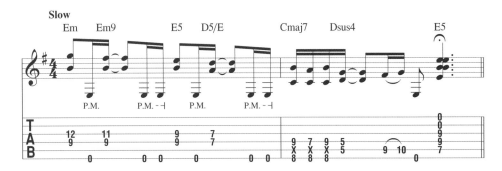

Lead Style

Joe's lead style is a bit more blues-tinged than the typical shredder, but that doesn't mean he shreds any less. It just tends to infuse his playing with a bit more personality than the average speed demon.

LEGATO TECHNIQUE

Satch is one of the undisputed all-time masters of the legato technique. He often constructs long lines with three-notes-per-string patterns that rise and fall within the scope of a larger melodic contour. This is usually done with a rhapsodic sense of rhythm; he's really aiming for certain notes on certain beats and just kind of cramming the rest of the notes in between along the way to create a flurry, as in this C major scale run. Notice that the only time you pick is when moving to a higher-pitched string.

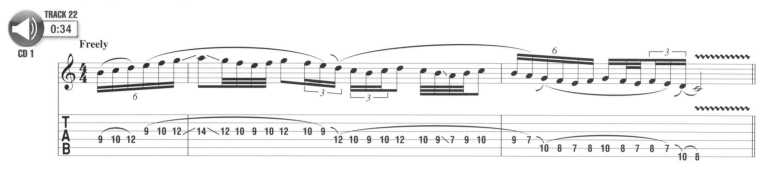

Other times, he'll use very strict rhythms with the legato technique and incorporate open strings to get lines that almost sound like a synth. Here's that type of idea in a Dorian line. Your left hand is, again, doing almost all the work here.

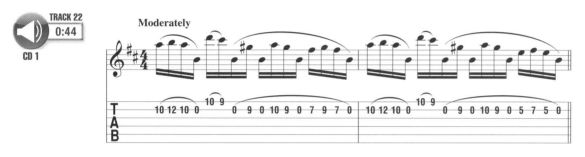

TAPPING

Satriani took the tapping technique that Eddie Van Halen popularized and gave it his own spin. One of his most striking applications is his pitch axis idea. He'll use an open string as a pedal tone and tap through various patterns, drawing from different parallel modes and scales. Here's an example in D where we're using D Ionian, D Lydian, D harmonic minor, and D Mixolydian.

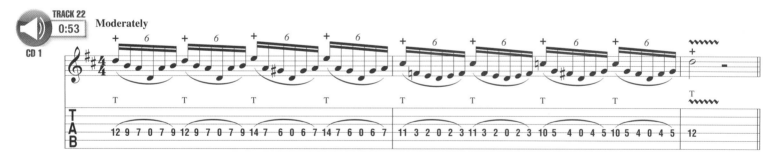

Another Satriani specialty is chordal tapping. He'll use several fingers of both hands on the fretboard to tap out chords—almost like playing a piano. Here's that idea in the key of E minor.

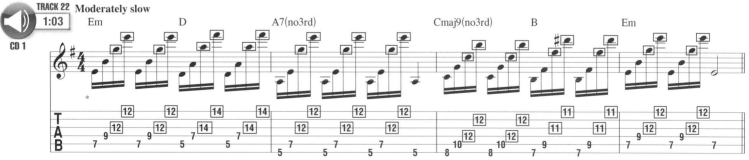

*All notes are tapped or hammered on. Squares indicate R.H. tapped notes

SIGNATURE HARMONIC TRICK

Finally let's take a look at one of Satch's signature moves: the Satch scream. This is accomplished with a pinch harmonic on the open G string while manipulating the whammy bar with the left hand. Check out the audio to hear a demonstration.

Since he arrived on the scene in the mid-eighties, Steve Vai has remained at the top of the heap in the rock guitar world. With tons of style and chops to spare, he has an extremely fertile imagination when it comes to guitar, and he's not afraid to use it. In this lesson, we'll take a look at some of the tricks he has up his sleeve that make him so uniquely inimitable.

Rhythm Parts

There's no denying that Steve turns most heads with his lead work, but he's also one hell of a rhythm player, so we'll start there. Let's check out a few of his favorite devices to use when he's not flailing away on the upper regions of the neck.

MIXING CHORDS WITH SINGLE NOTES

One of the ways Vai keeps his rhythm parts interesting is by mixing chords with single notes during a riff. Here's an example of this kind of thing in A.

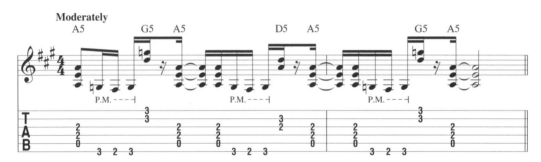

DRONING STRINGS

On clean rhythm parts, Steve often frets the lower portion of a chord on strings 6–3 and leaves the top two strings open to serve as drones throughout, resulting in some colorful harmonies.

Solo Style

Vai's been one of the most exciting soloists since the beginning. Let's take a look at a few ear-yanking concepts he's used along the way.

WIDE INTERVALS

Steve has a penchant for wide intervals and angular melodies. He'll often climb up 4ths or 5ths en route to a target note on the high E string, for example. Here's an example of this idea in an E minor lick.

This can be even more ear-grabbing as well. Check out this idea.

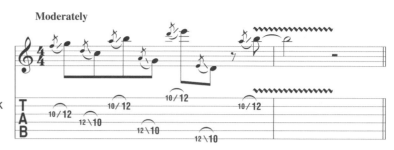

ODD RHYTHMS

Playing with Zappa in the early days certainly rubbed off on Vai, and he developed a strong command of odd rhythms, such as groups of five or seven. When played more slowly—as in five 8th notes in the space of four, for instance—the effect can be quite striking. Here's that idea in a D Dorian lick.

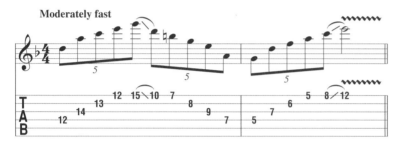

WHAMMY

You can't talk about Vai without mentioning the bar; he's pretty much the undisputed king of all things whammy. One of his favorite moves is the flutter. To create this effect, play a note and then quickly swat the end of the bar, as if trying to swat a fly, so that it quickly dips down and then snaps back into place.

TAPPING

And let's not forget Vai's formidable tapping skills; he's one of the scariest tappers around. He'll often skip strings, making use of two tapping fingers in the process, to create some scary lines like this one in D Dorian.

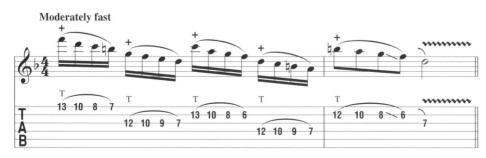

LESSON #24: BILLY GIBBONS STYLE

With a peso in hand and a Texas-sized beard, the Reverend Billy Gibbons and ZZ Top carved out their own unique blues-rock niche in the eighties. In the process, they ruled both the charts and MTV—not too bad for the "little ol' band from Texas."

Rhythm Style

For a blues band, ZZ Top mixed it up quite a bit, and Gibbons pulled out some inventive rhythm playing along the way, often mixing power chords, dyads, and other colorful voicings. Let's take a look at some of his rhythm guitar preferences.

BOOGIE RIFFS

Of course, it goes without saying that Billy could boogie. Here's a characteristic riff that borrows much from John Lee Hooker's brand of blues. Billy uses hybrid picking (pick and fingers) for this type of thing.

THE FUNKIER SIDE OF THINGS

He also had a funkier side too. Here's a riff reminiscent of his work in the late seventies.

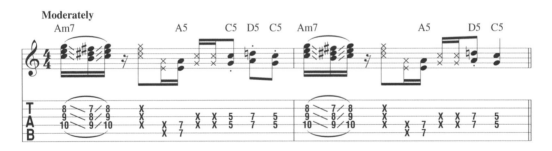

COMBINING DIFFERENT PARTS

Gibbons would also dress up a slow blues by combining different rhythm parts. For example, he might combine a muted power chord pattern (not shown here, but heard on the CD) with sustained chords, like this.

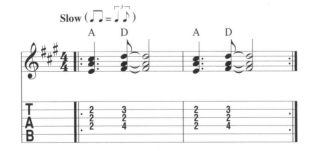

POWER CHORDS AND DYADS

In more of a rock context, Gibbons works his power chords and dyads into memorable hooks, like this riff in C. Notice the palm muting mixed in.

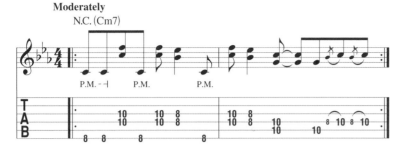

Lead Style

When it comes to lead playing, Gibbons is famous for his sublime tone, and, with his trusty "Pearly Gates" ('59 Les Paul) by his side, he milks every note for all it's got.

MINOR PENTATONIC HOOKS

He gets most of his mileage out of the trusty ol' minor pentatonic blues box, but he manages to craft some mighty memorable phrases from it, such as this one in C.

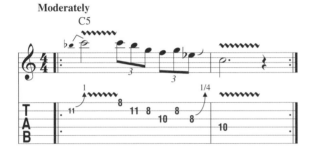

RINGING DYADS

Another favorite Gibbons-ism is the use of ringing dyads. Here's an example of this idea in the key of A. The minor 3rd and 4th are common intervals with this idea.

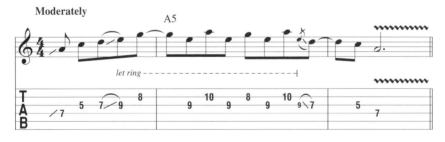

PINCH HARMONICS

Of course, you can't talk about Gibbons without mentioning the pinch harmonic. Choke up on the pick so that your thumb brushes against the string. You can move your pick along the length of the string to get different pitched harmonics to come out.

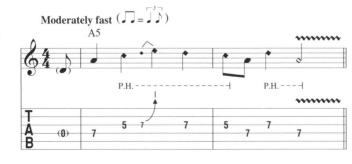

HYBRID PICKING FOR RHYTHM GUITAR

If you've never dabbled in hybrid picking before, you're missing out on a whole slew of possibilities. It can make many things easier to play, lend a different sound, or simply allow you to play things that are impossible with the pick alone. In this lesson, we'll take a look at the technique and how it applies to rhythm guitar.

The Basics

Hybrid picking refers to the use of both the pick and the pick-hand fingers to pluck the strings. To get started, try plucking these chords by using your pick on string 4, your second finger on string 3, and your third finger on string 2.

Now, we'll use the same picking hand method (pick, second, and third finger), but we'll move back and forth between two different string sets.

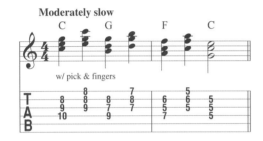

And finally, using the same pick-hand method, we'll arpeggiate through the chords, shifting between the two string sets. For each triplet, your plucking should be: pick, second finger, third finger.

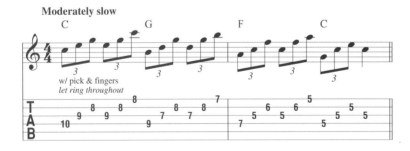

Now that you've got the basic idea down, let's check out how we can apply it in some different ways.

BOOGIE-STYLE RIFFS

Hybrid picking is excellent for those John Lee Hooker/ZZ Top-style boogie riffs. In this example in A, your second and third fingers remain on strings 4 and 3, respectively. The pick takes all the notes on strings 5 and 6.

ARPEGGIOS

As we briefly saw several examples back (with single-note triplets), hybrid picking can make arpeggios much less demanding on the picking hand. Here's a typical riff in E that demonstrates this. Since the pinky is smaller than the other fingers, it's rarely used to pluck the strings. Therefore, for this pattern, most people pluck strings 4 and 3 with the pick using consecutive downstrokes. The second and third fingers take the notes on the two high strings.

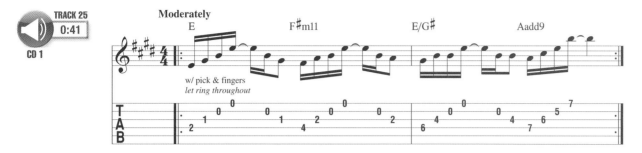

Along these same lines, hybrid picking makes an excellent choice when you need to move quickly between normal picking technique and the Travis picking style. In this example, the pick rocks back and forth between strings 5 and 4 throughout, the second finger handles all the notes on string 3, and the third finger handles the notes on strings 2 and 1.

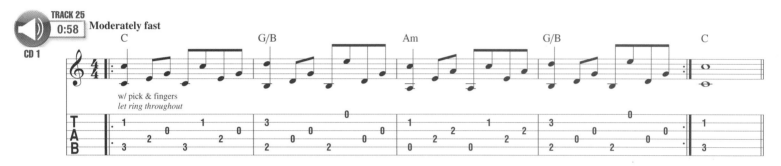

OPEN-VOICED TRIADS

Hybrid picking is also perfect for a "piano attack" on open-voiced triads—à la Eric Johnson. In this example, we're mainly using notes on strings 5, 4, and 2, but we have a few that use the 5–3–2 string group as well. This will give you some practice with shifting your pick-hand's second finger back and forth between strings 4 and 3. The third finger plucks string 2 throughout.

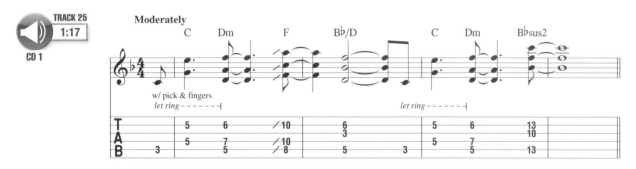

COUNTRY/SOUTHERN ROCK

Those snappy country rhythms are almost always the product of hybrid picking. Here's an example in B to demonstrate. Fingers 2 and 3 (of the pick hand) stay on strings 4 and 3 throughout. The pick plays the notes on string 5, but it also plays the dead notes on string 4 in between the finger-plucked dyads—chicken pickin' style. To achieve this sound, plant your fingers in plucking position on the strings to deaden them. When you pluck string 4 with the pick, you'll get the muted "cluck" sound.

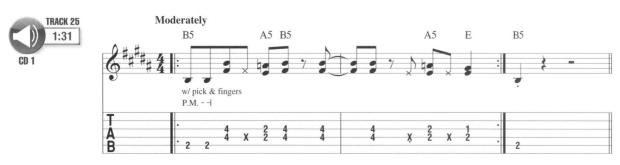

LESSON #26: HYBRID PICKING FOR LEAD GUITAR

We rock guitarists all love our picks, but we can help some of our licks out by using the technique of hybrid picking, in which both the pick and the fingers are used to pluck the strings. Besides providing a different sound—and an essential one for the country style—it also makes some licks much easier to play. With a well-developed hybrid picking technique, your lead possibilities expand exponentially. That's what this lesson is all about.

The Basics

Hybrid picking refers to the use of both the pick and the pick-hand fingers to pluck the strings. Generally speaking, when using the technique in a lead context, the pick hand fingers—almost always either the second or third, or both—take the place of upstrokes normally played with the pick. In other words, the pick normally picks down, and the fingers pluck up.

Exercises

Let's check out a few exercises to get a feel for it.

EXERCISE 1

In this first example, use your pick for all the notes on string 4, and use your second finger for all the notes on string 3.

EXERCISE 2

Now we'll bring the third finger in to play on string 2. Your second and third fingers should be acting like one double-bladed pick here, and the notes on strings 3 and 2 should be sounding absolutely simultaneously.

EXERCISE 3

You can do a lot more with this technique than just going back and forth between pick and fingers. When you employ hammer-ons or pull-offs, you can make excellent use of hybrid picking. Here's a simple example from A minor pentatonic to demonstrate this idea. The second finger is plucking the E note on string 2; the pick is plucking the notes on strings 3 and 4. At the end of the audio track, you'll hear this lick being sped up to show how easy it becomes for the right hand once you get the hang of it.

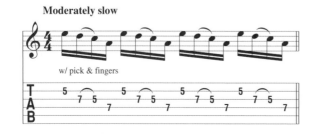

Licks

All right, now that you've gotten your feet wet, let's jump in with hybrid picking licks.

LICK 1

The picking on this first one is simple; the second finger plucks all the notes on string 1, and the pick does the rest.

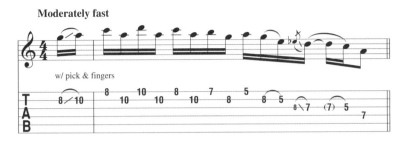

LICK 2

Here's a southern-fried lick in C that uses a syncopated three-against-four pattern. The pick plays all the notes on string 4 and the dead note on string 3 at the end; the fingers play all the double stops.

LICK 3

This is a quick, bluesy descending lick for which hybrid picking just seems to be made. You'll get some nice practice shifting down to different string groups with this one. The right-hand fingering is given in the music: P = pick, 2 = second finger, 3 = third finger.

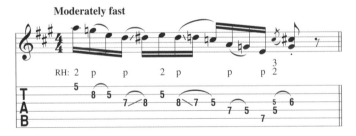

LICK 4

And to close out this lesson, let's check out a great country-ish ending lick in A that finishes with a pedal steel-type bend on the lower strings. Again, the right-hand fingering is shown.

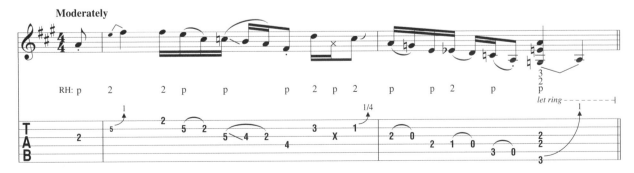

If this technique feels a bit unnatural to you, just give it some time. Eventually, it will feel as normal as standard picking. The real magic happens when you're able to switch back and forth smoothly between the two. This is also a specific skill, because you'll most likely be using slightly different hand positions for each. But you'll get there eventually, and you'll be happy you did. Have fun!

THE MINOR HEXATONIC SCALE

We're all familiar with the minor pentatonic scale. And even if you don't think you are, I guarantee you're familiar with its sound. It's been the melodic basis for more classic solos than you could shake a whammy bar at. Slightly more elusive, but incredibly expressive is the minor hexatonic scale. A favorite of such lyrical players as Eric Johnson, David Gilmour, and Mark Knopfler, it can add a whole new color to your tonal palette. In this lesson, we'll learn what it is and how to use it.

So What the Hex Is It?

Bad joke—cool scale. The minor hexatonic scale is, as the name implies, a six-tone scale. We can easily create it by adding the 2nd tone to the minor pentatonic scale. Therefore, its intervallic formula is 1–2–♭3–4–5–♭7. Let's check out a common fingering for A minor hexatonic around fifth position. In these diagrams, the root note (A, in this case) is shown as an open circle, and the 2nd tone (B, in this case) is shown as a gray dot.

 TRACK 27 0:00 CD 1

A MINOR HEXATONIC – SCALE FORM 1

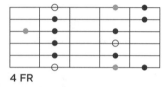

4 FR

Just as the minor pentatonic can be played all across the neck in five different scale forms, so can the minor hexatonic scale. (Even though it has six notes, there are really only five different scale forms, because beginning on either the 2nd or ♭3rd note results in the same fretboard position.) Here's another really common spot for it. If our first diagram was scale form 1, this would be scale form 4, which is in twelfth position.

 TRACK 27 0:16 CD 1

A MINOR HEXATONIC – SCALE FORM 4

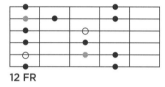

12 FR

As with any new scale you come across, you should take the time to learn it in every form. Here are the remaining forms for A minor hexatonic.

A MINOR HEXATONIC – SCALE FORM 2

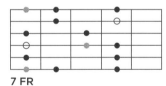

7 FR

A MINOR HEXATONIC – SCALE FORM 3

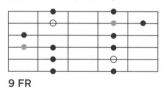

9 FR

A MINOR HEXATONIC – SCALE FORM 5

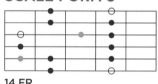

14 FR

How Do We Use It?

For the most part, any place you can use the minor pentatonic scale, you can use the minor hexatonic scale. It's simply a more colorful alternative and can really make the difference between a stock phrase and an incredibly melodic one. As with any scale, you don't have to use it exclusively. You could spend the majority of your solo in the minor pentatonic scale and then only use the minor hexatonic for a few chosen phrases. Again, the only difference between the two is the presence of the 2nd (or 9th) in the hexatonic, so they will sound identical until you make use of that note (which will make a big difference). Let's check out some licks so we can hear how it sounds.

LICK 1

This first one in A minor begins with a super stock pentatonic bending phrase and then moves into A minor hexatonic for the descent. We make use of a melodic 3rds sequence at the end: C–A–B–G–A.

 TRACK 27 0:31 CD 1

LICK 2

Here's one in D minor that makes use of the 2nd only once for a bend-and-release move on the high E string. After the two pentatonic phrases in the beginning, that 2nd really leaps out.

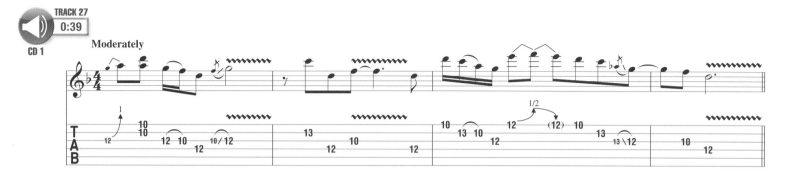

LICK 3

In this lick, the 9th is used more liberally throughout the line. It's in E minor and takes place in scale form 4, but notice how the 9th is also played on string 3 at fret 11 in order to facilitate the two-notes-per-string architecture during that portion of the lick.

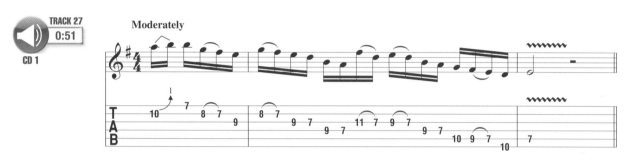

LICK 4

Here's another one from scale form 4. This one is in B minor and is a bit more angular, and we end on the colorful 9th.

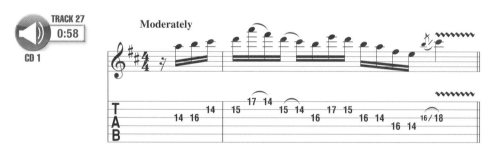

LICK 5

This final lick in C minor shows how the minor hexatonic is sometimes applied in a bluesier context. The 9th (D) is featured at the top of a quick sweep up the tonic minor triad (Cm). This sounds really nice in a mid-tempo minor blues shuffle.

LESSON #28: HARMONICS

With their brilliant tone and seemingly magical mechanics, harmonics have fascinated guitarists for generations. Due to space constraints, we won't be able to cover every type of possible harmonic—and there are a lot—but we will cover the ones that are essential to rock guitar, including natural harmonics, pinch harmonics, and tapped harmonics.

Natural Harmonics

Natural harmonics are normally the first type learned on the guitar. To play a natural harmonic, you touch the string—but don't push it down to the fretboard—at specific points (called nodes), pluck the string, and then quickly remove your finger. You can touch at different points along the string to produce different pitches. For the clearest tone, you should touch the string *directly over the fret wire*—not slightly behind it as in normal fretting technique. Touching the 12th fret harmonic produces a note one octave above the open string.

TRACK 28
0:00
CD 1

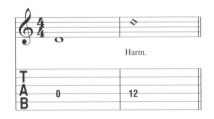

It's beyond the scope of this book to go into the science behind all of this, but the short story is that the available harmonic nodes on any string follow the harmonic series. Here are the most commonly used natural harmonics available on each open string and the note they produce relative to the open string.

Fret of Harmonic	Pitch Produced
12	One octave higher
7	One octave and a 5th higher
5	Two octaves higher
4	Two octaves and a major 3rd higher

Pinch Harmonics

With pinch harmonics (also known as "pick harmonic" or "squeal"), we're fretting notes normally with our fret hand and allowing the thumb of our pick hand to make contact with the string as we pick it. By picking in different spots along the string, you can create different pitched harmonics with the same fretted note. Listen to this example, where we're creating several different pitched harmonics all on this fretted A note.

TRACK 28
0:10
CD 1

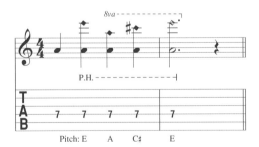

To hear absolute mastery of this technique in a metal context, listen to Zakk Wylde. For a bluesy take on the technique, ZZ Top's Billy Gibbons is the one to check out.

Tapped Harmonics

Another type of artificial harmonic is the tapped harmonic. Fret a note and then quickly and forcefully tap the string a specific distance of frets higher to sound a harmonic. Tap directly above the fret wire to sound the harmonic clearly, and don't push the string down to the fretboard; get off it instantly.

One variety of this technique, which is sometimes called a touch harmonic, involves picking a note normally and then touching or tapping the string at the specified fret to sound the harmonic.

TRACK 28
0:19
CD 1

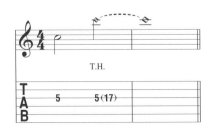

Alternatively, you can sound the harmonic right off by silently fretting and tapping the specified fret immediately. This is more difficult than the touch method.

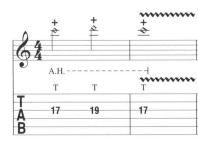

Licks

LICK 1

This first lick is in E minor and is typical of the chimey, bell-like melodies you can produce with natural harmonics.

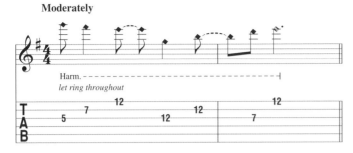

LICK 2

Here's a good example of the cool kind of quirky melodies you can come up with by mixing different natural harmonics from the 4th and 5th frets together.

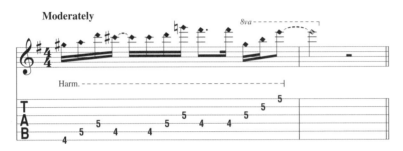

LICK 3

Now let's hear some pinch harmonics in action. This first one is a bluesy metal lick similar to something Satriani or Vai might play.

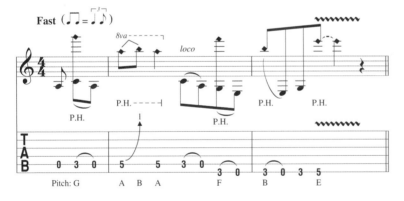

LICK 4

Finally, let's check out the tapped harmonic in this last C Mixolydian lick. You can obtain the same pitches without tapped harmonics, but it wouldn't have the same sound. I don't use the pick at all here. To sound the first note of the lick, I silently pluck the string with my tapping finger.

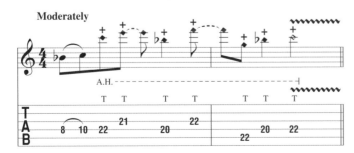

The world of harmonics is a vast one, and there are a number of types we didn't explore. If you enjoyed this introduction to the subject, I encourage you to further explore. There's much more fun to be had!

LESSON #29: ROCKABILLY STYLE

Rockabilly has always been synonymous with two things: slicked back hair and hot guitar licks. Traditionally played on hollow-body electrics, such as Gibsons or Gretschs, rockabilly players usually run through tube amps with a relatively clean tone. A slapback delay is often used to create a thicker sound, which is more audible when playing short notes. In this lesson, we'll learn how to rock around the clock and pick a few hot licks in the process.

Rhythm Playing

Since rockabilly is about more than just flashy licks, let's take a look at some rhythm concepts first.

CHORD FORMS

Guitarists mainly use a mixture of triads, seventh, ninth, sixth, 6/9, and even diminished chords on occasion. Let's take a look at some typical chord forms.

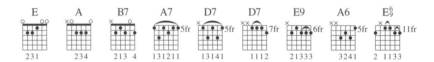

STOP-TIME

Stop-time hits are very common during the verses of a song. Barre forms are often employed here, and the I chord is usually approached by a half step below, like this example in G, which would be followed by the IV chord.

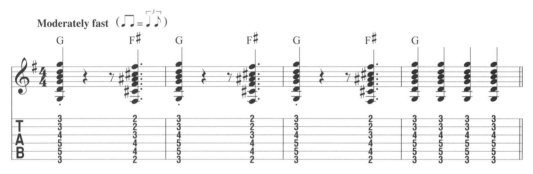

BOOGIE PATTERNS

Many songs use low-register boogie patterns to fuel the rhythm. Aside from the standard 5th-6th Chuck Berry-type riffs, you have these cool single-note bass line patterns.

CHORD STABS

Sometimes, the electric will highlight the rhythm with some syncopated chord stabs; sixth, seventh, and ninth chords are very common for this, as demonstrated here.

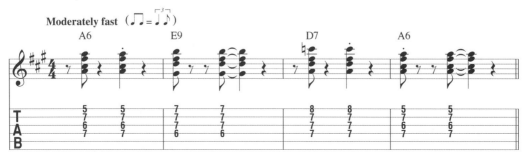

Lead Style

Ok, let's get to the solos. Rockabilly was one of the earliest styles to feature guitar solos as highlights of a song.

E MAJOR PENTATONIC SCALE

The major pentatonic scale is commonly used in rockabilly. Here's a moveable fingering in the key of E with circled root notes.

E MINOR PENTATONIC SCALE

The minor pentatonic is the other most frequently used scale. Here it is in E.

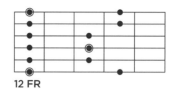

LICK 1

The notes from the major and minor pentatonic scales are combined all the time in rockabilly licks to get things like this.

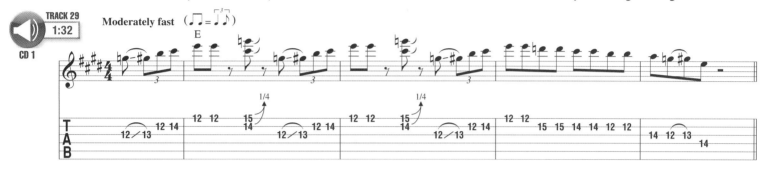

LICK 2

This one combines major and minor pentatonic scales in the key of A. It moves from the IV chord, D7, back to the I chord.

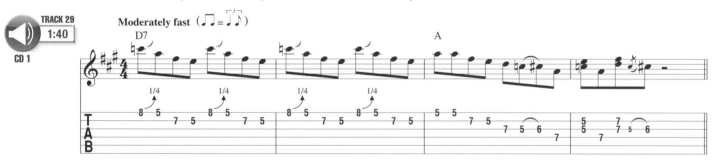

LICK 3

Since the key of E is so common, the open position is also used with rapid-fire pull-off licks such as this one, which finishes off with a couple of E9 chord jabs.

LICK 4

Let's finish off with a classic outro lick. This one's in D and concludes with a big D6/9 chord.

LESSON #30: GUIDE TO USING EFFECTS

Many players get hooked on effects pedals the moment they step on their first distortion box. Though there are plenty of purists out there, the majority of guitarists love their toys, and effects pedals are to guitarists what matchbox cars are to five-year-old boys. In this lesson, we'll take a look at some tips to get the most use out of those stomperiffic boxes.

Categories of Effects

Just about every pedal can be grouped within a larger category (though there are certainly some oddballs out there). Let's take a look at these now.

▶ **Distortion:** Overdrive, distortion, fuzz, and the like.

▶ **Dynamics:** Compressor, boost, volume pedal, and noise gate.

▶ **EQ/Filter:** EQ pedal, wah-wah, envelope filter, and talk box.

▶ **Modulation:** Broad category with chorus, flanger, vibrato, tremolo, ring modulator, etc.

▶ **Pitch Effects:** Pitch shifter/harmonizer, octave pedal.

▶ **Time-based:** Delay, echo, reverb, etc.

General Order of Effects

Here's a generally accepted order of effect types, which usually results in what most people consider a pure tone.

1. Filter type effects (wah, envelope filter, etc.)

2. Compressor

3. Distortion

4. EQ

5. Harmonizers, octave pedals

6. Modulation effects

7. Noise gates/volume pedals

8. Time-based (delay, echo, reverb)

This is only a guide, however, and there are no steadfast rules. Experiment!

Tips for Various Effects

TRACK 30 0:00
CD 1

COMPRESSOR

A compressor makes the loudest notes softer, which enables you to turn up the overall level. It reduces the difference between your loud and soft pick attacks. It's used often in country and funk styles and usually avoided by blues players. Here's an example of a riff played first without compression and then with.

TRACK 30 0:28
CD 1

DISTORTION/OVERDRIVE

Who hasn't stomped on a distortion pedal? Many use them to provide a bit of grit to an otherwise clean tone, some add even more distortion to a fully distorted amp, and others use them with a clean amp to achieve a fully distorted sound. Here's an example of a lick played three times: first clean, next with a hint of overdrive, and then with a good amount of gain from a distortion pedal. Notice how distortion naturally compresses as well.

TRACK 30 0:49
CD 1

NOISE GATE

A noise gate is kind of like your personal little minion, standing by your fully cranked amp and rolling off the volume when you stop playing. Listen to the difference it makes on the audio. Even with high gain, it's completely quiet during the pauses.

TRACK 30 0:58
CD 1

DELAY/ECHO

A delay or echo pedal generates distinct repeats of the notes you play. You can set the time or rate (measured in milliseconds), level, and the feedback, among other things. A very short delay time with one repeat (low feedback setting) is known as a "slapback" effect. Check out the audio to first hear a slapback effect and then a longer delay effect with higher feedback setting.

To create the famous "timed delay trick," set it for one repeat with a strong level. The time should be set to a dotted 8th note. When you play straight 8th notes, the delayed notes fall in between, creating a seamless 16th-note line.

TRACK 30 1:13
CD 1

REVERB

Reverb simulates the reverberation you hear in a cave, large/small room, concert hall, etc. It can be non-existent, very subtle, or extremely lush, as heard on the CD.

TRACK 30 1:31
CD 1

CHORUS/FLANGER/PHASER/TREMOLO

These are all slightly different ways to add dimension to the sound and are most common on longer notes. They can be subtle, drastic, or in between. Listen to hear a riff played clean and then with a chorus, flanger, phaser, and tremolo.

TRACK 30 2:31
CD 1

WAH/AUTO WAH/ENVELOPE FILTER

These are common for that seventies "waka-waka" funk sound. They basically sweep between a very bass-heavy tone to a very trebly one.

The bottom line with these effects is that your imagination is the only limit. Try them alone; try them all together. Do whatever makes a cool sound. I guarantee you'll have a lot of fun trying.

LESSON #31: RHYTHMIC IMITATION

Rhythm is one half of every melody, and it can create some striking effects when put to use in specific ways. One such method is rhythmic imitation—where one phrase imitates the rhythm of another. In this lesson, we'll talk about this powerful tool and how we can harness it to make a memorable statement in our solos or riffs.

What Is It?

With rhythmic imitation, the idea is to play one rhythm and then echo all or part of it with another phrase. In other words, the notes may change between phrase A and phrase B, but the rhythm will be nearly identical. We'll look at simple and advanced imitation.

Simple Imitation

Below we see the simplest form of rhythmic imitation. In the first example, play a certain rhythm in the first measure, and then we play the same exact rhythm in the second measure, only using a different melody. This helps create a rhythmic hook onto which the listener can grasp. In the second example, we're imitating a shorter rhythmic fragment that only lasts two beats, so the phrases begin every two beats instead of every measure.

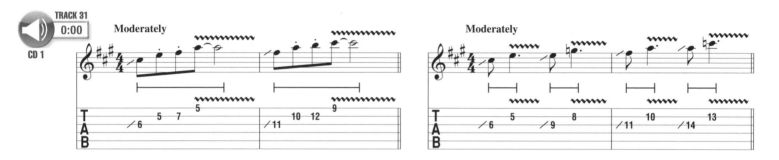

So, in simple imitation, we're repeating on the same exact place in every measure, every two beats, or every beat. There are no rhythmic surprises.

Advanced Imitation

With advanced imitation, we'll repeat the same rhythm, but it won't necessarily begin in the same spot with reference to the underlying beat. In Phrase A below, for example, we see simple imitation at work; the phrase is repeated every two beats, starting on the beat each time. In Phrase B, however, the phrase repeats every 1 1/2 beats, resulting in an on-the-beat/off-the-beat rhythm that's very stimulating. This is advanced imitation.

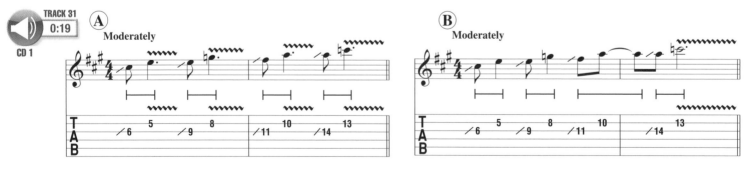

So, we're still imitating the same rhythm: one 8th note followed by a quarter note. But in Phrase B, instead of waiting an 8th rest so that the phrase starts on the beat each time (as in Phrase A), we're repeating it right away. This type of imitation can get as far out there and continue for as long as you want—just make sure you (and your band) are able to keep your place in the music! Next, let's check out a few licks that use imitation.

LICK 1 (SIMPLE IMITATION)

This first one is a classic example of simple imitation and is commonly used at the beginning of a solo to build a foundation.

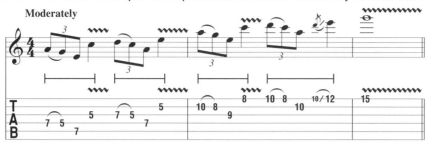

LICK 2 (SIMPLE IMITATION)

Here, we're still using simple imitation, but we're repeating two different phrase lengths. The first one lasts two beats and is repeated on beat 3 of measure 1. In measure 2, we speed up to a one-beat phrase that's comprised of four 16th notes. This phrase repeats on beat 2 of measure 2.

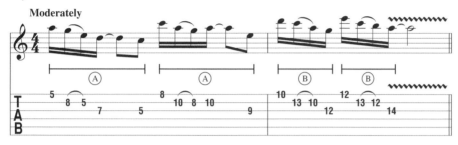

LICK 3 (ADVANCED IMITATION)

The rest of our examples use advanced imitation and are all set to a drumbeat so you can hear how they sit within the measure. This first one repeats a two-note phrase every fourth 16th note (each mini-phrase lasts three 16th notes).

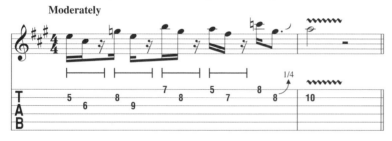

LICK 4 (ADVANCED IMITATION)

Here's one where we immediately repeat a mini-phrase from B minor pentatonic that lasts six 16th notes. Therefore, the phrases repeat every 1 1/2 beats.

LICK 5 (ADVANCED IMITATION)

This example is really stretching out. The first phrase, repeated twice, lasts a total of 3 1/2 beats. The second phrase, which begins on beat 2 of measure 3, lasts a total of 2 1/2 beats. It's repeated immediately one time before it gives way to a final conclusive phrase.

This works with riffs too. Check out the end of the main riff to AC/DC's "Back in Black" or the main riff in Stone Temple Pilot's "Vasoline."

LESSON #32: THE MINOR PENTATONIC SCALE

The minor pentatonic scale is the first scale learned by many guitarists and certainly the one most frequently used. It's provided the melodic foundation to some of the most classic solos and riffs of all time, and it continues to see just as much action today as ever. If scales were food, the minor pentatonic would probably be meat and potatoes. In this lesson, we'll learn what it is and what we can do with it.

Construction

The minor pentatonic scale is a five-note scale ("penta" meaning five) that can be built by omitting two notes from a natural minor scale. The formula for a natural minor scale is 1–2–♭3–4–5–♭6–♭7. An A minor scale, for example, would contain the notes A–B–C–D–E–F–G.

A MINOR SCALE

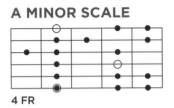

4 FR

To create the minor pentatonic scale, we simply remove the 2nd and ♭6th notes, which makes the formula 1–♭3–4–5–♭7. So, the notes of A minor pentatonic would be A–C–D–E–G. Since this scale form doesn't contain any open strings, it's a moveable form, meaning we can move the root anywhere on string 6 to play the scale in a different key. For example, if we move the form up two frets to seventh position, we have a B minor pentatonic scale.

A MINOR PENTATONIC SCALE

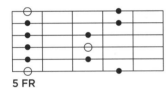

5 FR

B MINOR PENTATONIC SCALE

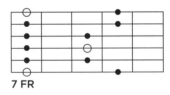

7 FR

This form is sometimes called the "box" position because of the box shape it resembles on the fretboard.

Box Position Licks & Riffs

Let's take a look at what we can do with this scale now.

LICK 1

We'll be moving the form around to different keys, but we'll start with an A minor pentatonic lick.

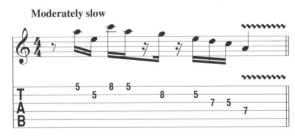

LICK 2

Here's one in D minor, which puts us in tenth position. This one includes some bends that are commonly used with this scale form.

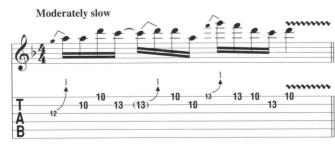

RIFF 1

This scale is great for riffs as well! Here's an example from C minor (eighth position).

Other Forms

Although many guitarists stick with the box form, the minor pentatonic scale can actually be played all over the neck. In fact, there are five forms that are all interconnected. Working in the key of A minor, here are the five forms laid out across the entire neck. Form 1 is the box position you already know.

A MINOR PENTATONIC – ALL FIVE SCALE FORMS

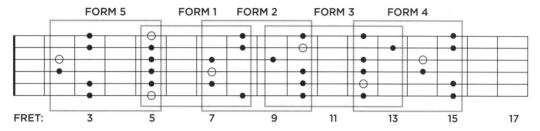

Let's close out with a few examples that use other forms. All of these will be in the key of A minor for simplicity, but these other forms can be transposed anywhere else just like the box position.

LICK 3

This lick is from scale form 4—probably the second most common pattern.

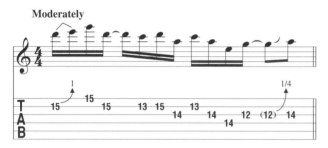

LICK 4

Here's one from scale form 2. Consequently, you may know this form by its other name: form 1 of C major pentatonic. (A minor is the relative minor of C major, so they share the same notes.)

RIFF 2

In this riff, we're connecting forms 5 and 1 with a slide. This is another very common maneuver.

THE MAJOR PENTATONIC SCALE

Though it's not quite as popular as its close relative, the minor pentatonic, the major pentatonic scale is a common source of melody found in rock, blues, and especially country, among other styles. It's got a bright, snappy sound, which is sometimes just what the doctor ordered. In this lesson, we're going to learn how to build the major pentatonic scale and what we can do with it.

Construction

The major pentatonic scale is a five-note scale ("penta" meaning five) that can be built by omitting two notes from a major scale. The formula for a major scale is 1–2–3–4–5–6–7. A C major scale, for example, would contain the notes C–D–E–F–G–A–B.

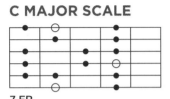

To create the major pentatonic scale, we simply remove the 4th and 7th notes, which makes the formula 1–2–3–5–6. So, the notes of C major pentatonic are C–D–E–G–A. Since this scale form doesn't contain any open strings, it's a moveable form, meaning we can move the root anywhere on string 6 to play the scale in a different key. For example, if we move the form up two frets to ninth position, we have a D major pentatonic scale.

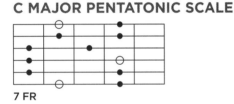

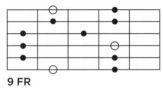

The major pentatonic scale can be played all over the neck in five different forms, which we'll look at in a bit. This is scale form 1.

Licks & Riffs from Form 1

Let's hear what we can do with this scale.

LICK 1

We'll move to different keys, but we'll start with a C major pentatonic lick.

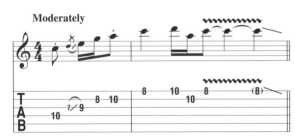

LICK 2

Here's one in D major, which puts us in ninth position. This one includes some hammer-ons and slides that are common in this form.

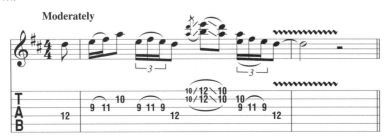

RIFF 1

This scale is great for riffs as well! Here's a Motown-sounding riff in B♭ (fifth position).

Other Forms

As previously mentioned, this scale can actually be played all over the neck; there are five forms that are all interconnected. Working in the key of C major, here are the five forms laid out across the entire neck. Form 1 is the one you already know.

C MAJOR PENTATONIC – ALL FIVE SCALE FORMS

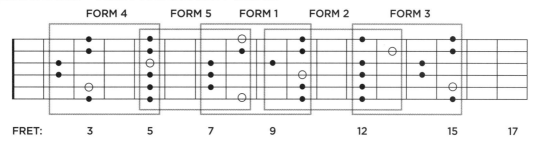

Let's close out with a few examples that use other forms. All of these will be in the key of C major for simplicity, but these other forms can be transposed anywhere too.

LICK 3

This first lick is from scale form 3—probably the second most common pattern.

LICK 4

Here's one from scale form 5. Consequently, you may know this form by its other name: form 1 of A minor pentatonic. (A minor is the relative minor of C major, so A minor pentatonic and C major pentatonic share the exact same notes.)

RIFF 2

In this riff, we're connecting forms 4 and 5 with a slide. This is another very common maneuver.

Many guitarists are intimately familiar with both the major and minor pentatonic scales, but not nearly as many are adept at combining them. Doing so increases your melodic repertoire significantly, and it will often feel as though a whole new world has opened up. Players like Eric Clapton, Jimi Hendrix, Angus Young, Steve Vai, and Zakk Wylde make regular use of this concept; in this lesson, we'll learn why.

Same Root–Different Notes: Parallel Scales

The first thing we need to make clear is that we're not talking about a relative minor relationship here. In other words, C major pentatonic, and its relative minor, A minor pentatonic, contain the exact same notes: C–D–E–G–A. The only difference is that C major pentatonic treats C as the root, and A minor pentatonic treats A as the root. "Combining" these two scales isn't really combining anything, since they're already essentially the same scale.

However, combining *parallel* scales makes a big difference. What's the difference between a relative minor and a parallel minor? Basically, it boils down to this:

▶ Relative scales share the same notes but have a different tonic.

▶ Parallel scales share the same tonic but have different notes.

So, the parallel minor of C major pentatonic is C minor pentatonic. That's the relationship we're looking at here. So let's check out the most common fingerings for each in the key of C; these would be scale form 1 of each.

C MAJOR PENTATONIC SCALE – FORM 1

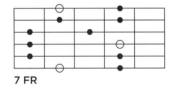

7 FR

C MINOR PENTATONIC SCALE – FORM 1

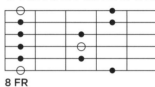

8 FR

Of course, since no open strings are used, these forms are moveable. By sliding the roots around on the sixth string, we can play these scales in any key.

When to Combine

As evidenced in the blues, our ears will accept the sound of a ♭3rd (as featured in the minor pentatonic scale) played over a major or dominant chord, provided we exercise a bit of discretion—i.e., we don't just flatly sustain the ♭3rd for days and let it clash with the chord's major 3rd. However, the opposite is not true. If you make a habit of playing major 3rds (as featured in the major pentatonic scale) over a minor chord, you're probably not going to get called back on very many gigs. Therefore, as a general rule, it's best to employ this combination concept in major key songs.

Licks from Form 1

Now let's check out a few licks that combine form 1 of the major and parallel minor pentatonic scales.

LICK 1

This first one is in the key of C.

LICK 2

This one's in the key of A, so our scale forms are down around fifth position.

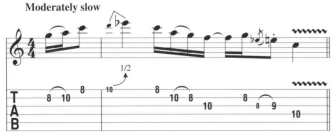

Other Scale Forms

Just as with any scale, it's highly beneficial to learn the major and minor pentatonic all over the neck. Here are full neck diagrams for C major and C minor pentatonic that show all five forms of each. Again, this whole system can be moved anywhere for other keys.

C MAJOR PENTATONIC – ALL FIVE FORMS

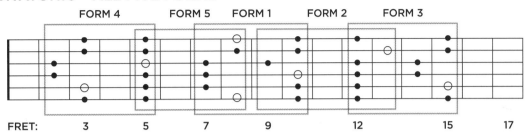

C MINOR PENTATONIC – ALL FIVE FORMS

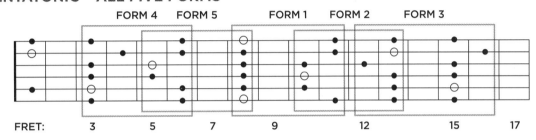

Let's wrap it up with a few licks that make use of the other forms.

LICK 3

This one's in E and is in the Eric Clapton vein—similar to what he played in "Badge."

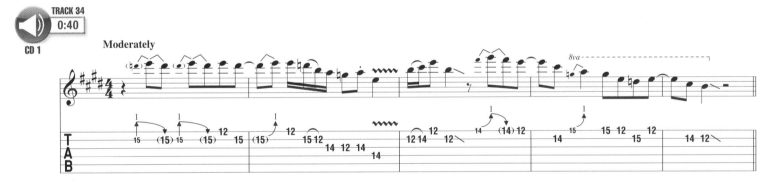

LICK 4

And here's one in G. Angus used a similar idea in "You Shook Me All Night Long."

LESSON #35: THE BLUES SCALE

Rarely do entire genres get scales named after them. However, the blues scale is a slight misnomer, because it's almost as frequently used in rock, country, and jazz as it is in blues. Regardless, it's an absolutely essential scale to know, and in this lesson, we'll learn how it's built and how it's used.

Construction

The blues scale is a six-note scale that can be built by adding one critical note to a minor pentatonic scale. The formula for a minor pentatonic scale is 1–♭3–4–5–♭7; in the key of A, this would be A–C–D–E–G.

A MINOR PENTATONIC SCALE

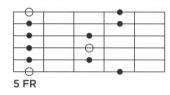

To create the blues scale, we add the ♭5th (or ♯4th), which results in a formula of 1–♭3–4–♭5–5–♭7. So, the notes of A blues scale would be A–C–D–E♭–E–G. Since this scale form doesn't contain any open strings, it's a moveable form, meaning we can move the root anywhere on string 6 to play the scale in a different key. For example, if we move the form up two frets to seventh position, we have a B blues scale.

A BLUES SCALE

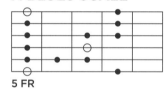

B BLUES SCALE

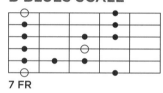

This form is sometimes called the "box" position because of the box shape it resembles on the fretboard.

Box Position Licks & Riffs

Let's check out a few blues licks from this position.

LICK 1

We'll be moving the form around to different keys, but we'll start with an A blues lick.

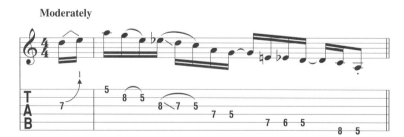

LICK 2

Here's one in D, which puts us in tenth position.

LICK 3

This one's in C and adds a few new elements. First, we bend to the blues note (G♭, in this case) on string 3—a common move. Then, we leap down from the tonic C note on string 4 to the blues note on string 5—a tritone away—continuing on down the scale.

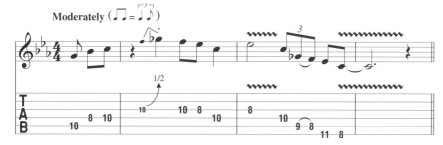

Other Scale Forms

Though many guitarists never tire of the box form, the blues scale can be played all over the neck. There are five forms that are all interconnected. Working in the key of A, here are the five forms laid out across the entire neck. Form 1 is the box position you already know.

A BLUES SCALE – ALL FIVE SCALE FORMS

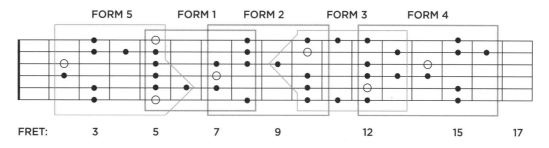

Licks from Other Forms

Let's close out with a few examples that use other forms. These will be in the key of A for simplicity, but these other forms can be transposed anywhere else, just like the box position.

LICK 4

This first lick is from scale form 5 and demonstrates two things: 1) Using the blue note only once colors the entire lick, and 2) You don't have to end on the tonic.

LICK 5

In this last example, we're connecting two forms (4 and 3) with a slide. This is another very common maneuver.

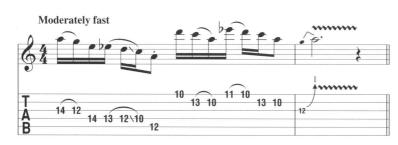

LESSON #36: THE COMPOSITE BLUES SCALE

If you've learned the major pentatonic, minor pentatonic, and blues scales, but you're still hearing some licks that seem to include other notes, it's most likely that these scales are being combined to create a more complex scale. This scale, called the composite blues scale (among other names), is the subject of this lesson, and it's what makes some licks and riffs sound much more colorful than the typical pentatonic lick.

Construction

The composite blues scale can be described as the combined notes from parallel major pentatonic and blues scales. The C composite blues scale, for example, contains the notes of C major pentatonic and C blues. The formula for a major pentatonic is 1–2–3–5–6, and the formula for the blues scale is 1–♭3–4–♭5–5–♭7. When we combine the two, we end up with the formula for the composite blues scale: 1–2–♭3–3–4–♭5–5–6–♭7.

So, a C composite blues scale would be spelled C–D–E♭–E–F–G♭–G–A–B♭. Here's a fingering for this scale around seventh position. We'll call this form 1.

TRACK 36
0:00
CD 1

C COMPOSITE BLUES SCALE – FORM 1

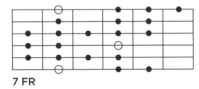
7 FR

Since this form contains no open strings, it's a moveable form, so you can slide the tonic anywhere along the sixth string to play the scale in other keys.

When to Use It

As our ears are more acclimated to accepting the ♭3rd over a major or dominant chord than accepting a major 3rd over a minor chord, it's best to use this scale when playing over a major chord progression. If you're playing over a song in the key of C major, or a blues in C, for instance, the C composite blues scale can sound great. However, if you're playing over a song in C minor, the major 3rd in the C composite blues scale, E, will clash pretty severely with the minor tonality, so it's best to avoid that note or work with another scale.

Licks from Form 1

Now let's hear what we can do with this scale.

LICK 1

As you'll no doubt hear in the solos of others, the chromatic notes (♭3rd and ♭5th) are often used as passing tones. This is demonstrated with this first lick in C.

TRACK 36
0:22
CD 1

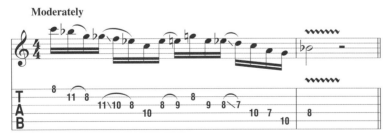

LICK 2

Here's one in A that mixes it up a good bit.

TRACK 36
0:30
CD 1

LICK 3

This lick in E really exploits the long string of chromatic notes from the 2nd to the 5th.

Other Scale Forms

As with the pentatonic scales, the composite blues scale can be played in five different forms across the neck. Due to the excess of chromatic notes, however, the forms aren't quite as clearly defined, as some players prefer to reach back for a chromatic note while others prefer to shift forward. Regardless, the forms shown below for C composite blues should be a good start. You can tailor them to your preference by moving a note or two to different strings if you'd like.

C COMPOSITE BLUES SCALE – ALL FIVE FORMS

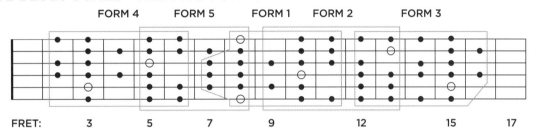

Now let's check out some licks from the rest of these forms. For simplicity, we'll remain in C, but try moving some of these up or down to other keys.

LICK 4

Here's one from form 3, which puts the long chromatic string of notes up on string 1.

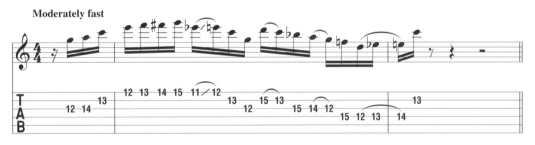

LICK 5

This lick is from form 5, which resembles the A blues scale box position. It's a bit out there.

LICK 6

And we'll close out with one that moves between forms 2 and 3.

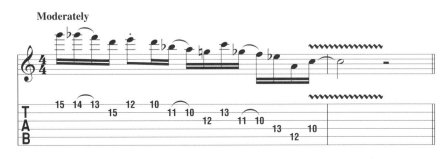

THE HARMONIC MINOR SCALE

Before Yngwie Malmsteen came along, the guitar and the harmonic minor scale made an odd pairing in rock. Of course, a few rock players had made occasional use of it, most notably Ritchie Blackmore and Randy Rhoads, but Yngwie is to the harmonic minor scale what Eddie Van Halen is to tapping; though he didn't invent it, he's certainly the one most responsible for bringing it to the masses. By the end of the eighties, almost every shredder had some harmonic minor runs under their fingers. In this lesson, we'll learn its construction and how to create some wicked-sounding neo-classical licks.

Construction

The harmonic minor scale is easiest thought of as a natural minor scale with a raised 7th. Whereas the formula for natural minor (or Aeolian mode) is 1–2–♭3–4–5–♭6–♭7, the formula for harmonic minor is 1–2–♭3–4–5–♭6–7. So the notes of A harmonic minor are A–B–C–D–E–F–G♯–A. Here's a fingering for each in A so you can hear the difference.

TRACK 37
0:00
CD 1

A NATURAL MINOR SCALE

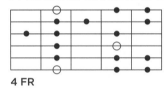

4 FR

TRACK 37
0:15
CD 1

A HARMONIC MINOR SCALE

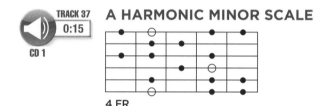

4 FR

When to Use It

This scale was created centuries ago when composers desired to hear a stronger V–i cadence in minor keys. Whereas the harmonized major scale, with its half-step leading tone between the 7th degree and the tonic, results in a major V chord, the harmonized minor scale, with its whole step interval between the ♭7th and tonic, results in a minor v chord. The latter creates a much less convincing resolution. Therefore composers started changing the v chord in minor keys to major (V), which essentially raised the 7th degree a half step from ♭7 to 7.

TRACK 37
0:32
CD 1

For example, in A minor, the ♭7th note is G. The normal v chord in the key of A minor is Em, which is spelled E–G–B. Notice that the G note is the ♭3rd of the Em chord. When we change the v chord (Em) to a major V chord (E), however, what we're actually doing is raising G a half step to G♯. Listen to the audio to hear the difference between an Am–Em–Am progression and an Am–E–Am progression. It's night and day.

All this explaining in a nutshell: if you're in a minor key, such as Am, and you see a major chord, such as E, that's the perfect place to use the harmonic minor scale.

A Harmonic Minor Scale – Other Scale Forms

As with any new scale, you should take the time to learn it across the entire neck. Here's A harmonic minor covering the full neck, with the five basic forms outlined.

A HARMONIC MINOR SCALE – ALL FIVE FORMS

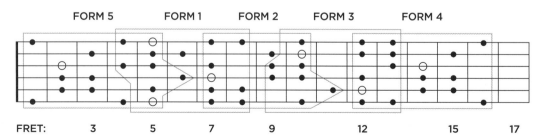

Now let's hear the scale in action.

LICK 1

We'll move to different keys here, but we'll start with one in A minor.

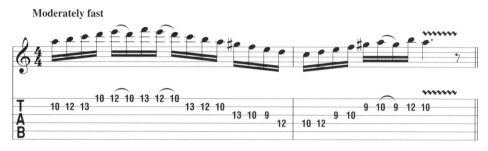

LICK 2

Here's one in B minor that makes liberal use of the legato technique.

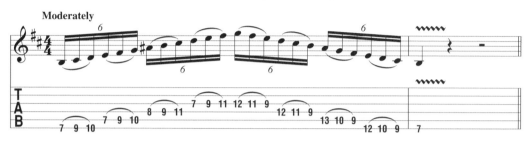

LICK 3

This lick in D minor makes use of one of Yngwie's favorite devices: the pivot note. In this case, we're pivoting off of the scale's ♭6th degree, B♭.

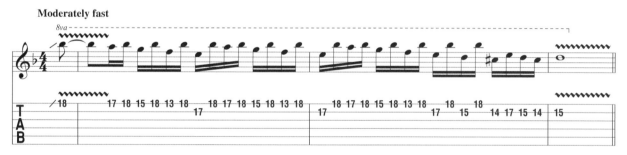

LICK 4

In this G minor example, we're moving up through several forms, repeating the same lick an octave higher each time.

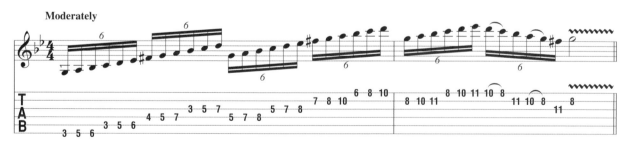

LICK 5

Finally, here's one in E minor that makes use of string skipping—something Paul Gilbert might do.

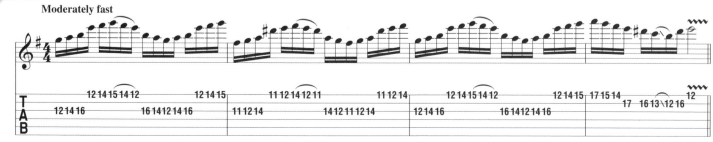

LESSON #38: SINGLE-NOTE RIFFS

Although the power chord has provided adequate fuel for many of the most classic rock songs of all time, sometimes nothing foots the bill like a single-note riff. Whether it's the stripped-down simplicity of Zeppelin's "Heartbreaker," the angular toughness of Living Colour's "Cult of Personality," or the bare-knuckled, in-your-face assault of Rage Against the Machine's "Bulls on Parade," the single-note riff has provided the single most captivating element of a whole song on more than a few occasions. In this lesson, we'll examine the concept inside and out.

Look Ma, No Power Chords!

The single-note riff is fairly self-explanatory; we're playing riffs comprised of single notes—not power chords, or other dyads, as is most often the case in rock. These are normally played on the lower strings, as they're thicker and therefore sound meatier, although there are numerous examples of higher register riffs as well. The higher the register, however, the blurrier the distinction between "riff" and "lick" becomes. We still have all the same technical devices at our disposal: palm muting, slides, hammer-ons, pull-offs, etc. And we're also more fleet-fingered, having shed the weight of needing to plant two or more fingers at one time.

Sources of Notes

Generally, single-note riffs are derived from a scale, arpeggio, or combination of both. There are those—particularly in prog rock or thrash metal—that defy any particular categorization and sound almost atonal. However, this is not the norm. Let's look at a few classic sources for single-note riffery.

The Minor Pentatonic or Blues Scale

This is the most common of all, and for good reason. It just sounds good. The only difference between the two scales is that the blues adds the ♭5th to the minor pentatonic.

A BLUES SCALE

Here's a fingering for A blues in fifth position to get you started—the ♭5 note is shown in gray—but be sure to learn the scale all over the neck as well.

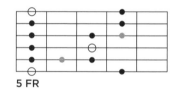

5 FR

RIFF 1

Here's a typical hard rock riff from the A minor pentatonic scale. Notice the quarter-step bends, which help lend some weight—especially when doubled by a bass or second guitar.

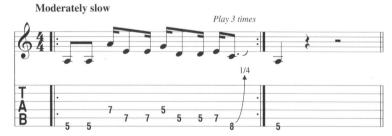

RIFF 2

This riff is from the E blues scale and works its way down to the open low E string. The syncopation in the beginning—starting on the upbeat—really kicks this one into gear.

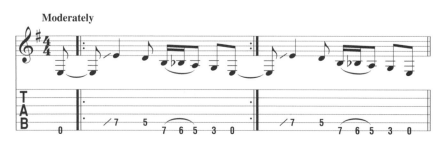

Major Pentatonic Scale

This one's not as tough sounding as the minor pentatonic or blues scale and is used more in classic rock or southern rock.

A MAJOR PENTATONIC

Here's A major pentatonic in fourth position.

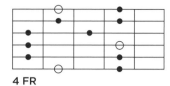

4 FR

RIFF 3

Here's a classic riff from the major pentatonic scale. In this example, we're playing a major pentatonic scale based off of each chord's root. So measure 1 is G major pentatonic, measure 2 is D major pentatonic, and measure 3 is A major pentatonic. The slides are key here for quickly shifting between forms like this.

RIFF 4

And here's an example from D major pentatonic that moves between fifth and seventh position throughout. I'm using fuzz and an octave pedal to really make the riff growl.

Natural Minor Scale

In the metal world, you have your fair share of natural minor riffs.

A MINOR SCALE (AEOLIAN MODE)

Here's A natural minor in fifth position.

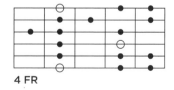

4 FR

RIFF 5

Here's a typical metal riff from the A minor scale. Notice the emphasis placed on the ♭6th tone (F). The pinch harmonic is another staple in this style.

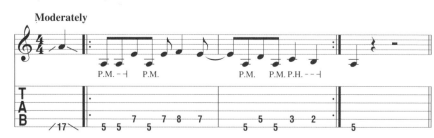

LESSON #39: CHUCK BERRY STYLE

John Lennon pretty much summed it up: "If you were going to give rock 'n' roll another name you might call it 'Chuck Berry.'" With his trademark double stops, syncopated bends, and duck walk, he casts a huge shadow across everyone who followed. One of the first great total entertainers—singer, songwriter, and guitar hero—Chuck was a force to be reckoned with. In this lesson, we'll find out why.

Rhythm Style

Chuck's rhythm style has been as influential as his lead playing, so let's start by looking at some of his trademark rhythm moves.

5TH/6TH BOOGIE PATTERNS

Berry fueled many of his songs with the classic alternating 5th and 6th boogie patterns on the lower strings.

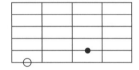 

Here's an example of this type of thing in A. It's a bit of a stretch for those sixth chords, so be sure to keep your thumb behind the neck.

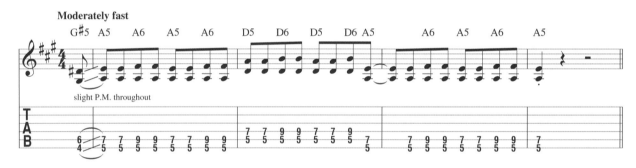

COUNTRY FEEL – ALTERNATING BASS

Chuck would also combine staccato chords with an alternating bass in some of his songs for more of a country feel. Here's an example of this type of thing in the key of D. We're alternating between the root and 5th on beats 1 and 3, respectively, and playing short, staccato chords on top for beats 2 and 4.

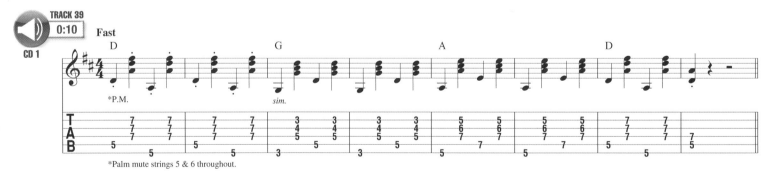

Lead Style

Now let's get into the meat of Chuck's playing—his revolutionary lead style. Like B.B. King before him and Jimi Hendrix after him, Chuck Berry rewrote the rule books for guitar with his many innovations.

DOUBLE STOPS

Without a doubt, his most signature sound was his use of double stops. A double stop is simply two notes played at the same time. They're usually on adjacent strings, but non-adjacent strings can be used as well. Next is a typical line in B consisting entirely of double stops. Try using one finger to barre each the way Chuck did.

He was also a master at bending double stops to get some crazy-sounding stuff. Here's an example of that idea in A. Notice that we're bending double-stop intervals of 3rds, 4ths, and tritones.

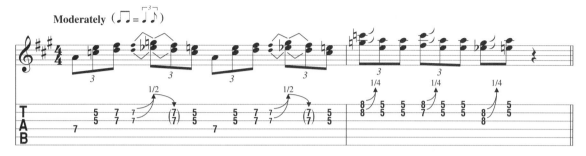

INTRO LICKS

Chuck's songs feature some of the most famous intros of all time. The most famous is an idea that mixed single notes and double stops and was mostly framed within the hybrid scale pattern we talked about earlier. Notice also the legendary syncopated unison bend move in measures 5–9 that you *can't* hear without thinking of Berry.

And here's another classic Berry-ism: the triplet-strummed augmented V chord. Chuck would usually follow this with the first line sung a capella before the band would join in. Since this is a D+, the song would be in the key of G.

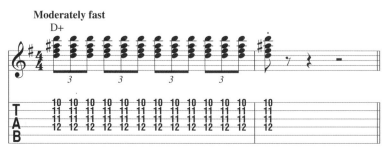

LESSON #40: BOOGIE RHYTHMS

From Chuck Berry to the Beatles to Stevie Ray Vaughan, boogie rhythms have been a mainstay in the world of rock guitar. In this lesson, we'll look at the many variations of this enduring concept and how they can be used in a variety of ways. (Duck walking is optional.)

Classic 5th and 6th Patterns

Perhaps the most classic of all boogie patterns are the alternated fifth and sixth chords, as popularized by Chuck Berry. Originally adapted by guitarists from piano players, the concept is simple, but the effect is a full-bodied accompaniment that's both interesting and groovin'.

The 5th portion is simply a good ol' power chord, shown here as an open E5 and a moveable form in third position as G5.

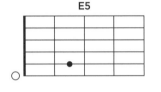
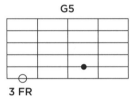

For the 6th portion, raise the 5th note a whole step to the 6th. This is no big deal in open position, but it's a healthy stretch for the moveable form.

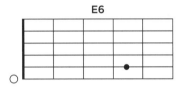
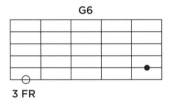

Riffs

Let's check some of these out in action.

RIFF 1

Here's a classic boogie shuffle pattern in the key of E. Open forms are used for the I and IV chords (E and A, respectively), but we're forced to use the moveable form for the V chord, which isn't all that comfortable.

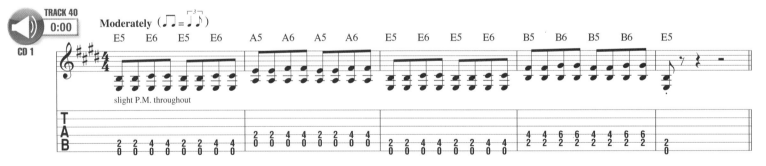

RIFF 2

Here's one with a straight feel in the key of B that adds another common element: the ♭7th extension. You'll have to stretch out one more half step from the 6th to reach the ♭7th interval. Since we're in B, it's not too bad of a stretch, but it's pretty serious down in G or F.

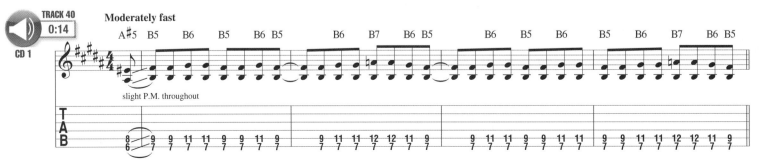

RIFF 3

Finally, here's another idea that's commonly used in open boogie patterns. We're adding a ♭3rd–3rd move every other time. Since we're in the key of A here, we can play the I (A), IV (D), and V (E) chords all as open patterns.

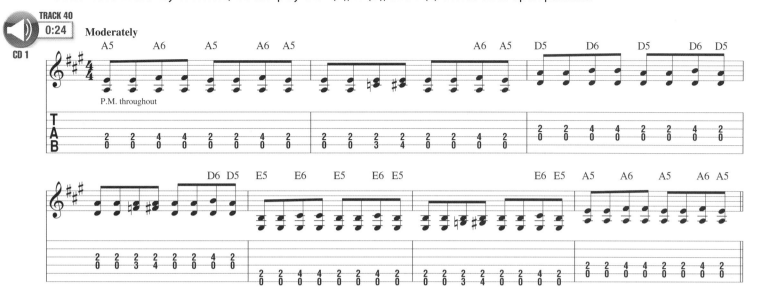

Single-Note Patterns

Now let's check out some boogie patterns that use mostly single notes. Many of these function as bass lines beneath the 5th-6th patterns we looked at above, but they sound great on guitar too.

RIFF 4

This first one is a classic idea in E that again makes use of the ♭3rd–3rd move. To make it sound really big, employ fret-hand muting to deaden every string except the one sounding. That way, you can strum through all six strings for added girth.

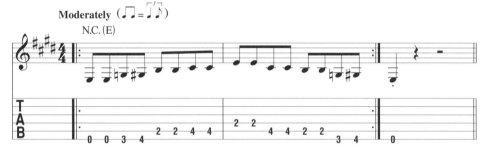

RIFF 5

Here's another classic one that's built using only the root, octave, ♭7th, and 5th.

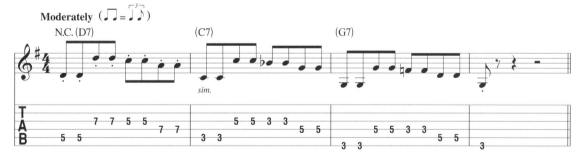

RIFF 6

Almost any of these patterns can be slightly altered to create an enormous amount of variations. For instance, we could alter the order of notes in the previous pattern, add a little triplet pull-off, and come up with something like this.

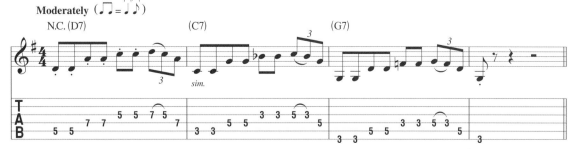

LESSON #41: INVERSIONS

One of the keys to inventive rhythm playing is having a nice chord vocabulary. After all, you can only do so much with a power chord. If you listen to someone like Keith Richards, Eddie Van Halen, Nuno Bettencourt, Steve Vai, or Eric Johnson, you'll hear all kinds of chords, and many of them are triads played in different areas of the neck using inversions. In this lesson, we'll learn what inversions are and how to incorporate them.

What Is an Inversion?

An inversion is simply a chord in which a note other than the root appears on bottom. Let's take a look at a C major triad as an example. A triad contains three different notes (hence the name): a root, a 3rd, and 5th. In a C major chord, this would be C (root), E (3rd), and G (5th), and the chord would be "voiced" (low to high) 1–3–5. We can play these notes in open position as the bottom three strings of our open-position C chord:

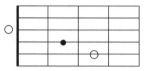

Since the root of this chord (C) is on the bottom, it's said to be in root position. But if we leave the 3rd and 5th where they are and transfer the C up an octave, the 3rd (E) becomes the lowest note, and the chord is voiced 3–5–1. This is first inversion.

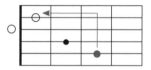

Likewise, if we repeat this process and shift the lowest note (now the 3rd) up an octave, leaving the 5th and root where they are, the 5th (G) becomes the lowest note, and the chord is voiced 5–1–3. This is second inversion.

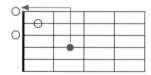

Major Triad Shapes

Obviously, we need to learn some moveable shapes that can be used for any chord. One efficient way to do this is to work with specific string sets and figure out the three different voicings on each. We'll work with a C root for now, but these shapes can be moved to any root. When we climb above fret 12, we'll bring the shape down an octave.

STRING SET 6-4: MAJOR TRIAD

We'll start with major triads on strings 6–4. You'll find that some of these shapes are easier than others (and consequently see more use).

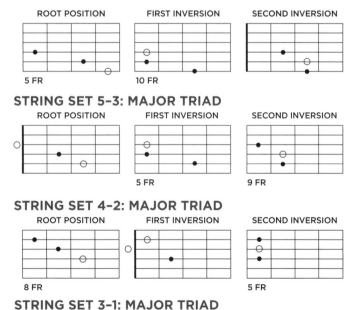

Minor Triad Shapes

Now let's check out C minor triads and inversions.

STRING SET 6-4: MINOR TRIAD

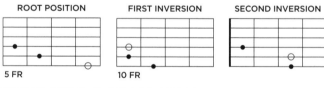

STRING SET 5-3: MINOR TRIAD

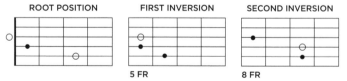

STRING SET 4-2: MINOR TRIAD

STRING SET 3-1: MINOR TRIAD

There are two other forms of triads as well—augmented (1–3–♯5) and diminished (1–♭3–♭5)—but they're rarely used in rock, so we won't look at them.

Riffs

Now let's check out how we can put these shapes to work for us.

RIFF 1

Often times, one chord will be alternated with another, where one or both will be inverted. A classic example is this idea on strings 4–2, containing a second inversion C chord and first inversion F.

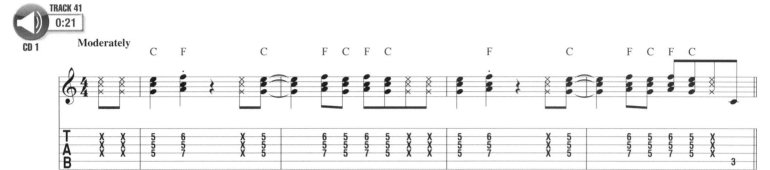

RIFF 2

The first inversion shape on strings 5–3 is also common:

RIFF 3

Here's another common approach: using different triad inversions on the top strings over a droning open string to get various harmonies. In this case, the triads are on strings 3–1, and we're using the D string as the bass drone.

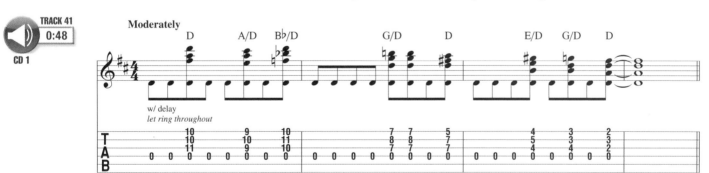

RIFF 4

Let's close out with another common riff on string set 4–2. This time, we're alternating second inversion chords with root position ones, with a first inversion shape thrown in for good measure.

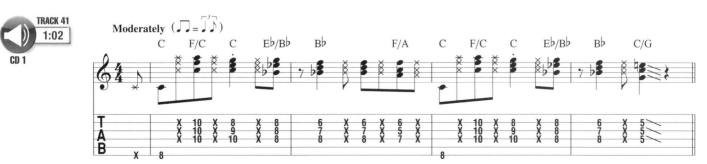

LESSON #42: POWER CHORDS

The power chord is to rock guitar what hot dogs are to a baseball game. You simply can not separate the two. Though we certainly make use of other chord types in rock, the simple truth is that, without the power chord, there would be no rock guitar. In this lesson, we're going to learn what makes a power chord and how it finds its way into so… many… riffs.

Construction

Power chords are comprised of two different notes: the root and the 5th. (Even if you play a power chord shape with more than two strings, you're still only playing two *different* notes.)

The root of the chord is simple; it's the note after which the chord is named. It's usually, but not always, the lowest note in the chord. We can find the 5th of a chord by counting up five notes from the root. For example, if we have a root note of C, then we say that C is the "1," and we count up the musical alphabet from there:

C (1)   D (2)   E (3)   F (4)   G (5)

So, we would say that G is the 5th above C. The number (5th in this case) represents the quantity of an interval. The other half is the quality, which is not quite as straightforward. We could get seriously side-tracked here and go into much more detail, but we don't have the space. So we'll just keep it as basic as possible. In a power chord, we need a perfect 5th from the root (perfect = quality, 5th = quantity). A perfect 5th is the distance of seven half steps (a half step is the distance between two adjacent frets on your guitar). Let's confirm this with our C and G example.

C   C#   D   D#   E   F   F#   G
 \ / \ / \ / \ / \ / \ / \ /
  1   2   3   4   5   6   7

So, the notes of C5, which is the chord symbol for a C power chord, are C and G. If you know your major scales (or have a way to access them), a shorter way to locate the perfect 5th is to simply find the fifth note of the root's major scale. For example, if you wanted to play B♭5, and you knew the B♭ major scale (B♭–C–D–E♭–F–G–A), then you can see that the 5th is F.

Many players don't know this theory behind power chords, but it's nice to be armed with this knowledge if you ever want to play an instrument other than the guitar (or bass), because it's universal and can be applied to any instrument.

Common Power Chord Forms

Since a power chord only contains two different notes, the most basic forms use only two strings. Here are these forms played off sixth-string, fifth-string, and fourth-string notes.

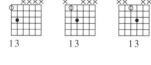

A common variation involves adding the root octave on top. That results in these shapes.

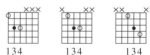

Power Chord Riffs

With only that much, you're armed with enough knowledge to write the next generation of classic rock riffs. Here are a few examples of what you can do with these shapes.

RIFF 1

TRACK 42
0:00
CD 1

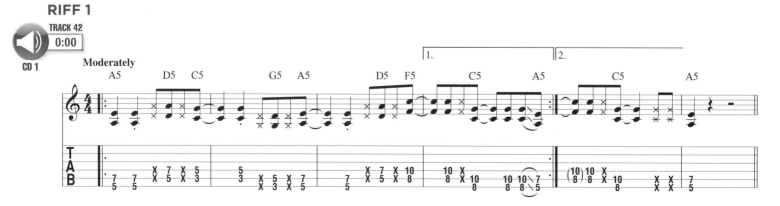

RIFF 2

Palm muting is also frequently used. Rest your palm on the strings near the bridge.

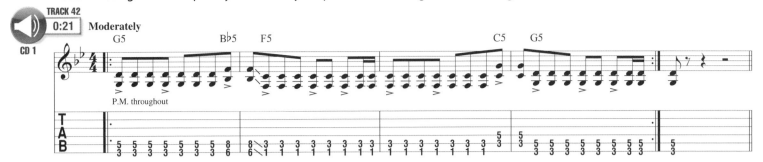

RIFF 3

Here's another common idea: the pedal tone riff. We're using the open low E string as a palm-muted pedal tone and playing different (unmuted) power chords on top.

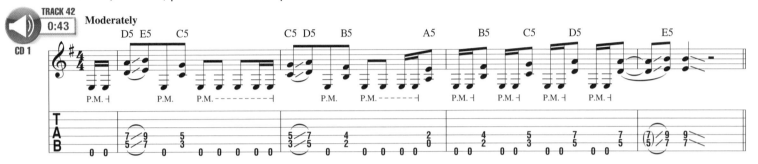

Inverted Forms

In addition to playing a power chord in a root–5th voicing, we can also invert the chord and put the 5th in the bottom. So, for example, instead of playing this C5 voicing:

Or we could move the root up an octave to string 3 to get this:

We could move the 5th (G) down to string 6 to get this:

And just as we doubled the root in our standard shape to create three-string voicings, we could double the 5th here to do the same thing, resulting in these shapes.

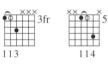

Inverted Power Chord Riffs

Now let's see how we can incorporate some inverted power chords into our riffs.

RIFF 4

In this first one, we're mixing root position and inverted power chords together.

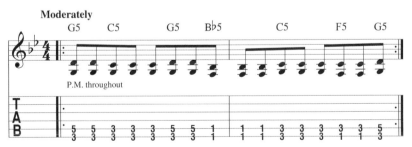

RIFF 5

Here's another pedal tone example using the inversion idea.

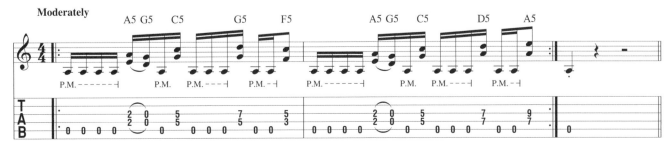

LESSON #43: DOUBLE STOPS FOR RHYTHM GUITAR

Although power chords and full-sounding open chords have populated many of rock's classic songs, the double stop sees its fair share of love as well from many players, including Eddie Van Halen, Angus and Malcom Young, Vito Bratta, Ritchie Blackmore, Randy Rhoads, and Steve Vai, just to name a few. In this lesson, we'll take a look at the double stop as a rhythm guitar device.

The Basics

A double stop is created when you play two notes at once. They're most common on adjacent strings, but non-adjacent strings are used as well. The musical term for the distance between two notes is the interval, and all double stops are comprised of a certain interval. The most common double stops on guitar are 3rds, 4ths, 5ths, and 6ths. It's beyond our scope to thoroughly explain the concept of intervals, but here are some basic qualities that apply universally.

▶ There are five interval qualities: major, minor, augmented, diminished, and perfect

▶ 2nds, 3rds, 6ths, and 7ths are normally major or minor

▶ 4ths and 5ths are normally perfect or augmented; 5ths can also be diminished, and 4ths can also be augmented

▶ A major interval is one half step larger than a minor interval—e.g., a major 2nd is one half step larger than a minor 2nd

▶ A diminished interval is one half step smaller than a perfect interval—e.g., a diminished 5th is one half step smaller than a perfect 5th

▶ An augmented interval is one half step larger than a perfect interval—e.g., an augmented 4th is one half step larger than a perfect 4th

For those that don't know, a half step is the smallest interval in Western music. It's the distance of one key to the very next (black or white) on a piano and the distance of one fret on a string of the guitar or bass.

Shapes on the Guitar

On the guitar, these double stop intervals create shapes that are easily memorized. Here are the shapes for the most common double stops on the lower adjacent string sets.

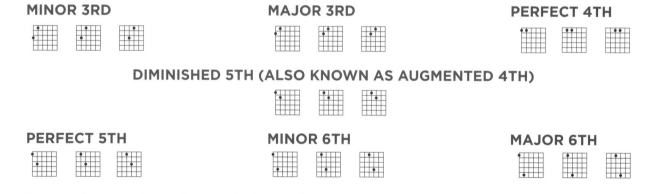

Basically, these shapes can be used to provide the 3rd of a chord that's lacking in a power chord, or they can simply provide a thicker alternative to a single note line.

Riffs

Let's hear how these double stops can be used to create some great rock riffs.

RIFF 1

This first one is a typical metal-sounding riff in Am that puts several different double stops on top of a muted A pedal tone.

RIFF 2

This riff makes use of mostly 4ths, but there are a few major 3rds as well.

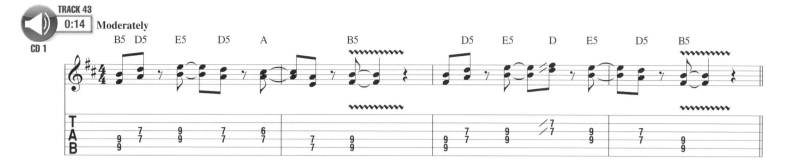

RIFF 3

Here's a Van Halen-style riff that works with 4th and 3rd double stops on strings 4 and 3.

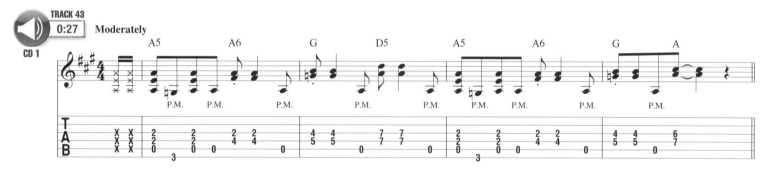

RIFF 4

For that Motown or Stax soul sound, 6ths will go a long way. Notice that we're using non-adjacent strings for the 6th intervals, which is also very common on the higher strings.

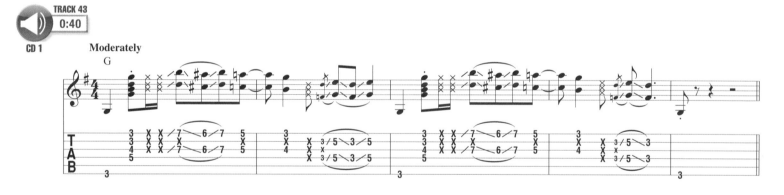

RIFF 5

And let's not forget the Hendrix style—itself an outgrowth of the soul style—which made constant use of double stops treated to slides, hammer-ons, and pull-offs.

The next time you find yourself chugging along on a simple power chord riff, think about trying out a double stop riff to change things up. Chances are you'll stumble onto something you really like.

LESSON #44: DOUBLE STOPS FOR LEAD GUITAR

From Chuck Berry to Jimi Hendrix to Steve Vai, double stops have been constantly exploited in the world of lead guitar with memorable results. Though they're not usually as flashy as the single-note stuff, they often provide the hookiest part of the lead, and that alone makes them worthy of study. In this lesson, we'll look at what double stops are and how they can add a new dimension to your solos.

The Basics

A double stop is created when you play two notes at once. They're most common on adjacent strings, but non-adjacent strings are used as well. The musical term for the distance between two notes is the interval, and all double stops are comprised of a certain interval. The most common double stops on guitar are 3rds, 4ths, 5ths, and 6ths. It's beyond our scope to thoroughly explain the concept of intervals, but here are some basic qualities that apply universally.

▶ There are five interval qualities: major, minor, augmented, diminished, and perfect

▶ 2nds, 3rds, 6ths, and 7ths are normally major or minor

▶ 4ths and 5ths are normally perfect or augmented; 5ths can also be diminished, and 4ths can also be augmented

▶ A major interval is one half step larger than a minor interval—e.g., a major 2nd is one half step larger than a minor 2nd

▶ A diminished interval is one half step smaller than a perfect interval—e.g., a diminished 5th is one half step smaller than a perfect 5th

▶ An augmented interval is one half step larger than a perfect interval—e.g., an augmented 4th is one half step larger than a perfect 4th

A half step is the smallest interval in Western music. It's the distance of one key to the very next (black or white) on a piano and the distance of one fret on a string of the guitar or bass.

Shapes on the Guitar

Here are the shapes for the most common double stops on each set of adjacent strings.

MINOR 3RD

MAJOR 3RD

PERFECT 4TH

DIMINISHED 5TH (ALSO KNOWN AS AUGMENTED 4TH)

PERFECT 5TH

MINOR 6TH

MAJOR 6TH

Licks

Let's check out what we can do with these in a lead context.

LICK 1

This first example answers a single-note phrase in G with a descending double-stop line in 3rds from the G Mixolydian mode.

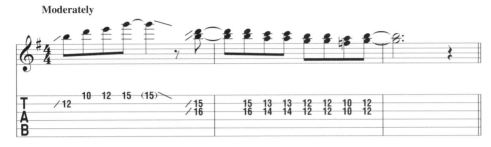

LICK 2

Here's a Chuck Berry-inspired line that gets a lot of mileage out of double stops.

LICK 3

This is a bluesy take on double stops in A, making use of several double stops on the upper strings. In measure 1, make sure you're only bending string 2!

LICK 4

Our final lick is similar to something Steve Vai might do. We're sliding 5ths and 4ths around on the top two strings to get a slightly Eastern flavor.

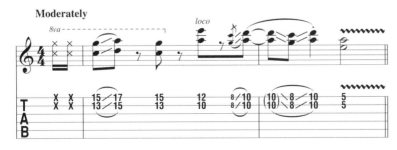

Double stops can sometimes be a breath of fresh air, and can help you break out of a rut, because they force you to abandon your go-to fingerings and licks. You can't help but start thinking more melodically. Go on! Give the double stop some love!

LESSON #45: BASIC STRING BENDING

Rock guitar solos without any string bending are certainly few and far between. Bending is one of the most expressive techniques we have on the guitar, and though it takes a bit of effort to master, it's well worth the effort. In this lesson, we'll take a look at the basics of string bending and learn some classic licks.

The Basic Idea

Bending (or stretching) a guitar string always raises the pitch. The farther you bend, the higher the pitch is raised. It takes time to develop the strength to bend strings, but with practice, you'll be bending all over the neck without a single wince. You'll find that the closer you are to the 12th fret, the easier it is to bend. Bends on frets 1–3 are extremely difficult and will require serious finger strength.

You can use all four fingers to bend, but the third finger is most commonly used. Usually, when bending a string with the third finger, the first and second fingers help out "behind the scenes" by pushing up as well. This makes maintaining a constant pitch much easier and also aids in keeping unwanted noises from popping out. When bending with other fingers, the same concept applies. The remaining fingers help out behind the bending finger.

In the music, the distance of the bend is described in steps. On the guitar, a half step is the distance of one fret on a string, a whole step (also "full step" or just "step") is the distance of two frets, and so on. Wider bends of 1 1/2 steps, two steps, or more are not unheard of. In rock, we also make frequent use of microtonal bends—i.e., bends smaller than a half step. The quarter-step bend is half the distance of a half-step bend and is extremely useful in bluesy styles.

> ### BENDING LOGISTICS
> Generally speaking, for bends on strings 1–3, which are the most common, the strings are "pushed" up toward the ceiling (or toward the sky if you're communing with nature), while bends on strings 4–6 are "pulled" down toward the floor. There are exceptions to this rule, but it's certainly a good place to start. The reasoning is quite simple. You can't pull down very far—and therefore raise the pitch—on string 1 before the string pops off the fretboard!

Exercises

Let's look at a few basic exercises to get started.

EXERCISE 1

We'll start with possibly the most common bend of all: a whole-step bend on string 3. Listen closely to the pitch of the unbent note and make sure you're matching that with your bend. Try bending first with your third finger (supported behind with the others). Then try it with each other finger.

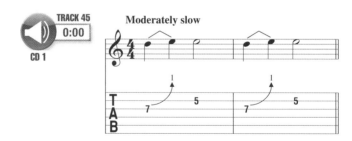

EXERCISE 2

Now we'll follow the same process on strings 2 and 1, adding a half-step bend. Notice that, when bending on string 1, we need to move out of position in order to hit the unbent target note. Take your time with this; we're just checking the accuracy of the bend.

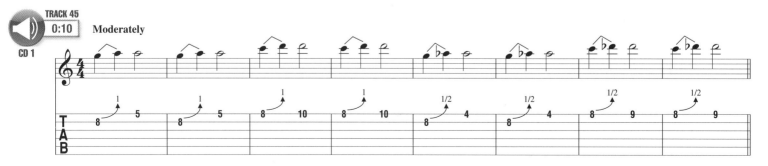

EXERCISE 3

Finally, we'll use the same procedure with bends on the bottom three strings. For these bends, pull the strings down toward the floor. Remember to try it with all four fingers.

Licks

Now that we've got our feet wet, let's get going with some classic bending licks.

LICK 1

This first one in A is one of the most classic rock licks of all. Notice that we're using a grace-note bend here, meaning we bend up to pitch immediately.

LICK 2

Here's one from D minor pentatonic that contains a whole-step bend on string 1—another extremely common move—and quarter-step bends on strings 3 and 4.

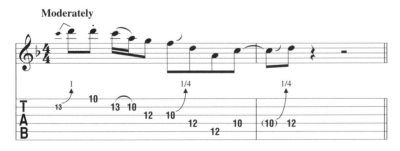

LICK 3

Let's finish off with one in E that uses a cool effect: the gradually released bend. After bending up a whole step, keep picking the string as you gradually release the bend.

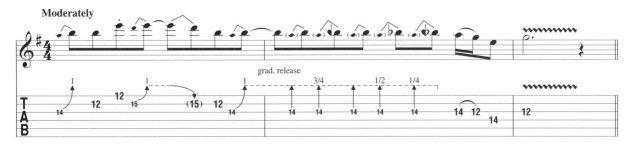

String bending is an incredibly expressive tool on the guitar, and we can employ the technique in various ways to achieve different results. This lesson will look at some more advanced concepts and will assume you're familiar with basic string-bending concepts.

The Pre-Bend

With a pre-bend, you'll be bending the string before you even pluck it. This means you'll really need to have those bends down cold! Go back and forth with the pre-bent note and the unbent target pitch to make sure you're accurate. Let's start with an exercise.

EXERCISE 1

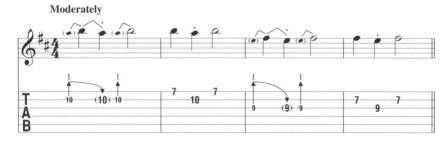

The Oblique Bend

With an oblique bend, you're playing a double stop in which one string is bent and the other remains stationary. This one is extremely common in Southern rock. It takes a little practice to develop the coordination, so in these exercises, make sure you're keeping the unbent note absolutely still.

EXERCISE 2

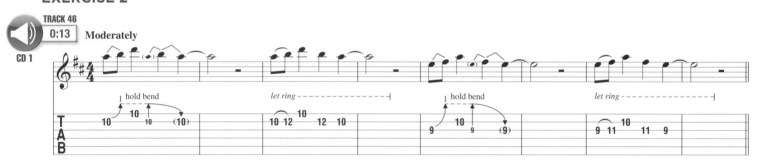

EXERCISE 3

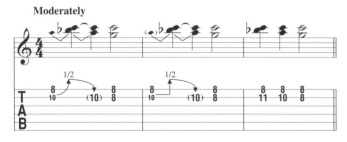

The Unison Bend

In a unison bend, you play a target pitch on one string and a bent pitch a string lower at the same time, so that both the unbent and bent string are both sounding. If you don't get the accuracy of the bend right, this can sound pretty gritty and kind of ugly. When done properly, however, a thick tone is achieved. Here's an exercise.

EXERCISE 4

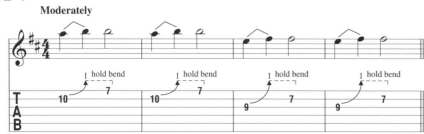

Licks

Now let's check out some licks that make use of these advanced concepts.

LICK 1

This first one will test your pre-bending skills, including a whole-step bend on string 4 executed with the first finger.

LICK 2

Here's a workout on the oblique bend concept. We begin with one on the top two strings right off the bat, bending string 2 up a whole step beneath string 1. In measure 2, we see a variation on this idea. We first bend string 3 up a whole step and then hold it while playing a note on string 2. Make sure the bend doesn't fall when you add the higher note!

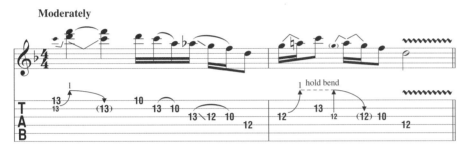

LICK 3

This lick makes use of several unison bends in a common scenario: ascending up a scale to a climax. Note that, although the notes on string 1 (the target notes) are all part of A minor pentatonic, the notes from which we're bending are not all in key, so grace-note bends work best for this type of thing.

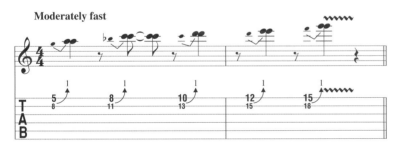

LICK 4

Now let's check out a final lick that makes use of all three concepts. As contrived as this idea may seem, it's actually not all that uncommon to see something like this.

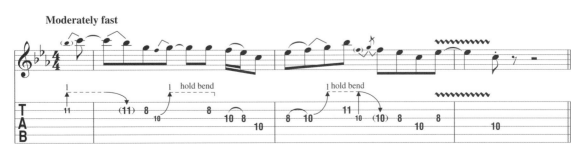

That does it for this lesson. Be sure to check out your favorite players to hear how they each make use of these different concepts. Then try to come up with some ideas of your own. Enjoy!

LESSON #47: DROP D TUNING

Ever since the Seattle crowd discovered Neil Young's precursor to the grunge sound with his seventies rock classics, Drop D tuning has been a mainstay in modern rock. It's been the perfect vehicle for not only the sludgy half-time riffs of Soundgarden, but also the frenzied, chaotic precision of bands like System of a Down. If you've never messed around in Drop D tuning before, be warned: the hours can quickly get away from you!

Getting There

Drop D is by far the easiest of all alternate tunings. All we have to do is drop the low E string down a whole step to D. You can use a chromatic tuner for this, or you can simply use your open D string as a guide and match that pitch (albeit an octave lower). Bingo! You're in Drop D tuning.

What We Can Do With It

This tuning has seen plenty of use throughout the years in various styles. Let's check out some of the more common ways of using it.

THE ONE-FINGERED POWER CHORD

In rock guitar, Drop D tuning is often exploited via the one-finger power chord. By barring strings 6–4, we have a root–5th–root power chord. This enables you to play power chord riffs with ease. Here are just a few examples of this type of idea.

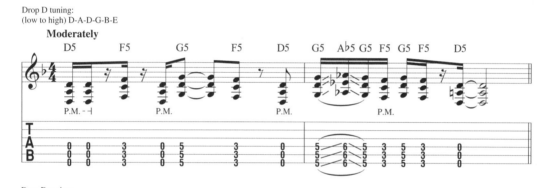

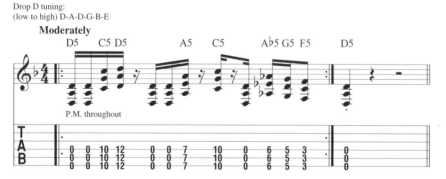

In this example, we demonstrate the ease in playing a sus2 chord on the bottom strings in Drop D tuning. In standard tuning, this requires an unpleasant stretch.

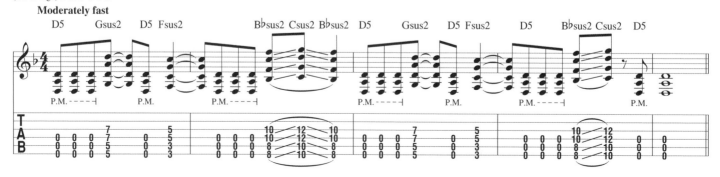

ARPEGGIO RIFFS

Those octave open D strings provide an excellent opportunity to create some awesome arpeggio riffs on the lower strings. Here are a few takes on that idea.

OTHERWISE UNPLAYABLE CHORDS

Drop D tuning shortens the physical distance between the notes on string 6 and the notes on all the others, enabling some previously impossible—or at least very difficult—chords to lie comfortably under the fingers. Check it out.

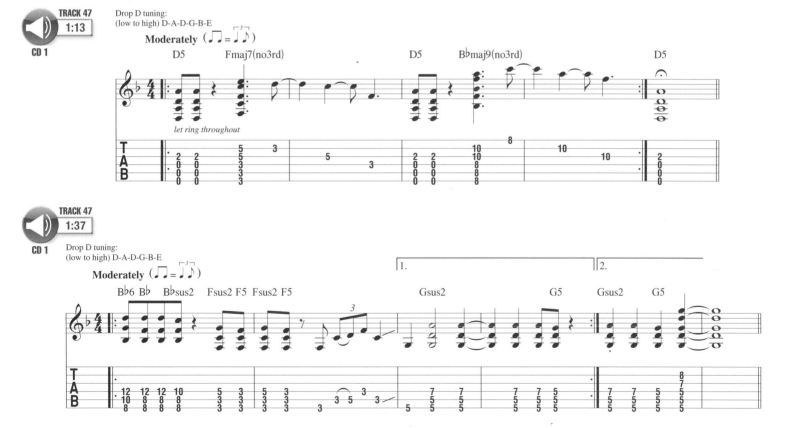

I'm sure that you'll discover your own benefits to the tuning with a bit of experimentation. It can really help if you're feeling in a rut. Enjoy the discovery!

If you've listened to much Iron Maiden, Thin Lizzy, Boston, Steve Vai, or, more recently, Avenged Sevenfold, you've no doubt heard your share of harmonized lead lines. This concept can provide a healthy dose of ear candy when your solo needs a pick-me-up, and it's simply a nice skill to have in general. In this lesson, we'll take a look at how it's done.

The Basic Idea

With a harmonized lead line, you begin with one line that functions as the melody. This is usually (though not always) the line that's composed first. For example, let's start with this basic melody in the key of G major.

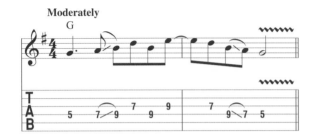

Now we want to add a harmony to that line. We have several options, but let's start with the most common.

HARMONIZING IN 3RDS

Playing 3rds above (or below) a given melody is fairly easy, provided you're familiar with the harmonized major scale. Since our example is in G major, the scale is G–A–B–C–D–E–F♯. So, to harmonize a 3rd above this line, we'd take it note by note and play a diatonic (meaning "of the key") 3rd above each note. For example, if the melody note is a G, we'll play a B: G (1) A (2) **B** (3). If the melody note is an A, we'll play a C: A (1) B (2) **C** (3)—and so on. A 3rd above our given melody would sound like this:

We could also play a 3rd below our melody line. The same concept would apply; we'd simply play a diatonic 3rd below each individual melody note. That would sound like this.

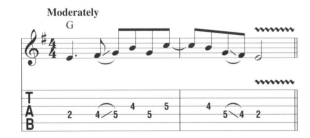

You may have noticed that the latter sounded a bit odder than the first. This has to do with the melody note and how it relates to the chords beneath it. If the melody is the root of the chord, then playing a 3rd above will sound nice, because you'll be playing the 3rd of the chord. However, if you play a 3rd below, you'll be playing the 6th, which is not always as stable sounding. This brings us to our next topic.

Making Adjustments for the Chords

You'll most likely find that harmonizing strictly in 3rds will rarely fit the bill. Most often, a note or two of the harmony line will be adjusted to better align with the chords. This is especially the case on longer sustained notes, when a particularly "colorful" harmony note would stand out the most. Let's take a look at another melody in the key of G as an example.

TRACK 48 0:28 CD 1

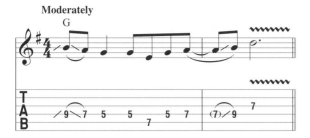

Notice that the melody ends on the note D, which is the 5th of the G chord sounding beneath it. Now let's harmonize this melody with strict diatonic 3rds above.

TRACK 48 0:38 CD 1

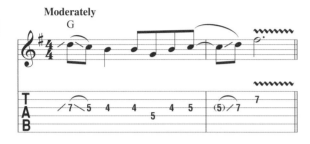

That final sustained note is quite bright, huh? I'm not saying that you wouldn't ever want this sound—you certainly may at some point. But most of the time, by adjusting the top harmony part to the closest chord tone, we can get a sound that's more stylistically appropriate. In this case, the chord below is a G triad, which is spelled G–B–D. The melody is on D, and the harmony is on F♯ at that point. What's the closest chord tone to F♯? It's G. So, for that final note, we may end up harmonizing in 4ths—D (1) E (2) F♯ (3) **G** (4)—so that it sounds a bit more stable.

TRACK 48 0:48 CD 1

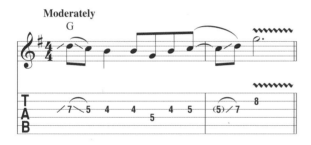

We can apply the same idea to other parts of the line, too, if we experience anything that doesn't seem to work very well.

Choosing Specific Harmonies for Effect

Sometimes, you may want to choose a specific harmony interval because you want a particular effect. The intervals of 4ths or 5ths are common in this regard, but any one is a possibility with this approach. Here's an example of both approaches. Notice how we alter the C note in the former to avoid a particularly dissonant moment.

TRACK 48 0:58 CD 1

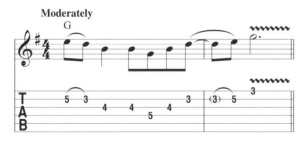

TRACK 48 1:08 CD 1

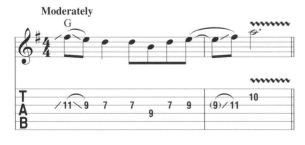

To really get a feel for this idea, listen to the above-mentioned artists as well as the Allman Brothers Band, Joe Satriani, and the Eagles for different takes on it. It's a whole lot of fun and can really make a melody shine.

MODAL MIXTURE RIFFS

If you've listened to much Rolling Stones, (early) Van Halen, Nirvana, or the Beatles, you've heard plenty of mode mixing. This is a powerful writing device that can really create some colorful riffs. In this lesson, we'll take a look at the modal mixture idea and see how it can apply to riffs.

What Is Modal Mixture?

Modal mixture is the combining of major and parallel minor tonalities. In other words, if you combine the notes from the C major scale with the notes from its parallel minor, C minor, you're engaging in modal mixture. This is normally used as an isolated incident rather than a continuous scalar application. In other words, it's common if you have a song in C major to "borrow" a chord or two from the parallel C minor, but still retain the overall major feel, particularly with regards to the resolution of phrases. By the same token, if you have a song in C minor, you may borrow a few chords from the parallel C major. The former is definitely more common, but it does happen both ways quite often.

Let's listen to an example to hear the basic idea. This is a progression in C major, but we have two borrowed chords from C minor: B♭ (♭VII) and Fm (iv).

Now let's look at the opposite. Here's a C minor progression with two chords borrowed from the parallel C major: F (IV) and G (V).

That's the basic idea. Here's a chart detailing the most commonly borrowed chords from the parallel modes.

COMMON CHORDS BORROWED FROM PARALLEL MINOR KEY

i
♭III
iv
v
♭VI
♭VII

COMMON CHORDS BORROWED FROM PARALLEL MAJOR KEY

I
ii
IV
V

Riffs

Now let's check out some riffs using this idea.

RIFF 1

This first one presents a common application: using combinations of inversions to access different harmonies. This is a big-time part of the sound in many Rolling Stones classics.

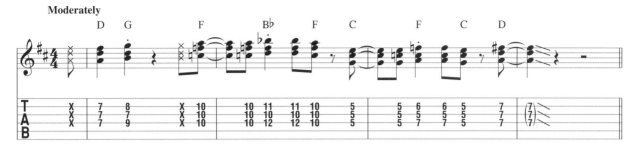

RIFF 2

Here's something Eddie Van Halen loved to do. Against a palm-muted pedal tone on the open low E string, we're playing triads from E major and the parallel E minor modes.

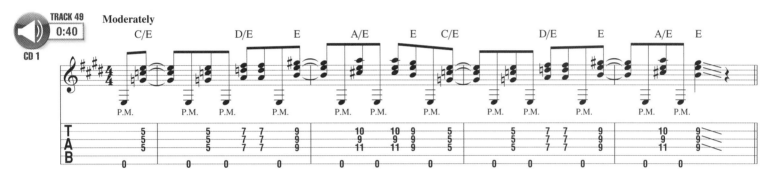

RIFF 3

This is another classic example: a minor key song making use of the borrowed major IV chord. You can hear this idea in the work of Tom Petty, among many, many others.

RIFF 4

And let's close with a nod to the Beatles. The minor iv chord in a major key is one of their signatures.

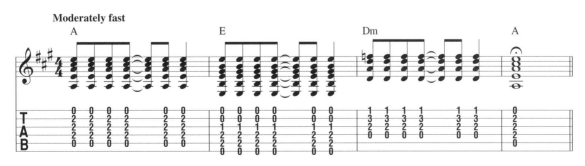

You'll be surprised by how frequently this idea comes up when you listen to your favorite bands. There's certainly nothing wrong with I–IV–V, but if you feel like stepping outside a little bit, try using a little modal mixture in your next riff.

LESSON #50: SYNCOPATION

Rock music may not be the most rhythmically complex music on the planet, but it's a good deal more complex than people often give it credit for. Sure, there are plenty of examples of the constant, stream-of-8th-note bass lines and the barrage-of-steady-16th-note guitar solos, but there's a great deal of syncopation as well, and that's the study of this lesson.

What Is Syncopation?

To put it simply, syncopation is the act of stressing a weak beat. In 4/4 music, each beat is normally stressed as a strong beat, with beats 1 and 3 often described as the strongest. Beats 2 and 4, known as the "backbeat," aren't stressed quite as much. When we divide the beats even further, such as the "and" between beats 1 and 2, we find that there's not really any inherent stress placed there at all.

When we purposely play rhythms that accent these normally unstressed notes, we're employing syncopation. It may sound complicated, but you hear it all the time. In fact, many songs would sound flat-out square if you took away the syncopated elements.

Examples of Syncopation

Let's check out a few examples to demonstrate the concept. We'll start by simply strumming a chord once on each beat:

Now, we'll syncopate on beat 4 by playing the chord on the upbeat and sustaining it through to the second beat of measure 2:

It suddenly comes to life! Granted, this example is still very academic, but the difference is palpable. We can take this idea as far as we want by stressing more or less of the normally unaccented parts of the measure. Here are a few more ways we could syncopate the first example:

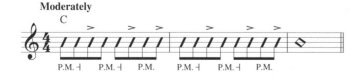

So you see, the sky's the limit when it comes to syncopation.

Riffs & Licks

Now let's check out a few examples that make use of varying degrees of syncopation. For each example, try tapping your foot on the beat as you play so you don't get lost within the measure.

LICK 1

RIFF 1

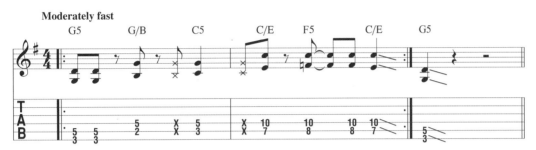

LICK 2

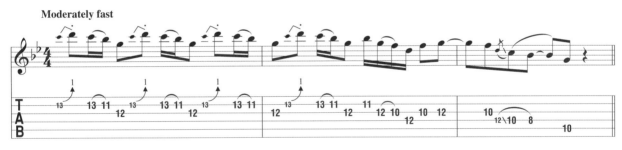

RIFF 2

Watch out for this last one; the rhythms are pretty tricky. Subdivide the count into 1-e-&-a, 2-e-&-a if necessary.

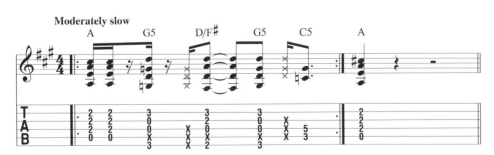

The more you experiment with syncopation, the more ways you'll find to apply it. Moving a chord or note by an 8th or even by a 16th note in either direction can sometimes make all the difference. Have fun trying it out!

LESSON #51: WARM-UP EXERCISES

Playing the guitar is a physical activity. It may not feel as strenuous as going for a jog or playing in a pickup game of hoops, but to the muscles in your fingers, hands, and forearms, it can be rather trying. So, just as you'd stretch your legs or start at a slow jog before hitting full pace in a run, it's best to do the same prior to playing your instrument. In this lesson, we'll show you some effective ways both on and off the fretboard to get properly warmed up.

Stretch 'Em!

Before you even pick up your guitar, there are things you can do to facilitate your playing. Muscles control the movement of your fingers, but tendons, which connect muscle to bone, also play a major factor, so it should make sense that you'll want to effectively stretch to help avoid repetitive strain injuries like tendonitis or carpal tunnel syndrome. Before you start on these stretches, though, heed these three rules:

1. If it hurts, *STOP*. Pain is a sign that there's already an injury, which will only be aggravated by further stretching.

2. Stretches should be performed slowly, and then held for 15–20 seconds.

3. Don't "bounce" the stretch; this can cause injury.

FOREARM STRETCHES

First, we'll stretch your forearm muscles. Perform these stretches on both hands.

 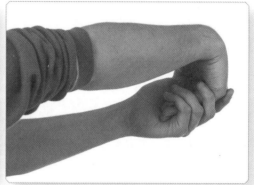

FINGER & THUMB STRETCHES

Now we'll stretch your fingers and thumb. Again, do these on both hands.

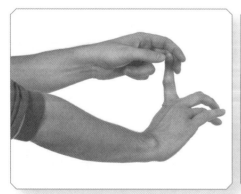 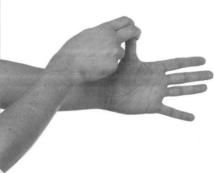 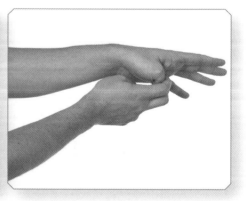

Fretboard Exercises

Now that you're properly stretched, let's get started with some actual warm-up exercises.

EXERCISE 1

The first exercise is probably familiar to you, but it's an old standby for a reason. It gets your fingers moving and, if done with a metronome, it can help your time-keeping and rhythm immensely. Repeat the pattern up and down the neck, and then try the same pattern using hammer-ons for ascending lines and pull-offs for descending ones.

EXERCISES 2A–D

Next, we'll break up that pattern into three-notes-per-string exercises, using various combinations of fingerings and both legato and alternate picking attacks. Again, play each of these four patterns up and down the neck. Feel free to intermingle them to help keep it interesting.

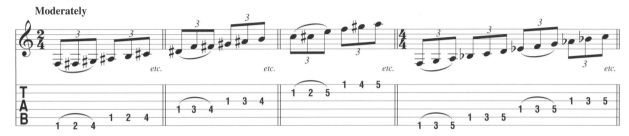

EXERCISE 3

This next one focuses on your fret hand, using extended legato phrases on each string. Strive for evenness in timing and volume.

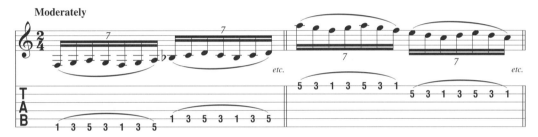

EXERCISE 4

I got this one from Joe Satriani. You may have seen this exercise in its arpeggiated form, but Joe takes it up a notch, requiring you to grab the "chord shapes" much more quickly. This is a great warm-up for your fret hand and helps to build accuracy in changing chords quickly. Use all three string sets (6–3, 5–2, 4–1), and strive for economy of motion.

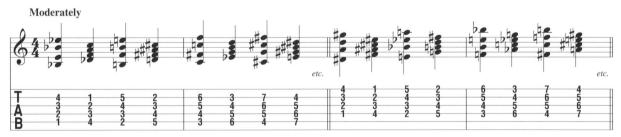

EXERCISE 5

Finally, here's a scale exercise that spans the entire fretboard using a four-notes-per-string pattern. This example is an E major scale. Try creating this sort of pattern using all the modes of E major, and then try the same exercise using a fifth-string root. Also, be sure to try it using both noted fingering approaches.

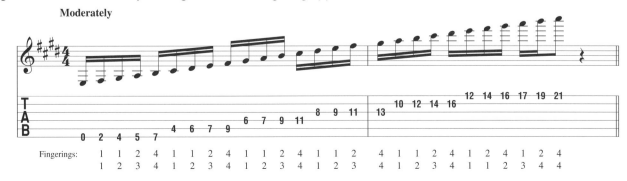

LESSON #52: SEVENTH CHORDS

On your way to becoming a rock rhythm guitar master, you've probably pummeled some power chords, bashed some barre chords, and tinkered with tons of triads. But have you experienced the dominant force of the seventh chord? Not just for bluesmen and jazzbos, the seventh chord—in all three of its qualities—can be the secret ingredient you need to take a song to an all-new level. In this lesson, we'll look at how major, minor, and dominant sevenths are used to best effect in a rock guitar setting.

Quality Chords

There are three categories of seventh chords: major, minor, and dominant. Major seventh chords comprise the root, 3rd, 5th, and 7th notes of a major scale (1–3–5–7). Dominant seventh chords contain the root, 3rd, 5th, and flatted 7th notes of the major scale (1–3–5–♭7). Minor seventh chords use the root, flatted 3rd, 5th, and flatted 7th notes of a major scale (1–♭3–5–♭7).

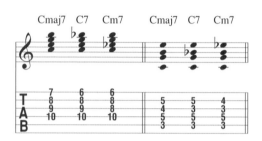

Using C as the root, the adjacent example shows first what these chords look like in stacked 3rds on the notation staff; however, these are neither very common nor finger-friendly shapes. So we've also presented the three chord types in a much more commonly used barre-chord basis.

Dominant Leader

Best known as being the harmonic basis for the blues, dominant sevenths have also played a significant role in rock and pop music. The Beatles, for instance, frequently used dominant seventh voicings, rather than simple triads, for the V chords in their songs.

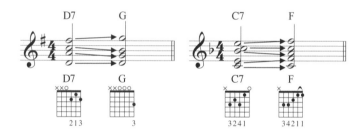

In most forms of Western music, including rock, the V chord leads back to the I, or tonic, and the dominant seventh chord helps to amplify the natural pull of the V–I progression. Take a look at these two adjacent examples.

As you can see, the chord tones in both changes either stay the same or move only one half step, with just one exception (A–G, in the D7–G progression). Using the flatted 7th results in a tighter shift in voice leading, which in turn makes for a more pleasing listening experience.

Check out this progression first with a simple major triad as the V chord (D), then using a dominant seventh (D7) on the repeat, to hear the difference in resolution to the I (G).

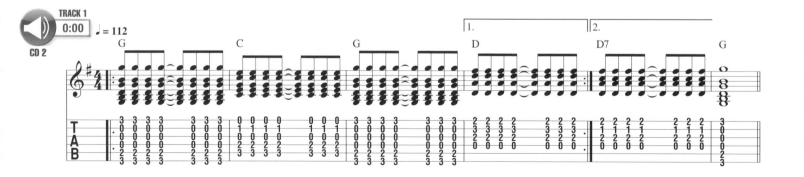

A dominant seventh chord can also be useful when moving between IV and V chords. The simple triads in a IV–V move contain no common tones, but by making the V chord a V7, that flatted 7th note matches the root of the IV chord. Famous examples of this include Supertramp's "Give a Little Bit" and the Beatles' "Here Comes the Sun."

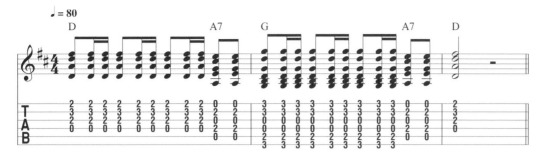

Color Your Chords

Major and minor seventh chords are excellent tools to add color to your rock-based progressions. Bands such as the Red Hot Chili Peppers, Incubus, the Eagles, and Led Zeppelin have made excellent use of these colorful chords to create timeless sounds and riffs.

You may have heard the commonly used description, "major chords sound 'happy,' while minor chords sound 'sad.'" The seventh adds even more depth, and in the case of major sevenths, restrains the "happiness," sometimes to the point of melancholy. Compare this IV–I progression using triads (F–C) and major sevenths (Fmaj7–Cmaj7).

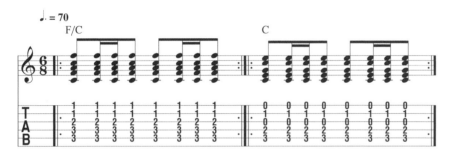

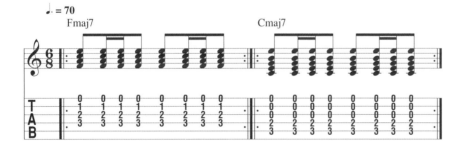

Finally, here's a progression you might hear in a rock ballad (albeit with a "surprise" ending). Try it first using triads (i.e., Em–Bm–C–Am, etc.), then as written to hear the greater harmonic depth and color.

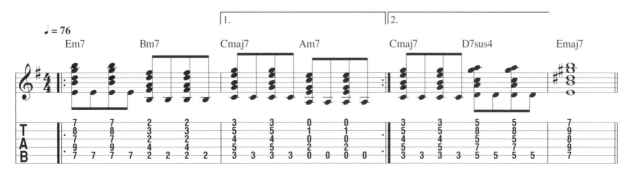

In practice, you'll most likely find seventh chords intermingling with triads in a rock context. The next time you're trying to find the right chord change in one of your songs or arrangements, consider a seventh chord. It will open a whole new world of sonic possibilities.

A popular way to add color and harmonic depth to traditionally triad-based rock progressions is with "suspended" (or "sus") and "add" chords. In this lesson, we'll explore how these suspensions and embellishments facilitate voice leading and common tones, resulting in more coherent chord progressions.

Sus vs. Add

Although suspended and add chords are often lumped together, there is a very distinct and important difference between them. Suspended, or sus, chords replace the tonality-defining 3rd, resulting in a chord that is neither major nor minor, but can serve in either role. An add chord maintains the 3rd, but adds another note to the triad to create a richer harmonic experience.

"Sus" It Out

The two types of suspended chords you'll most often play are sus2 and sus4. A sus2 chord replaces the 3rd with a 2nd. For instance, to play a Dsus2 chord, you take the D triad D–F♯–A, remove the 3rd (F♯), and replace it with the 2nd (E) to get a D–E–A chord (1–2–5). Similarly, if you remove the 3rd (C♯) from an A chord and replace it with the 2nd (B), you get an Asus2 chord.

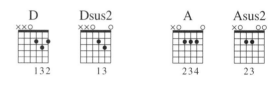

Here's a Led Zeppelin-inspired chord riff based on D and A chords, using their sus2 and sus4 forms to give it melodic contour.

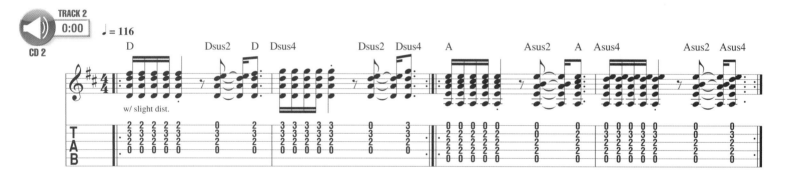

You can also suspend a seventh chord for even greater harmonic richness. Perhaps the most well-known instance of this is the ringing G7sus4 that opens the Beatles' "Hard Day's Night." (Yes, we know that's only a composite approximation of what a 12-string electric, 6-string acoustic, bass, and piano played, but it's also the best summary chord.) Our example, which features two big, ringing suspended seventh chords at the start, is reminiscent of prog rock legends Rush and prog-pop masters the Police.

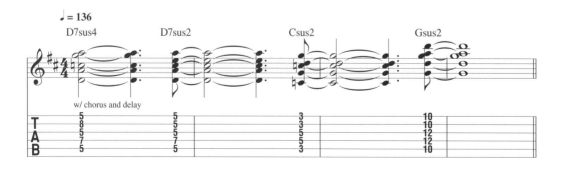

"Add" It Up

As mentioned earlier, an add chord maintains the 3rd and thus its major or minor tonality. Because the root, 3rd, 5th, and 7th are the chord tones that result from stacking 3rds, it leaves the 2nd, 4th, and 6th as notes that can be "added" to the triad.

Here are some of the more commonly used open-position add chords.

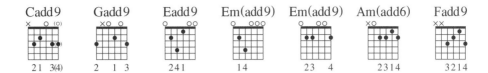

> ## IF 2 WAS 9?
>
> You've probably come across a chord labeled "add9" when the 2nd scale tone is added, and perhaps you wondered why it's "add9" instead of "add2." Technically speaking, the chord could be named either way, Cadd2 or Cadd9, depending on the octave in which the added note falls. In the Cadd9 chord above, the added D note falls an octave and a 2nd above the root, C; therefore, we call it Cadd9. If instead you were to play a basic open C major chord and remove your second finger from the E note on the fourth string, so that the open D note is allowed to ring out, you'd be playing a Cadd2 chord. In most guitar music, it doesn't matter in which octave the added note appears—unless it serves as the bass note.

This riff is typical of a hard rock ballad. Note the "double add" Dadd4/add9 chord in bar 4, which is just an open C chord slid up two frets. Sliding "cowboy chord" shapes like this up and down the neck while allowing open strings to ring can create many interesting sus and add sounds.

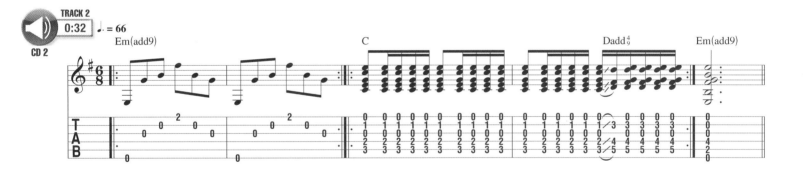

The add chords in that riff function primarily to add color, but add and sus chords are also quite useful for compositional tools like voice leading. The next chord riff *could* be played with simple triads (i.e., G–C–Em–D), however, using the Cadd9, Em7, and a strategically placed Dsus4 provide voice leading via the G5 chord (G–D–G) on the top three strings throughout the progression.

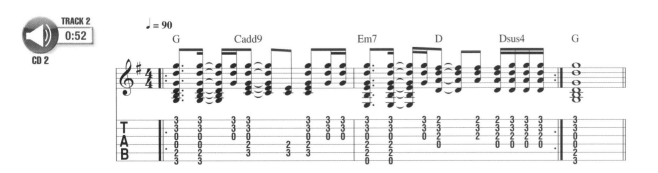

LESSON #54: OCTAVES

Mention octaves to a guitarist, and most will immediately respond with "Wes Montgomery," the legendary jazz guitarist and acknowledged master of the octave-soloing technique. But this perfect interval has had a huge impact in the world of rock guitar as well, especially in the metal and punk realms. In this lesson, we'll learn essential octave shapes and the various ways in which they're used for both riffs and melodies in a rock context.

The Perfect Interval...

An octave is the interval from a given root note to its matching root seven scale steps, or the interval of an 8th, away. Along with the unison, 4th, and 5th intervals, the octave is called a perfect interval, because of its perfect consonance, or harmonic stability.

On the guitar, the octave interval lies in some pretty convenient shapes, shown here.

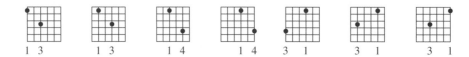

Octaves can be played linearly (one note at a time); but more commonly, they are played vertically (as dyads). Because of the way the octave lies on the fretboard, you typically have one string between the octave notes, so you either need to pluck the two fretted notes to cleanly articulate the octave, or you have to mute the string between using the fleshy underside of the finger fretting the lower-pitched note. In tablature, this muted string is shown with an "x."

This first riff is a heavy rocker in the style of 1990s grunge and early 2000s rock. Note how the muted A octaves in measures 3–4 produce a "muted harmonic" at the 7th fret of the G string—a very cool effect resulting from the physical layout of the octave shape.

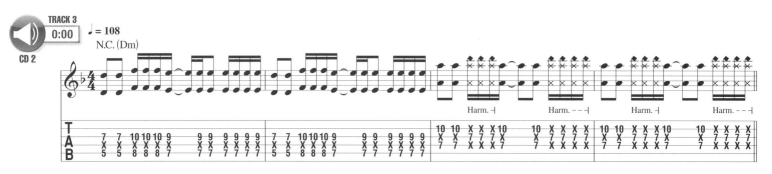

...Is Perfect With Drones

In a rock context, one of the most effective uses of the octave interval is in conjunction with a drone—typically an open string. Here's a riff in the key of E set against an open low-E string drone and beginning on the major 7th, à la the Smashing Pumpkins' "1979."

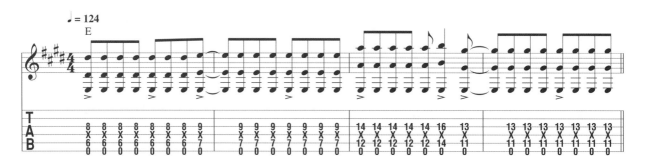

In that last riff, the droning note fell in the bass voice, but you can also place the drone *between* the octave notes. This next riff uses the less common octave fingering that places two strings between the fretted notes, which makes it easy, in this case, to use an open G drone. Be sure to mute the D string with the underside of your ring finger, which is fretting the notes on the A string.

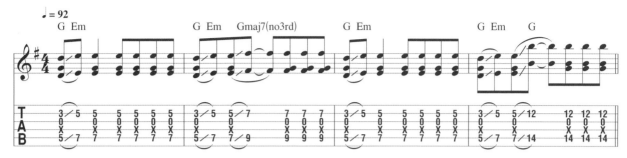

Double Down (or Up)

On a standard-tuned 22-fret guitar, there are *five* octaves between the lowest note (open low E) and the highest easily attainable note (full-step bend at the 22nd fret on the high E string). So why limit yourself to single-octave shapes?

The two-octave shape used in this next riff isn't all that common, but it has been used to great effect in some early rock tunes—particularly the blues-rocker "Train Kept A'Rollin'."

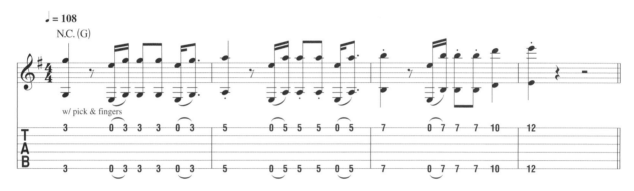

You can also use octaves in a more conceptual manner, such as repeating a phrase or arpeggio across one or more octaves. This final example is a Steve Vai-inspired shred phrase alternating an E major arpeggio in two octaves followed by a closing four-octave barrage of E notes. Whew!

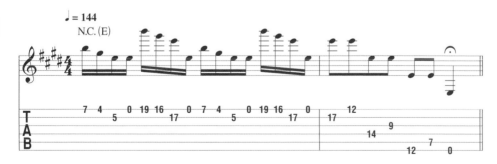

This overview of octaves in rock guitar covers most of the common uses of this perfect interval, but there is much more to explore. For the first four octave shapes shown in this lesson, try adding the 4th on the middle string instead of muting it. Or, experiment with various scale- and arpeggio-based patterns that repeat on each successive octave—a favorite technique used by Paul Gilbert. You're limited only by your imagination.

LESSON #55: 3RDS AND 6THS

The world of rock guitar is abundant with full-on chords and single-note licks and solos. The tasteful world of intervallic play falls between, from enriching fills and riffs to electrifying harmonized guitar solos. For these purposes, the 3rd and 6th intervals reign supreme. In this lesson, we'll show you how these related sounds can help generate more exciting and sophisticated phrases.

3rds Theory

You're probably familiar with how stacked 3rds are used to create diatonic chords. The same concept applies in working with diatonic 3rds intervals, except you're isolating dyads. Below you'll find three one-octave C major scales harmonized in 3rds (the third scale begins on E, so you could also call this E Phrygian).

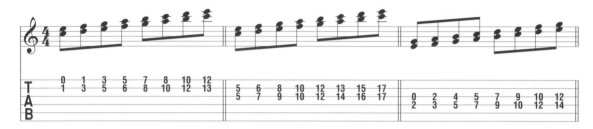

The tab for these three scales depicts the fretboard locations for the harmonized 3rds on the three most commonly used string pairs. Look closely, and you'll see a pattern emerge. On string sets 2–1 and 4–3, major 3rds are *one* fret apart and minor 3rds are two frets apart, and ascending the scale you get a M–m–m–M–M–m–m (M=maj; m=min) diatonic pattern. On string set 3–2, the same diatonic pattern holds true, but because of the guitar's tuning, the fingering changes so that major 3rds are on the same fret and minor 3rds are one fret apart.

Getting this diatonic pattern under your fingers is critical to successful use of 3rds whether in riffs or licks, so practice the pattern on all string sets starting not only on the root, as you do in the first two scales of our previous example, but also on other scale tones, as you do in the last scale.

One popular 3rds riff is from the laid-back blues-rocker "Heaven," by the Los Lonely Boys. This first example is in the style of that riff. When fretting the major 3rds dyads, experiment using your index and middle fingers or your middle and ring fingers. You should be able to do both, as each will have its advantages depending on the direction of the phrase and the target notes.

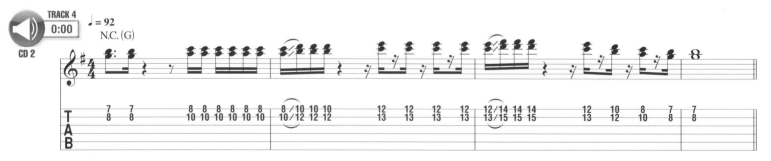

Of course, using only 3rds intervals can be limiting. But using them along with the more common 4ths and 5ths heard in rock guitar can really give a riff some character. Here's one in the style of AC/DC that covers the middle string set.

Sister 6ths

In the previous examples, we harmonized the C major scale by adding the 3rd above the root. But if you find that 3rd, and then drop it one octave, the resulting interval is a 6th—and a very effective musical tool. Here is the C major scale harmonized in 6ths.

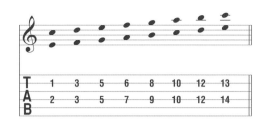

As with the 3rds, the 6th intervals also follow a pattern with regard to fingerings. Major 6ths are one fret apart, whereas minor 6ths fall on the same fret. Work out the fingerings on all the string sets so you can whip out your 6ths licks at will.

This next example shows a 6ths riff in the style of Led Zeppelin.

The 6th interval is also highly effective in an arpeggiated format. One of the most popular rock examples of this is the intro riff to Bon Jovi's "Wanted Dead or Alive." Our next example mines similar territory.

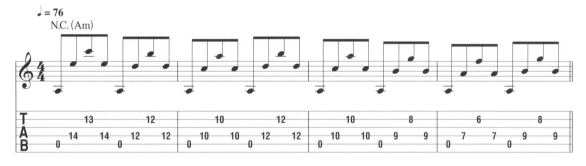

Terrific 10ths

We went up a 3rd then down an octave to create 6ths. If you were to instead go up a 3rd and then *up* another octave, you get a 10th, or an octave plus a 3rd. Famous examples of 10th interval riffs include the Beatles' "Blackbird" and the Red Hot Chili Peppers' "Scar Tissue." This final example draws inspiration from the latter. Your best approach is to use hybrid picking, though using just a pick offers a nice exercise in moving across wide intervals.

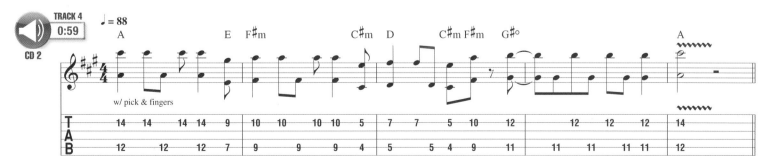

This may be a rock guitar book, but when it comes to 3rds—and especially 6ths—few guitarists do it better than country pickers. Check out some country 3rds and 6ths licks and try to work them into your rock arsenal.

LESSON #56: CONNECTING PENTATONIC SCALES

The foundation of Western pop and rock music is the seven-note major scale. But there can be no doubt that through the influence of the blues, the most important scale in rock guitar has become the five-note pentatonic scale. From Jimi Hendrix and Eric Clapton to Eric Johnson and Joe Bonamassa, this little scale has evolved from a mostly one-position box to an all-encompassing fretboard roadmap to soloing success. In this lesson, we'll show you the five box patterns of the pentatonic scale and more importantly, how to create lines that break their boundaries.

Penta Patterns

As you may have heard, the word pentatonic comes from the Greek words penta, meaning "five," and tonic, meaning "note"; thus, "five-note" scale. Because there are five notes in a pentatonic scale, there are also five scale patterns, or fingerings associated with it. Here are the five patterns as they lie in the key of G.

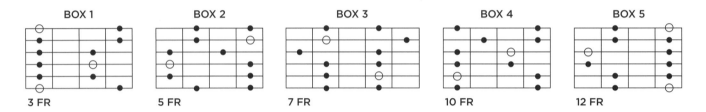

Most of you are probably *very* familiar with box 1; in fact, it's probably the most commonly used scale pattern in all of rock and blues guitar. But if the remaining four boxes are new to you, you'll want to start getting those under your fingers right away, as that facility will open a whole new world of soloing opportunities.

Here's what those five patterns look like across the entire fretboard, again in the key of G.

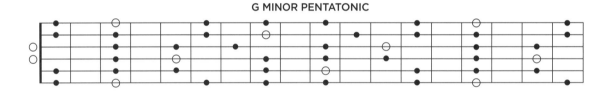

Connecting the Dots

Now that you know where the notes lie on the fretboard in all five positions, let's take a look at some licks that use notes from two adjacent boxes. For simplicity's sake, all the licks in this lesson are presented in G minor pentatonic. Make sure you learn how these patterns connect in all keys.

LICK 1

This first one is based in box 1, but extends back to box 5 on strings 5 and 6. The B♭ note on the 1st fret of string 5 is the same pitch as the B♭ that would normally be played by the pinky on string 6 in box 1, so the only "new" note is the low F (1st fret, string 6). This is a very common move in blues-rock and rock soloing, so you'll want to become very comfortable with this position shift.

LICK 2

Using the same basic lick, this time we extend the phrase up into box 2 on the top three strings. As with the previous lick, this particular position shift is a *very* common move in rock guitar, so it's essential to get it under your fingers. The slide on string 3 that serves as a connector between the two boxes is most often executed with either your middle or ring finger of the fret hand.

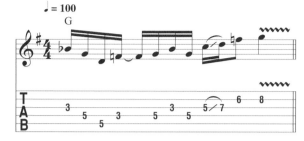

LICK 3

Now we'll get into likely new territory for most guitarists—bridging boxes 2 and 3. This Jimi Hendrix-style double-stop lick features several position shifts to hit notes from the two scale patterns and will really test your knowledge of boxes 2 and 3.

LICK 4

This next lick, a Claptonesque gem from his Bluesbreakers days, begins in box 4 and shifts down to box 3 at the end of the first measure.

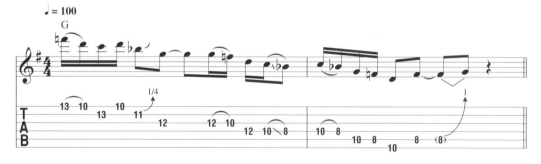

LICK 5—PENTATONIC PATTERNS GONE WYLDE

The final lick in this lesson is a hard-rock shred lick borrowed from guitarist Zakk Wylde—a master of the pentatonic scale. It climbs all five boxes on the top two strings in a blazing sextuplet pattern.

ALTERNATE PICKING

One of the biggest challenges that rock guitarists face is the ability to produce clean and evenly articulated notes when playing a melody or solo. One way to conquer that challenge is by using alternate picking. In this lesson, we'll show you several exercises to help you develop stellar alternate picking techniques.

Ups and Downs

Alternate picking strictly alternates between downstrokes and upstrokes on the guitar. This strict alternation is used regardless of string change or melodic direction (ascending or descending). The simplest exercise to get started is to use the alternate picking technique on open strings.

EXERCISE 1

In this exercise, begin with a downstroke and play two bars on each string, beginning on the high E and continuing down to the low E. Start at a slow tempo like 60 bpm, making sure to nail the rhythm—downstroke on the downbeat, upstroke on the upbeat—and not to pause when switching strings.

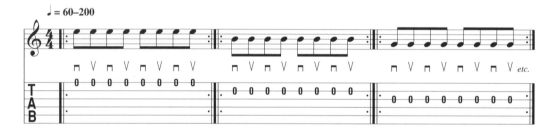

EXERCISE 2

This second exercise, which uses four notes per string with one finger per fret, also may look familiar. Although it seems simple, the key is to strive to play it in perfect rhythm with perfect left- and right-hand coordination. Once again, begin with a downstroke on the downbeat and play upstrokes on the upbeats. But then play it again, this time beginning with an upstroke on the downbeat and using downstrokes on the upbeats. Repeat the pattern all the way up to the 12th fret.

BE A HUMAN METRONOME

The best alternate pickers in rock guitar are the best because you can set a metronome by their lines. That's because they all used a metronome in every practice session, going as slowly as necessary to play the exercise or phrase cleanly and in perfect rhythm, and then gradually working up to tempo. Listen to the alternate-picked lines of John Petrucci (Dream Theater) and Paul Gilbert (Mr. Big, Racer X), in particular, to hear examples of perfect time. Moreover, both guitarists also achieve flawless articulation, where the pick strikes the string at the precise moment that the note is properly fretted—another priceless benefit of regular metronome use.

EXERCISE 3

Rock guitar instructor Troy Stetina—one of the best alternate pickers in the business—has identified four distinct picking mechanics. These are given their own measure in the following exercise. The first involves moving to the next lower-sounding string with an upstroke. The second moves to a higher string with an upstroke. The third moves to a new string with a downstroke. Finally, the fourth picking mechanic crosses back between two strings.

Work on each of these patterns until they're all comfortable, and try to extend the patterns shown all the way up and down the minor pentatonic scale.

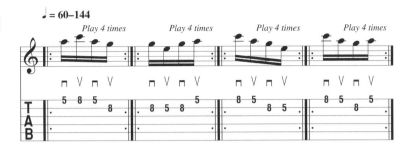

Sequences

Playing scales and chromatic patterns are great exercises, but at some point you need to make it musical. That's where sequences come in.

EXERCISE 4

This first sequence is a diatonic exercise from John Petrucci. It moves through three positions of an A minor scale, but you can extend it over the entire neck and in all keys.

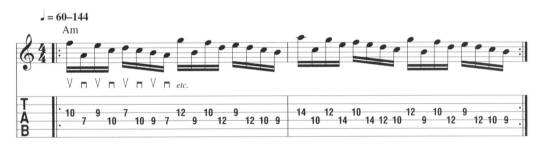

EXERCISE 5

This final sequence is a favorite of Paul Gilbert. It climbs (and later descends) the first six notes of the A minor scale in three successive octaves in a 16th-note triplet rhythm, then offers a final burst of A harmonic minor before downshifting to 8th-note triplets on an open string. It's the shift in rhythm that is key here. The ability to maintain a steady and even alternate picking attack across varying rhythms is absolutely essential.

LESSON #58: ECONOMY PICKING

The word "economy" is defined as the efficient and concise use of nonmaterial resources, such as energy or motion. And although alternate picking is sort of the gold standard when it comes to shred guitar, proficiency in economy picking can only help if playing fast is your thing. In this lesson, we'll show you how economy picking can be used to play scales and licks at breakneck speeds.

Economic Advisors

Long espoused by jazz guitar titans like Kenny Burrell and Jimmy Bruno and brought to mass popularity by jazz-rock fusion super-picker Frank Gambale, economy picking is equally appropriate for rock guitar lines. The essence of the technique is to waste no motion. Think about it: if you use strict alternate picking on a three-notes-per-string ascending pattern starting on a downstroke, when you switch to the next higher string, you're supposed to attack it with an upstroke. But to do so, you've got to *pass over* the string and come back *up* to execute the attack. Why not strike the note on the way *down*?

Let's take a look at how this works using a one-octave A minor scale.

Instead of playing this:

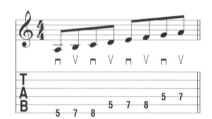

Play this:

As your picking hand moves physically toward the floor to each higher-pitch string, you hit the note—simple!

Now, if you've been an alternate picker all your life, this technique may feel awkward at first, as it conflicts with some well-ingrained habits. But don't worry—once you get used to it, you'll have *both* techniques available and be a better player because of it.

To get started, try playing this popular three-notes-per-string major scale pattern (shown in A) up and down the fretboard using economy picking. One key thing to remember as you embark on the economy picking technique: use a metronome. If you don't pay close attention to your rhythm, your lines may end up sounding a little lopsided.

Thrifty Yet Nifty

Let's take a look at some licks that take full advantage of this technique's economy of motion.

LICK 1

The first lick is a descending A harmonic minor run in the style of Yngwie Malmsteen—who has arguably the greatest economy of motion in rock guitar.

TRACK 7
0:00

CD 2

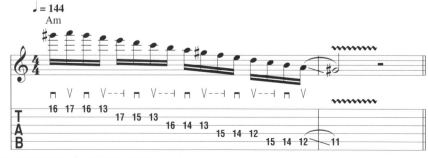

LICK 2

This next lick, reminiscent of a John Petrucci line, descends the C♯ minor scale in a three-notes-per-string pattern and starting on an upstroke, but the order of the notes has been altered to give the line greater melodic intrigue.

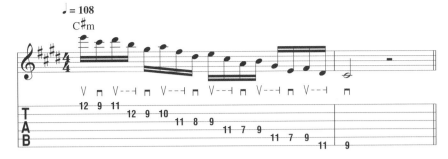

LICK 3

We've focused on three-notes-per-string patterns thus far, as they are not only popular in the rock guitar realm, but also friendly to the economy picking technique. But you can also use the technique on certain two-notes-per-string patterns, like this Zakk Wylde-inspired minor pentatonic fretboard ascent.

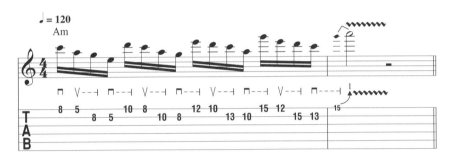

LICK 4

In this next example, a popular repeating blues-scale lick climbs the fretboard in minor 3rds. For most efficient execution, play a downstroke on the top string, then successive upstrokes on the second and third strings. Because there's a pull-off on the second string, be careful not to rush the upstroke on the third string.

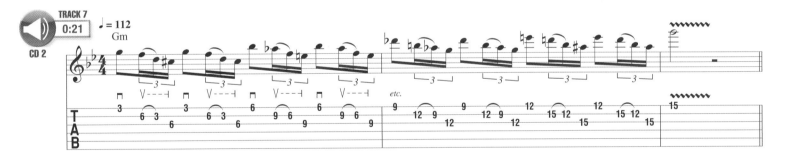

LICK 5

Finally, we present a minor pentatonic scale pattern that alternates between three and one note per string, as developed by Frank Gambale. This arrangement of notes requires some pretty big stretches, but it's also the most efficient way to climb the scale. As per Gambale's design, we've placed an even number of notes (four) on the top string, which allows you to turn the pattern around for an equally efficient descent. Start really slow with this one, and again, *use a metronome.*

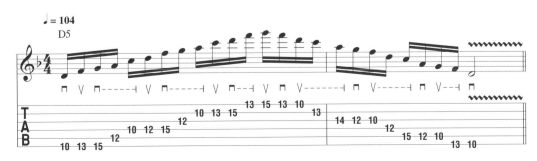

LESSON #59: INTRO TO LEGATO TECHNIQUES

One of the most important melodic devices a rock guitarist needs in his arsenal is a strong legato technique. An Italian term most simply translated as "smooth," command of this technique will give your lines a fluid, liquid-like flow, whether you play in the classic rock style of Jimi Hendrix and Eric Clapton, the Southern rock style of the Allman Brothers and Lynyrd Skynyrd, or the shred approach of legato legends like Eddie Van Halen and Joe Satriani. In this lesson, we'll introduce you to the three key components—hammer-ons, pull-offs, and slides—that consitute legato technique.

Hammer-Ons

The hammer-on gets its name from the action taken by your fret-hand fingers to produce the note—you "hammer" a finger down onto the string to sound a note. This is most often done using your middle or ring finger, and the preceding note is typically picked. The primary minor pentatonic box with its two-notes-per-string pattern is perfect for practicing hammer-ons. Play through the A minor pentatonic scale here, using your ring or pinky finger to hammer onto the second note on each string. Note that you have the option of using either your pinky or ring finger on the top two strings, and strive for a steady, flowing rhythm; in other words, don't rush the hammer-ons!

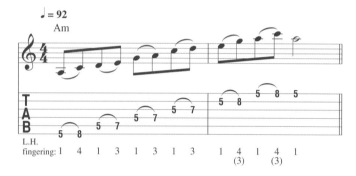

Essential to a strong hammer-on technique is the ability to use any combination of fingers. This exercise will help you build consistency and strength. Make sure that all notes—both picked and hammered—have the same volume.

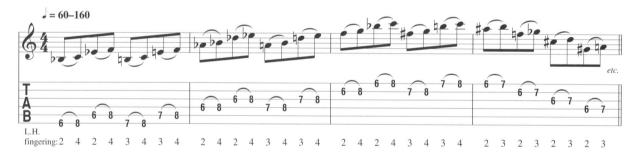

Here's a hard rock riff in A that incorporates hammer-ons in a much more musical setting, plus an essential hammer-on lick, also in A.

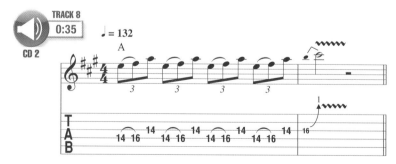

Pull-Offs

Opposite to the hammer-on, the pull-off requires you to first sound a higher-pitched note and then pull that fret-hand finger off the string to sound a lower pre-fretted note. Following is the A minor pentatonic (in this case, C major pentatonic) box pattern again, only in descending pull-off fashion.

Just as with hammer-ons, it's essential that you learn how to execute pull-offs using any combination of fret-hand fingers. Go back to the hammer-on exercise in Example 2 and play it again, but this time reverse each note pair so that you're pulling off; for example, place your pinky finger on the 8th fret, sixth string, pick the note, and then pull off to your middle finger at the 6th fret, sixth string, and so forth.

Here is an essential rock guitar repeating lick in the style of Led Zeppelin, featuring pull-offs as a key element.

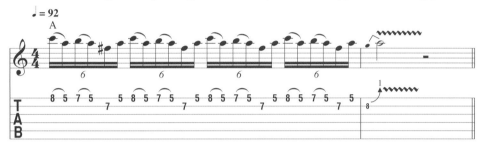

Of course, you can use hammer-ons and pull-offs together, where you strike the first note, hammer onto the second, and then pull off to the third. This approach is clearly used in the first lick below. Beat 4 of the second lick uses a technique called a trill, which is the rapid alternation of hammer-ons and pull-offs between two notes.

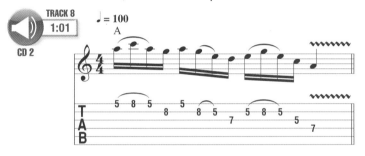

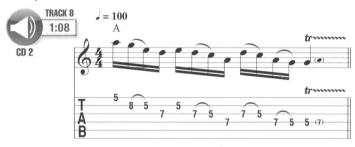

Slides

Slides involve striking a fretted note and then sliding up or down along the same string to a target note. There are two types of slides. The first and more commonly used is a slurred slide, where you strike only the initial note and then slide to the second without a second attack. The other type is called a shift slide, which is the same move except you strike the target note, too.

Here's a sliding lick you might employ over a big ringing Em or E5 chord. The first half features shift slides whereas the second half uses the slurred version.

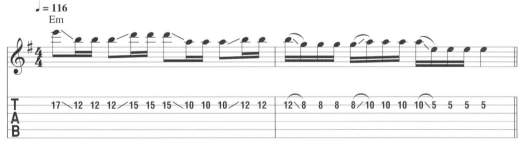

And here's an Allman Brothers-style minor pentatonic phrase incorporating hammer-ons, pull-offs, and slides, to pull it all together.

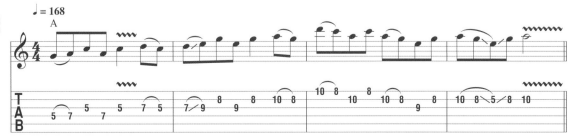

THREE-NOTES-PER-STRING PATTERNS

If you've ever wondered how guitarists pull off those lightning-fast runs up and down the neck, odds are they were using three-notes-per-string patterns from the major or minor scale. That's because this particular configuration is extremely friendly to the fretboard's intervallic structure and physical layout. In this lesson, we'll show you essential three-notes-per-string patterns for the major and minor scales as well as some useful sequences built from them.

Major Scale

When guitarists learn the major scale, most learn a single-position box pattern that places either two or three notes on each string. Although this is an essential pattern to know and have comfortably under your fingers, it's not particularly friendly to playing fast rock passages—which is where the three-notes-per-string pattern comes in.

PATTERN 1

Beginning with your index finger on the sixth-string root, this scale pattern features a string-pair symmetry that makes it easy to learn and play. Here it is in the key of G:

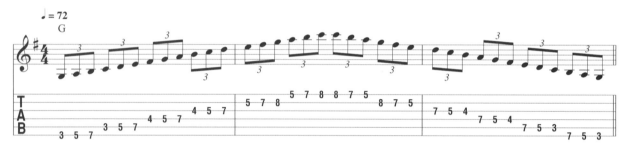

PATTERN 2

A second must-know three-notes-per-string major scale pattern has its root on the fifth string. Here's that pattern, with the sixth-string notes shown on the descending portion of the scale.

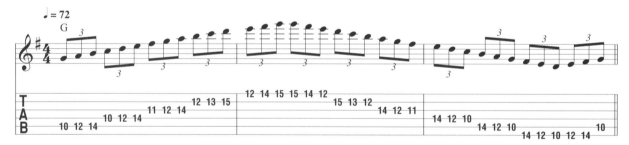

Minor Scale

Because such a large proportion of rock tunes are played in minor keys, it's essential to have a few three-notes-per-string minor scale patterns under your fingers. For these patterns, we're going to change things up a bit. First, each pattern features the root note as the second note on the starting string. Second, when you reach the top note, you're going to shift up to the next scale tone and then begin a new three-notes-per-string minor scale pattern. You can simply go straight up and down a single pattern, and in fact, you should do so for practicing purposes. But both patterns presented in each example represent popular choices, and we wanted to fit both in.

PATTERN 3

Here are the two sixth-string root patterns.

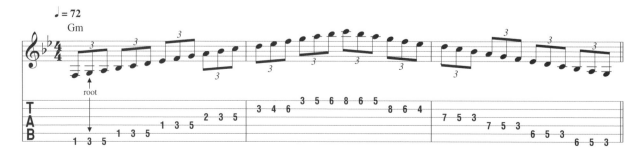

PATTERN 4

And now for the two fifth-string root patterns.

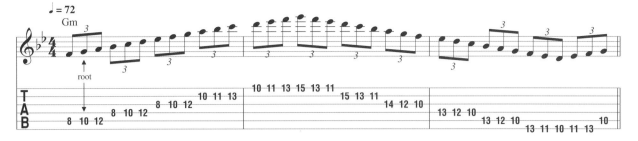

Sequences

It's not often that you'll be required to simply play up and down a scale pattern. To make things more musical, rock guitarists often use sequences.

SEQUENCE 1

This first one is an ascending six-note pattern. It's imperative that you accent the first note of each six-note sequence, to give the phrase rhythmic life. Try reversing the phrase into a descending pattern, too; again, accent the first note of each six-note sequence.

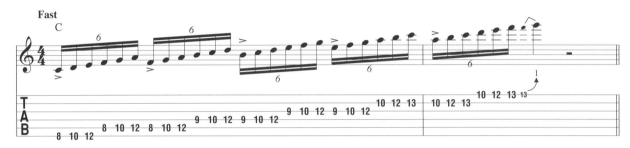

SEQUENCE 2

Here's another major scale sequence, this one consisting of a nine-note pattern using a legato articulation.

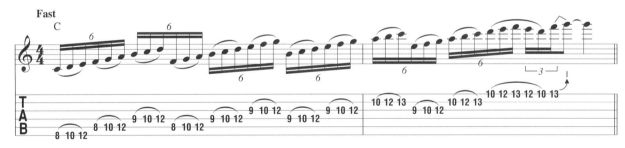

SEQUENCE 3

Here's a minor scale sequence inspired by George Lynch. This one climbs linearly up the fretboard along the top two strings. Be sure to start slowly and use a metronome. You should also try this pattern in descending fashion.

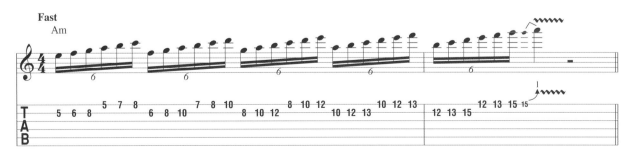

The scale patterns and sequences presented here merely scratch the surface of what's out there using three-notes-per-string patterns. Practice all of these patterns and sequences in all keys, up and down the neck, while using a metronome. You should also try using a legato articulation for the picked patterns, and picking on the legato patterns.

From Eddie Van Halen and Randy Rhoads to Joe Satriani and Steve Vai and beyond, the fine art of legato shred technique has left an indelible mark on the world of rock guitar. Although those and other legato masters have created distinct and exciting styles of their own, many of those scorching, "liquid" lines are based on specific fretboard patterns. In this lesson, we'll show you some popular and useful patterns you can use to develop your own incendiary legato technique.

Single-String

Legato shred lines can be played either up and down a single string or across multiple strings. We'll first take a look at a couple of single-string patterns.

PATTERN 1

This first phrase climbs the high E string using a combination of hammer-ons, pulls-offs, and slides. Although you'll more likely use just portions of this ascent in a real musical setting, this extended line also works well as a legato exercise, as you pick *only* the first note. Strive to generate even volume and duration for each note of the phrase.

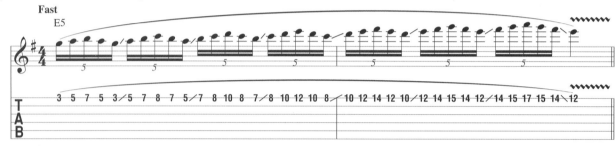

PATTERN 2

What goes up can generally also come down. This next single-string legato pattern descends the high E string, again using pull-offs, hammer-ons, and slides. Here, you'll pick only the first and final notes.

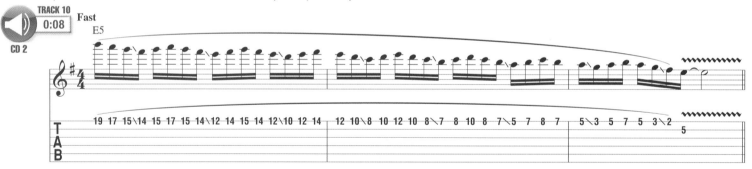

Up, Down, and All Around

Whereas single-string patterns are both useful and a good starting point, your bread-and-butter shred legato lines traverse the entire neck across all six strings. Though it may seem intimidating at first, there are some patterns that will help you along the way.

PATTERN 3

In this extended descending E minor legato pattern, you'll use the exact same fret-hand fingering (1–2–4) for every three-note grouping in the sequence. When moving to the next lower string, you'll lead with your pinky finger and use a "hammer-on from nowhere" to sound the first note. This is a challenge for new legato players, as the pinky tends to be the weakest finger, but if you practice slowly and strive for equal volume across all notes, it will come to you rather quickly.

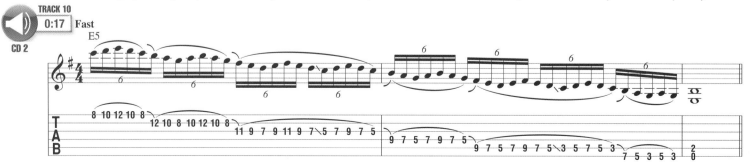

PATTERN 4

This one also uses a 1–2–4 pattern, but with only a half step from finger 1 to 2. Note the wide-interval slide used to shift positions along the third string in the first measure. Again, be sure to lead with your pinky finger when going to the next lower string. For this pattern, it requires a slight position shift, but it's the most efficient move.

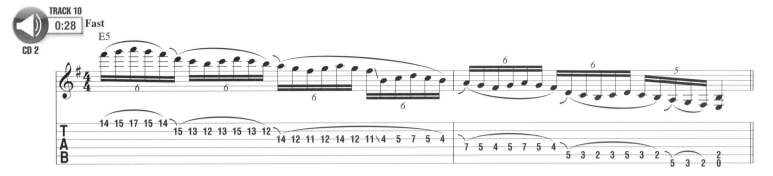

PATTERN 5

Now let's take a look at a couple of ascending legato shred patterns in E minor. For these ascending patterns, you'll pick the first note on each new string. The first one has its root on the fifth string, 7th fret, and climbs two full octaves.

PATTERN 6

This one covers all six strings and climbs an impressive three octaves. Note the shift slide, rather than a slurred one, up to the high E to end the line.

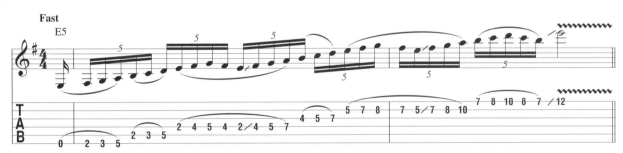

Pentatonic Legato Shred

Although major and minor scales (or their modes) using three-notes-per-string patterns are most commonly used in legato shred phrases, you can create some rather thrilling pentatonic legato lines using three notes per string. This results in some repeated notes, but that just adds a little intrigue to these lightning-fast lines.

PATTERN 7

Here's an example in E minor pentatonic that also includes a tapped note to cap the melodic zenith of the line.

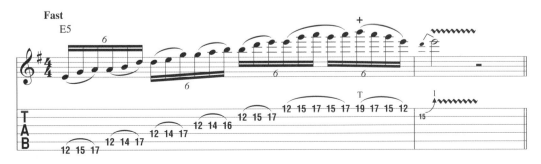

As you work on your legato patterns, you should also listen to the work of the masters, from Joe Satriani and Steve Vai to Reb Beach and Mark Tremonti, and for some truly jaw-dropping material, check out Allan Holdsworth.

LESSON #62: SWEEP PICKING

In the world of shred guitar, there is one technique that reigns supreme for "wow" factor: sweep picking. It's a simple and logical concept for playing single notes across adjacent strings, yet it requires lots of patience and practice if you want to execute it properly. In this lesson, we'll break down the key elements of the technique and show you essential arpeggio patterns on which you can use it.

Ups and Downs

As its name implies, sweep picking involves "sweeping" your pick across the strings, typically to play arpeggios consisting of one note per string. For ascending arpeggios, you'll play consecutive downstrokes, and for descending arpeggios, consecutive upstrokes. It's important, however, that you don't treat these pick strokes as separate actions, but rather allow your pick to "fall" to the next string in a single, smooth action.

Further, it's imperative that each note of the arpeggio sound clearly and *individually*; you do not want the notes to ring together. This requires some nifty fret-hand work, in which you need to lightly lift off each fretted note immediately after you play it. Coordinating that momentary fretting precisely with when the pick hits the string takes a lot of practice, but the rewards are worth it.

EXERCISE 1

Here is a basic sweep-picking exercise across the top four strings. Focus on a steady, singular sweep stroke in each direction, making sure to allow only one note at a time to ring. And use a metronome! It's way too common to hear guitarists "rush" the sweep picking technique.

Pick 'n' Roll

When you encounter notes on the same fret of adjacent strings, you need to roll your finger to effectuate the fretting-muting technique.

EXERCISE 2

This exercise alternates between Am and Bm arpeggios, both requiring the "roll" technique to assure sounding just one note at a time. Logically, you'll use your index finger for the Am triads and your ring finger for the Bm triad, but try using your middle finger as well.

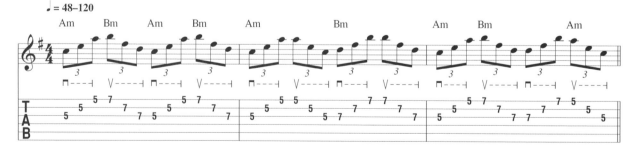

Essential Shapes

Now that you've got a basic understanding of how the sweep picking technique is executed, let's take a look at some vital arpeggio shapes.

On the following page are the popular three-string triad shapes and inversions, in both major and minor tonality, and with an added note on the top string (open circle indicates the root). To play these, sweep across the top three strings with a downstroke and play the second note on the top string with an upstroke.

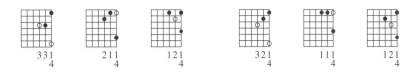

3 3 1   2 1 1   1 2 1   3 2 1   1 1 1   1 2 1

EXERCISE 3

Here are the primary major and minor four-string shapes, inserted into the chord progression from Pachelbel's "Canon in D." Note the picking directions between the staves. As before, strive for even volume and attack, sounding just one note at a time.

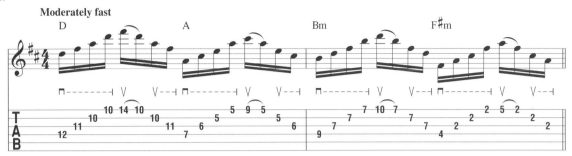

EXERCISES 4 AND 5

Taking the level of difficulty up a notch, the next two examples depict the most popular major and minor arpeggio shapes using five strings. Again, note the picking directions between the staves to help you navigate the pull-offs and hammer-ons.

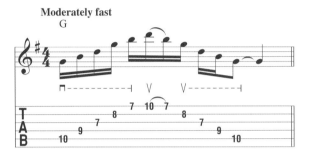 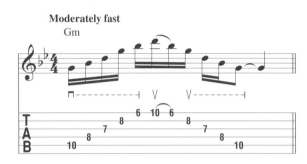

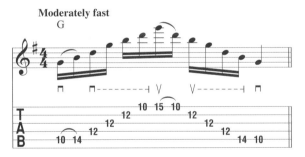 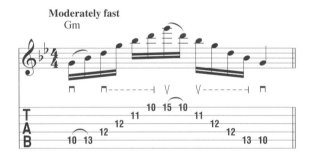

EXERCISE 6

Finally, here are the two most commonly used six-string arpeggio shapes for sweep picking. These are based on the popular sixth-string-rooted barre chord shapes, only with the major 3rd added to the bottom and top strings. As you speed up, it gets tricky to make that third string sound clearly between the rolled notes on strings 5–4 and 2–1. Take your time and focus on getting each note to ring clearly.

A highly developed sweep picking technique requires much dedication and focus, which is why, perhaps, so few guitarists really stand out with this technique. Listen to the work of shredders like Yngwie Malmsteen, Paul Gilbert, Jeff Loomis, Tony MacAlpine, and Vinnie Moore, to hear the technique performed correctly. You can also check out Greg Harrison's excellent instruction in *Shred Guitar* from MI Press/Hal Leonard for more on this thrilling technique.

LESSON #63: STRING SKIPPING

If sweep picking is shred guitar's vanguard technique, string skipping is its secret weapon. With it, the capability to produce wide-interval melodic contours enables you to create memorable and, if so desired, jaw-dropping lead guitar lines. In this lesson, we'll explain the basic elements of string skipping, provide some exercises for perfecting it, and top it all off with some downright scary licks.

Jump Right In

As its name implies, the string skipping technique involves playing notes or a phrase on non-adjacent strings. Because most rock melodies or licks don't use intervallic leaps greater than a 6th, string skipping isn't commonly utilized. But by developing command of the physical aspect of the technique, you open a whole new world of intervallic opportunity.

EXERCISES 1A & 1B

The most elementary way to develop speed and accuracy using string skipping is to start with a short and basic idea, playing it slowly with a metronome and gradually speeding up. These first two examples ascend and descend, respectively, notes from the A minor pentatonic scale on the third and first strings. It is generally recommended that you use strict alternate picking when string skipping.

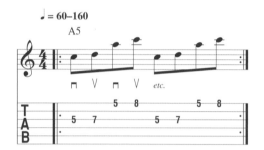 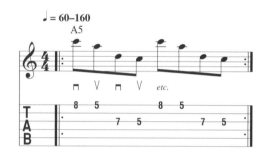

EXERCISE 2

This next exercise climbs up and back down the fretboard through all five boxes of the A minor pentatonic scale. Again, use your metronome first at a slow tempo to ensure accurate attacks, then gradually increase the speed.

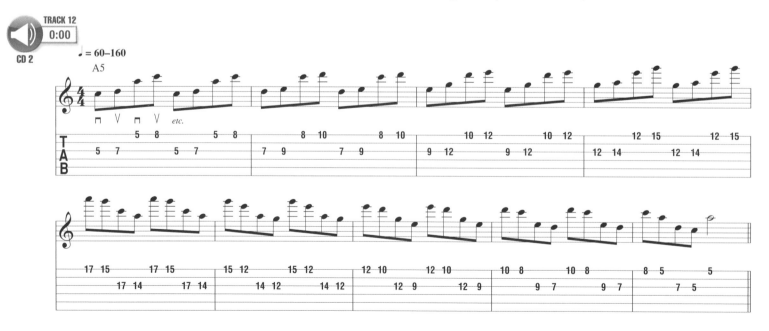

Although that example is shown here as an exercise, there are melodic possibilities as well. For example, the first four bars would work very well as a solo-capping two-octave ascending line over a progression in A minor, especially if you bend that final high G note up to an A and give some sweet, singing vibrato.

EXERCISE 3

Here's a string-skipping exercise that uses the ever-popular three-notes-per-string scale pattern. As usual, start slowly and gradually increase the tempo, making sure to work with a metronome. Be sure to play this one in all keys, up and down the neck, and vary the pattern—perhaps by skipping two strings.

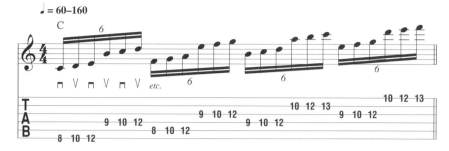

Lickety Skips

Once you become comfortable with the string skipping technique itself, you can try out some licks that employ it.

LICK 1

Here's a John Petrucci-inspired string-skipping phrase using a three-notes-per-string approach and covering a few different scale fingerings.

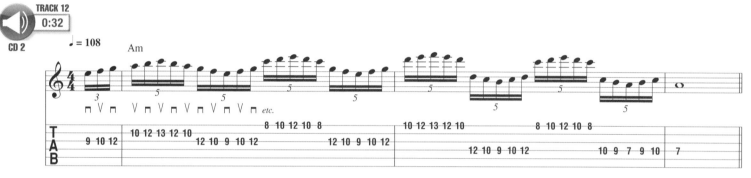

LICK 2

The undisputed king of string skipping in rock guitar is Paul Gilbert, and these final two licks come straight from his gangly digits. This first one is a descending legato phrase that contains a whole lot of notes, yet requires you to pick only once per string in each position.

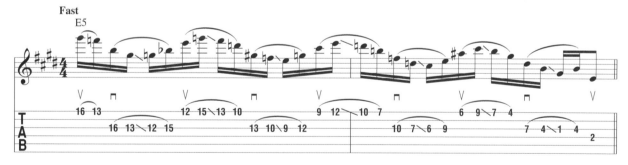

LICK 3

The final lick is a Gilbert classic. I'm pretty sure his metronome has a setting called "ridiculous" at the very top, which exactly describes this lick when Gilbert rips it off. Unless you have large hands and long fingers like Gilbert, this one will take quite a bit of woodshedding, as the stretch is quite difficult. But the reward is well worth it. Pay close attention to the picking instructions; they will help you conquer the lick with maximum efficiency.

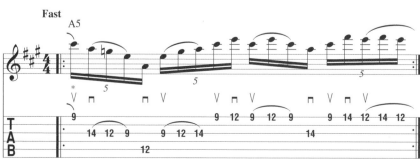

*Pick note 1st time.

LESSON #64: INTRO TO TAPPING

Though Eddie Van Halen is credited with making the technique both popular and part of rock guitar standard repertoire, other rockers were attacking their fretboards with both hands well before Ed's time. Steve Hackett (Genesis) is one of the most celebrated early adapters, while others such as Harvey Mandel (Canned Heat), Brian May (Queen), and Leslie West (Mountain) also experimented with the technique. In this lesson, we'll explore the essential elements of this exciting two-handed technique.

On Tap

Essentially, tapping is a hammer-on executed with one or more fingers of your pick hand, and is typically used in conjunction with pull-offs and occasionally slides. In fact, after you tap onto a note with your pick hand, you'll need to perform a pull-off with your tapping finger to adequately sound the next note (assuming it's lower in pitch—which it almost always is).

EXERCISE 1

Let's get started with this arpeggio exercise in which you begin each triplet with a tapped note and then pull off to an open string. Start slowly and strive for even volume and duration across all notes.

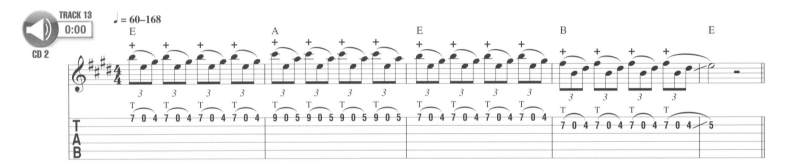

WHICH FINGER?

The tapping technique is performed with a finger from your picking hand, but which finger should you use? Eddie Van Halen famously "wedges" his pick between the joints of his middle finger and uses the index finger of his picking hand, while his thumb anchors the top of the neck and his ring and pinky fingers the bottom, for stability. But if your music requires rapid switching from picking to tapping and back again, using your pick hand's middle finger (while still holding the pick between your thumb and index finger) is a much more efficient strategy.

INDEX FINGER TAP (PICK POSITION)	MIDDLE FINGER TAP

You can use whichever method feels more comfortable, but you really should work to be proficient in both.

EXERCISE 2

Using the same progression from Exercise 1, we're now going to change the order of the notes. In addition to evenness of volume, it's also essential that you mute all unwanted string noise. While this is easy to do when tapping on the high E string, moving to interior strings, like the B string in these examples, presents opportunity for inadvertent noise. As you "pull off" the notes—whether with your tapping finger or fret-hand finger—use a downward motion and let that finger come to rest against the next adjacent string to help facilitate muting.

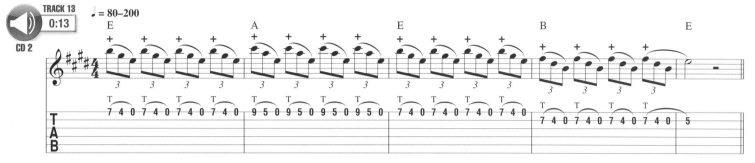

EXERCISE 3

Next we'll try a more linear line while maintaining an open-string anchor. This one requires frequent position shifts up and down the high E string.

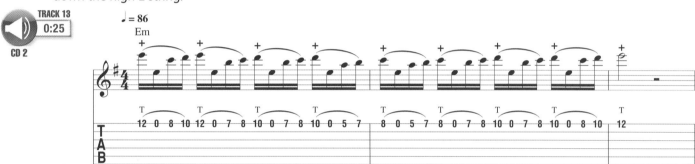

Eruption on Tap

Now that you've got a feel for the basic technique, let's move onto the tapping style that essentially has defined the technique—the Eddie Van Halen-style tapped arpeggio pattern made popular in his iconic "Eruption" solo.

LICK 1

Notice how we cover four different chords in a single position by moving your tapping finger just one fret and moving between the E and B strings. This is where a strong command of harmony and the fretboard can help your tapping lines stand out.

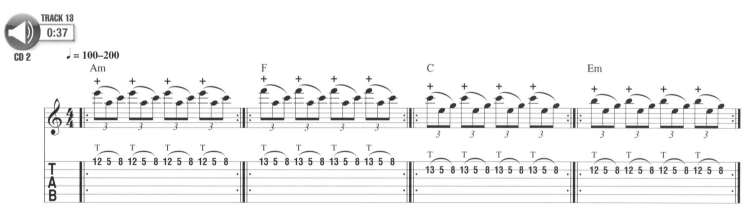

LICK 2

Here's a Nuno Bettencourt-inspired diminished seventh arpeggio sequence that climbs four octaves across all six strings.

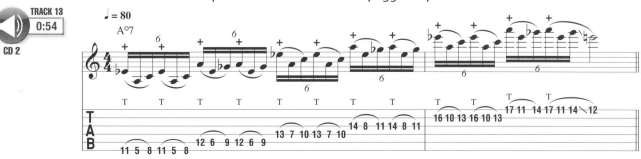

LESSON #65: ADVANCED TAPPING

Eddie Van Halen's tapping technique may have mesmerized the guitar-playing world—and still does—but many players since have taken Ed's technique to some pretty extreme places: multi-octave arpeggios, multi-finger tapping, and even a little something called "nubbing" among them. In this lesson, we'll explore techniques and licks that will help you tap into downright scary fretboard territory.

Scale Sequences

The first advanced tapping technique we'll examine involves expanding scalar phrases. This first example descends four octaves of the E minor scale in legato fashion, using taps and slides to generate momentum. You'll also see "hammer-ons from nowhere" employed for each string change. In this lick, these are performed with your fret hand's pinky finger. Strive to achieve even volume between these hammer-ons, the tapped notes, and the pull-offs.

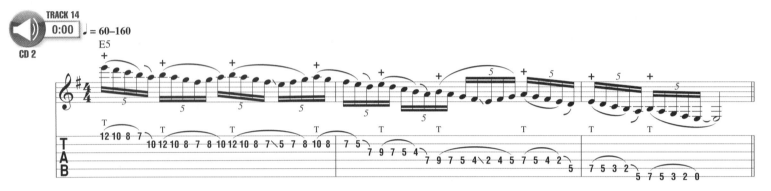

But… what if you want your tapped ascending legato line to be in stepwise fashion? You *can* perform those hammer-ons from nowhere using your index finger, *or* you can use this advanced Reb Beach tapping technique. Using his middle finger to tap notes, when he reaches the final tapped note on a string, he frets the first note on the next string and simultaneously "plucks" the string using his ring finger. This approach requires some rapid-fire position shifts and precise coordination, but I think you'll be surprised at how quickly it will come to you if you already have intermediate tapping skills.

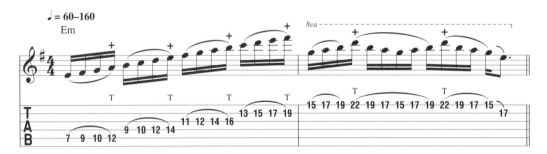

Tapped Arpeggios

When Extreme's "Get the Funk Out" hit the airwaves in 1991, guitarists everywhere were scrambling to figure out what Nuno Bettencourt was doing in the middle section of the solo. Turns out he was using a combination of tapping and string-skipping to create some truly amazing-sounding arpeggios. As usual, muting unwanted noise is essential, and much of that can be done with the palm of your tapping hand as you ascend. Use the underside of your fretting fingers as you descend.

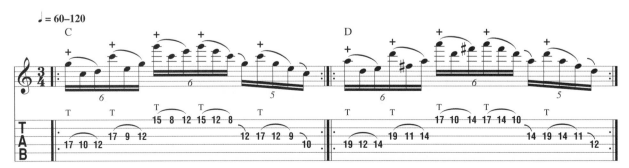

Here's a tapped arpeggio sequence that requires hammer-ons from nowhere using your fretting hand. This sequence, which I learned from shredder Toshi Iseda, combines adjacent inversions of a G major arpeggio. Be sure to follow the tapping directions ("T") between the staves very closely for best execution of the lick. Once you're familiar with the pattern, it's meant to be played ridiculously fast, so buckle up!

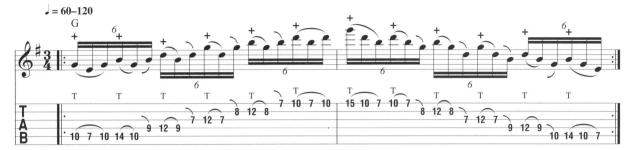

Two, Three, and Even Four Fingers Are Better Than One

While Eddie Van Halen was getting all the glory (and deservedly so), a young guitarist from Seattle named Steve Lynch was working on his own two-handed technique, inspired by Harvey Mandell and Emmett Chapman (the Chapman Stick). In fact, Lynch published an instructional book, *The Right Touch*, on the topic in 1979. His most famous use of multi-finger tapping is heard in Autograph's 1985 hit, "Turn Up the Radio," which inspired this next example.

Although you can easily bounce your index finger back and forth to tap the notes, do it Steve's way by using your index finger on the lower-pitched tapped note and your ring finger on the upper.

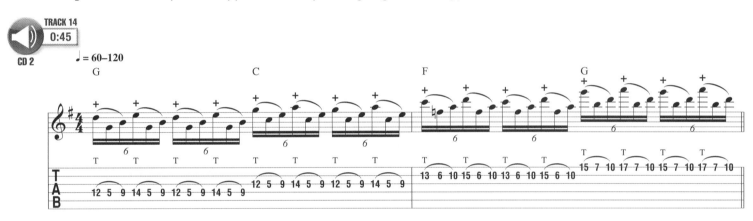

Although tapping makes up just a small part of his arsenal, former Night Ranger guitarist Jeff Watson wowed the world with his spidery *eight-finger* finesse. Truth be told, he never really used all eight fingers, but he did use all *four* pick hand fingers for blazing legato lines in "(You Can Still) Rock in America," similar to this next example.

Place your pick hand's thumb along the top edge of the neck, for stability, and keep your hand perpendicular to the fretboard. Aside from training your fingers to hit the right frets, the biggest obstacle is muting unwanted notes and noise. A key method for doing so is keeping all tapping fingers on the string as you hammer "up" the line, pulling them off one-by-one as you descend. In this manner, when you pull your pinky, ring, and middle fingers off the string (in upward fashion), your index finger, which remains in place fretting its note, mutes the strings physically above it (lower pitch strings) via the fleshy underside.

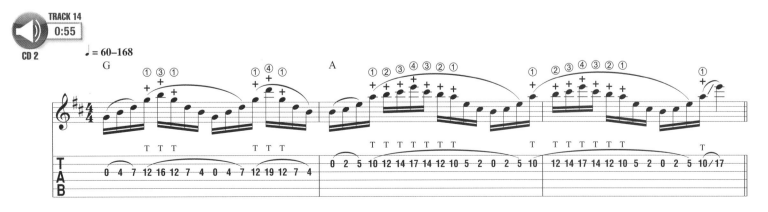

LESSON #66: MODERN SHRED TECHNIQUES

The term "shred guitar" typically brings to mind such luminaries as Yngwie Malmsteen, Steve Vai, Joe Satriani, Paul Gilbert, and Steve Morse, and although each and every one of these guys is as relevant as ever, the genre is being pushed to ever-expanding boundaries by exciting players like Buckethead, John 5, Guthrie Govan, and Tosin Abasi, among others. In this lesson, we'll explore some of the new shred techniques used by this forward-thinking group of super pickers.

Pentatonic Power

For decades, the minor pentatonic scale has been a defining sound of rock guitar. So it shouldn't be too surprising that some adventurous guitarists have found a way to make this five-note favorite a key part of the shred arsenal. One such player is Rusty Cooley, who has taken the minor pentatonic scale—and as a result his scary phrases—to a whole new level of extreme.

LICK 1

In this example, Cooley extends the standard "box" shape of the minor pentatonic to a three-notes-per-string version and then uses string skipping and legato techniques in combination with a sequence to form this blistering phrase in E minor.

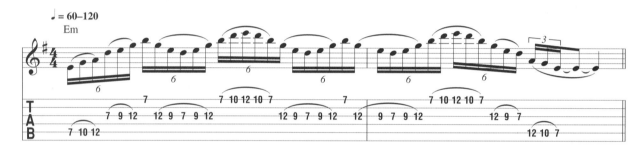

Chromatic Chaos

The minor pentatonic scale isn't the only one modern shredders have adapted to their art; borrowing from classical and jazz idioms, some guitarists have gone to the chromatic well with refreshing results.

LICK 2

This first line comes from Guthrie Govan, who craftily utilizes chromatic passing tones in the style of a jazzer, but in a rock-fusion context.

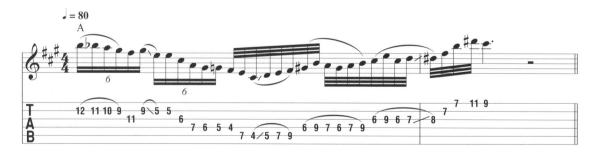

LICK 3

Whereas Govan draws from rather accepted jazz practices for his chromatic devices, other modern shredders go to this stepwise scale for a more dramatic—and chaotic—sounding effect. In the following John 5 lick, an augmented arpeggio leads to a chromatic descending line which in turn kicks off a major 7th arpeggio capped by more chromatic chaos.

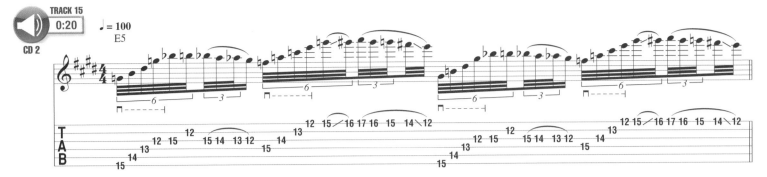

LICK 4

Still other guitarists have "tapped" into the power of chromatic lines in two-handed ways, like Buckethead's famous "nubbing" technique, which he performs with two, three, and even four tapping fingers. Essentially, he mirrors his left- and right-hand fretting patterns, and when played at Buckethead-worthy warp drive speed, it creates a very cool "video-game" sound effect.

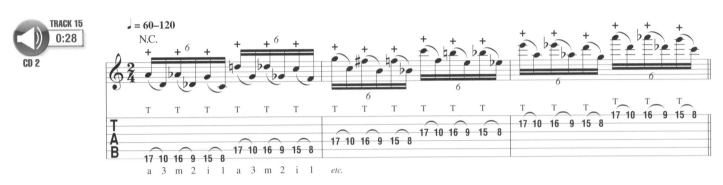

LICK 5

Guns N' Roses guitarist Ron Thal (a.k.a. "Bumblefoot") is one of the few guitarists who can go toe to toe with Buckethead—both in nicknames and outrageous guitar techniques. Known for using a sewing thimble on his pick-hand pinky to access notes beyond the fretboard, Bumblefoot also likes to manipulate chromatic phrases in tapping fashion. In this tapping extravaganza, he takes a chromatic sequence of B–Bb–B–C, adds a colorful (if dissonant) major 7th to each tone, and taps it out across four strings for one crazy-sounding shred sequence.

And For the Sweep ...

Sweep picking may be a fairly stock shred technique, but in the nimble hands of guitarist Tosin Abasi, it becomes a whole new animal.

LICK 6

Using suspended chord voicings for a progressive metal slant, Abasi takes this requisite shred approach to an exciting level of "suspense." Start slowly using a clean tone to make sure you're hitting all the notes cleanly, and note how you have to reset your sweep motion on the fourth 16th note of beat 3 in the first bar.

LESSON #67: INTRO TO THE CAGED SYSTEM

One of the eternal quests of rock guitarists everywhere is to master the entire fretboard. This is especially true of advanced beginner and early intermediate players who soon tire of the box patterns typically learned at that stage and are looking for ways to break out of those patterns. In this lesson, we'll introduce you to a popular fretboard learning system that will enable you to instantly identify root notes, chord tones, and scales in any key, anywhere on the neck.

C–A–G–E–D

Imagine having the ability to effortlessly navigate the entire fretboard as you rip off that killer 16-bar solo. There are several schools of thought when it comes to choosing the best way to learn and navigate the fretboard, but one of the most enduring, popular, and effective ways is the CAGED system. The five letters in "CAGED" represent the five open-position chord shapes, and mastery of these five shapes represents the key to locating any chord, scale, or arpeggio in any position on the fretboard.

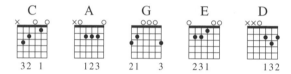

Now, as you probably are aware, each one of those chord shapes can be turned into a movable shape that can be played anywhere on the fretboard, in any key. For example, below you'll find each of the CAGED shapes played as a D major triad. Note the numerals placed above each grid. While many CAGED devotees will talk in terms like "D major chord of the C shape," you can see how that could be confusing. So as an alternative, many modern proponents of the system instead would say, "D major, pattern 1."

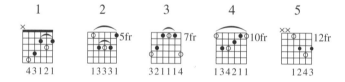

As you can see, these five shapes cover over 12 frets of the neck (the pattern repeats to continue up the neck). Upon closer inspection, you may have noticed too that each adjacent pair of chords contains at least one overlapping note. The result is complete fretboard coverage in the given key, using just these five shapes.

Roots, Arpeggios, and Scales

One of the most important parts of the CAGED system is the pattern formed by the root notes when you lay the five chord shapes across the fretboard. When overlapped end to end, these root-note patterns show you every occurrence of that root on the entire neck. Here's what the root shapes look like in D.

ROOT SHAPES IN D

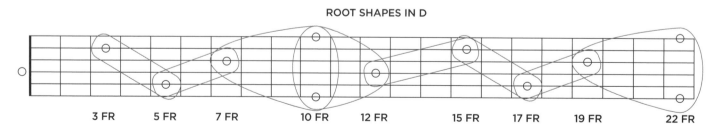

One very effective exercise you can do on your own is to map out the root shapes for all 12 notes of the chromatic scale. Choose keys randomly, so you're not just moving the patterns up one fret for each half-step increment.

In addition to root notes, the CAGED system, using the five movable chord shapes, provides a fast and relatively compact way to learn essential arpeggio shapes across the fretboard. This is essential knowledge for using the chord-tone soloing approach.

Deriving from the five shapes shown earlier, here is an arpeggio exercise in the key of D that ascends shape 1, descends shape 2, ascends shape 3, descends shape 4, and ascends shape 5.

Each chord shape of the CAGED system also has an associated scale pattern as well, which, when mastered, makes key center soloing across the entire fretboard a much easier task. Here are the five scale patterns associated with each of the CAGED shapes.

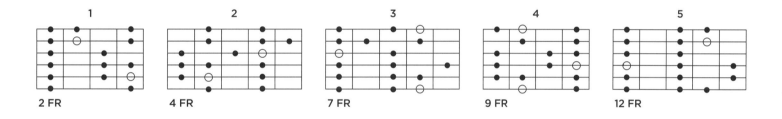

Finally, here's a scale exercise using the same "ascending 1, descending 2, etc." pattern used in the arpeggio exercise above.

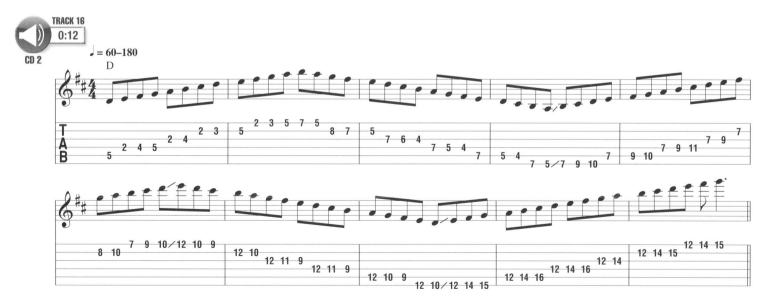

LESSON #68: CAGED LICKS

The five letters in "CAGED" represent the five open-position guitar chord shapes, and mastery of these five shapes represents the key to locating any chord, scale, or arpeggio in any position on the fretboard. But playing scales and arpeggios won't get you the gig; you've got to turn that knowledge into useful and entertaining phrasing. In this lesson, we'll show you some constructive rock licks culled from the five arpeggio and scale patterns of the CAGED system.

C-Shape

The first lick in this lesson lies within the C-shape pattern. This double-stop gem in the key of G major is written in the R&B-rock style championed by Jimi Hendrix and Curtis Mayfield. It works great as a closing phrase to a solo or interlude section. Note the use of grace notes—an essential element to this style.

A-Shape

Moving on to the A shape, or pattern 2, this Allman Brothers-inspired lick features a ♭7th (F) degree, to give the lick a bluesy vibe. It kicks off with a G major arpeggio, thus hammering the chord tones. The heavy syncopation is certainly *not* very Allman-like, but it helps to demonstrate how you can borrow from one sound and make it your own.

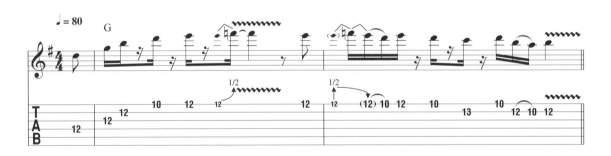

G-Shape

At a glance, this lick may look like a stock E minor pentatonic blues-rock lick, which is understandable given that E minor is the relative minor of G major, and the G-shape scale pattern contains the notes of E minor pentatonic in their familiar box pattern. But any tonal ambiguity that exists is soon resolved when the lick ends on the sustained G root note. Be careful not to rush this one!

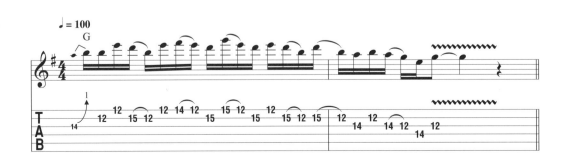

E-Shape

This E-shape, or pattern 4, lick in the key of G is built from one of my favorite Mark Knopfler licks (measure 1). In measure 2, we extend the pattern up a whole step to reach the high B note.

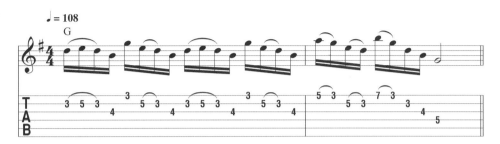

D-Shape

This pattern 5 lick was inspired by Joe Satriani's inventive legato approach. For phrasing's sake, I've moved the F♯ and B notes in beats 1 and 2, respectively, to the 4th fret, as opposed to the 9th fret one string lower. Strive for even duration and volume across the phrase.

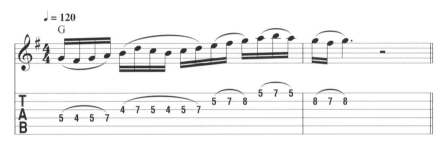

Crossing Patterns

The whole point of the CAGED system is complete fretboard mastery, whether that means being able to play in any key in any position, or being able to move fluently across patterns. The licks presented thus far have all been intra-pattern phrases. For our final lick, we're going to ascend through all five patterns in an alternate-picked shred run comprising descending triplet sequences. Yeah, the language is confusing, but you'll see what we mean below.

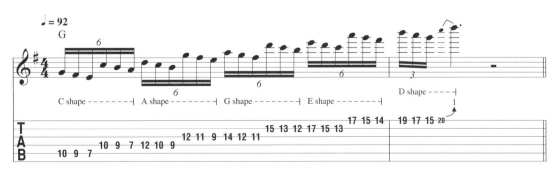

For practice purposes, you can turn those descending triplets around and ascend. It's another valuable rock phrasing device and makes for an excellent alternate picking exercise.

LESSON #69: KEY CENTER SOLOING

One of the great quests that all rock guitarists undertake at some point in their lives is determining which scale to play over a given chord progression. With a dash of theory and a sprinkle of harmony, you can glance at a chord progression and usually (and quickly) find one scale common to all the chords. In this lesson, we'll explore the concept of key center soloing and how it will make your solo spot much more comfortable.

Getting to the Roots

Before you can jump into key center soloing, you've got to have a basic understanding of scale theory and harmony. Working on the assumption that you already know how to build or spell a major scale, let's get to the harmonization. Here is the C major scale, followed by the harmonized C major scale, which shows all of the triads diatonic to that scale, or, diatonic to the key of C major.

With this knowledge, you can easily identify a song's or progression's key. A musical key is defined as the principal tonality of the song; thus, once the key of the song is identified, you only need to play that key's associated scale. For example, here is a two-bar I–vi–IV–V progression in the key of C. Rather than changing scales over each chord, you can simply play the C major scale over the entire progression as shown here.

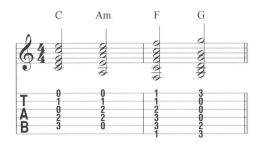 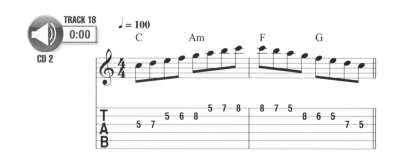

LICK 1

Let's stretch the previous progression to four bars and give an actual solo phrase using the key center soloing approach; that is, using just the C major scale over the whole progression.

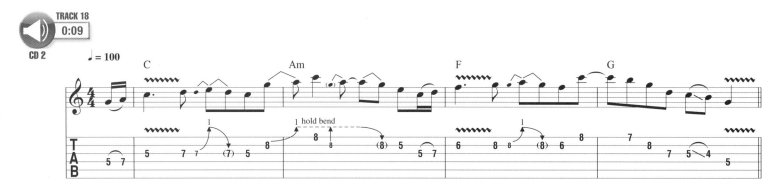

The Key Is NOT the Only Key

Key center soloing is *not* just about looking at the key signature and letting loose, for the key signature only tells part of the story. The first and most common hitch in this approach is the key's relative minor. For example, the seven notes that compose the C major scale also compose the A minor scale. As a result, the two keys share a key signature. So after you discern the key signature, you'll need to look at the progression itself to see or hear where the tonic lies.

LICK 2

In the previous example, we played C major over a C–Am–F–G progression, because it resolved to C. In this next example, we rearrange those same four chords, and now you can clearly hear that A is now the tonic, so we'll play A minor.

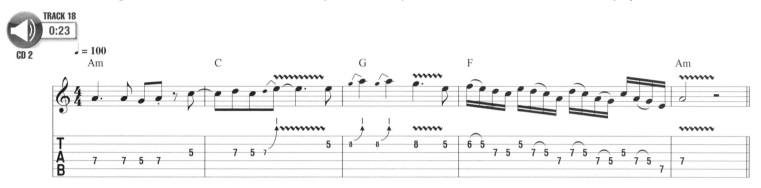

"But the notes of C major and A minor are the same, so why can't I just play the C major scale over this progression, too?" I hear you, and while that's *technically* correct, the difference lies in which notes get the most focus. In the phrase above, you'll note that it starts and ends on an A note, to emphasize its role as the tonic.

LICK 3

Sometimes, the chords in a given progression don't fit squarely or obviously into a single key. One example of this is a modal progression. When you come across a modal progression, you can still use the key center approach—you just need to be able to identify the appropriate mode. Our next progression, A–E–G–D, is presented with a key signature of A major, even though the G major chord isn't in the key. To account for this rogue chord, we use the A Mixolydian mode, which is just an A major scale with a G natural note instead of G♯.

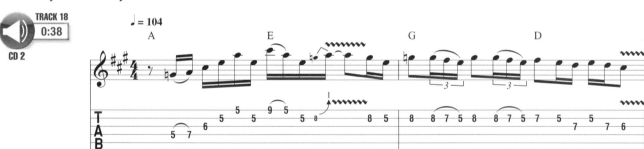

LICK 4

Given that we're talking *rock* guitar soloing, there's some wiggle room to break some rules—which is exactly what we do in the final example. Using the exact same progression played in the exact same way, we give the "ol' reliable" A minor pentatonic a spin, and it works!

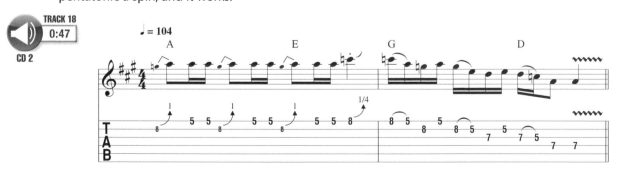

As to *why* it works, you need to look to rock's roots in the blues, where using a minor 3rd (C) in place of a major 3rd (C♯) offers the musical tension. Aside from that note, every other note of the A minor pentatonic scale used here is common to the A Mixolydian mode, so it's really not as big a stretch as it seems. The bottom line is that you need to use your ear, and if it sounds good, play it!

CHORD TONE SOLOING

With key center soloing, you find the tonal center of a given song or progression and then identify a single scale that you can use to solo over it. But if you really want your licks and lines to stand out, you need to be even more selective in your note choices. In this lesson, we'll show you how to best exploit the notes that make up each chord of a given progression.

Putting Notes in Focus

Too many rock guitarists learn how to identify a song's or progression's tonal center, determine the matching scale, and let loose. Although this key center approach works and is perfectly acceptable, if you really want your solos to shine, you've got to know which notes to play where. A great way to approach this is to use the arpeggio shapes from the CAGED system. Here they are:

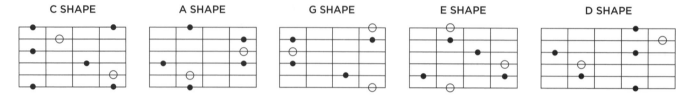

As a rock guitarist, you'll often find yourself soloing in minor keys. Here are the three most commonly used minor arpeggio shapes, from the three open-position minor chords.

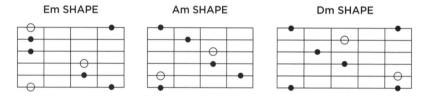

Now, you *could* just play arpeggios over each chord in a given part, as in this popular A–E–F#m–D (I–V–vi–IV) progression.

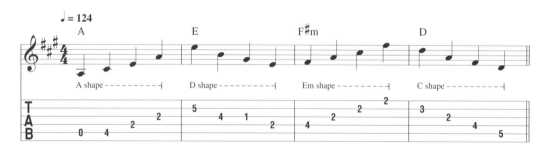

But as you can hear, that would get boring in a hurry. Instead, you'll want to use those chord tones as the skeleton, or bones, of your phrasing.

LICK 1

In this next example, see how I've incorporated the chord tones from the previous example into a much more musical phrase.

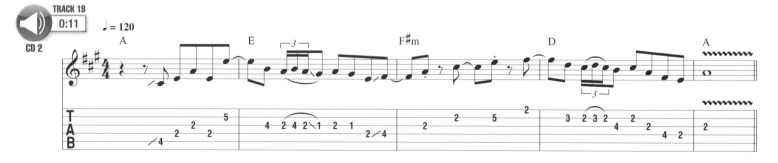

LICK 2

Here's another example that makes significant use of arpeggios, this one inspired by guitarist Mark Knopfler's keen sense of chord tone soloing.

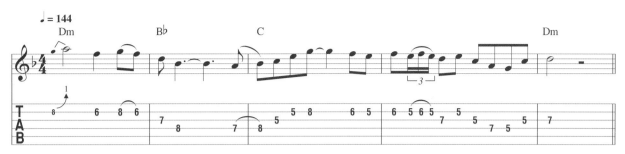

More Than Arpeggios

Though Licks 1–2 contained plenty of scale tones, they were constructed primarily of arpeggios. It's also possible and often desirable to construct more scalar-based lines, making sure to hit chord tones either on the change or in anticipation of the change, and on the strong beats (1 and 3).

LICK 3

This next example, inspired by the highly melodic phrasing in Lynyrd Skynyrd's "Sweet Home Alabama," kicks off with a D major arpeggio, but the remainder of the phrase is composed primarily of a descending scalar sequence. Note the chord tones on beats 1 (D, root) and 3 (C, root) in measure 1 and on beat 1 (B, 3rd of G) in measure 2. A scale tone (A, 2nd/9th of G) is played on beat 3, but I chose that over a B note because it better fits the overall motif of the phrase, and it's more or less a passing tone in this instance.

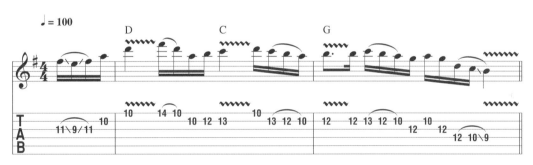

LICK 4

Even if you just want to rip key center-style through a minor pentatonic pattern, there's no reason you can't hit the chord tones while you're doing it. This final example sits in the twelfth-position E minor pentatonic box pattern, using familiar licks and devices yet finding plenty of chord tones for each underlying chord: unison E notes for the Em chord, D and B notes (5th and 3rd) for G major, E and G notes (3rd and 5th) for C major, and G and B notes (root and 3rd) for the final G major chord.

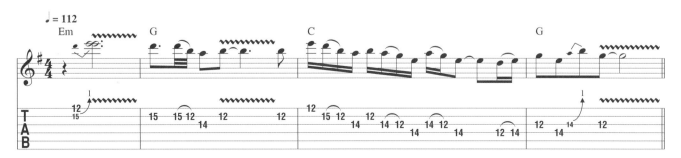

Many rock guitarists live to solo in minor keys, but when it comes to major keys, they fall apart at the seams. Yet it's that ability to effectively navigate major key soloing that has helped to make guitarists like Neal Schon, Steve Lukather, Tom Scholz, and Brian May such icons of melodic savvy. In this lesson, we'll explore some of the tools you can use to create highly melodic major key rock solos.

Major Key ID

First, you need to be able to identify when a progression calls for a major key solo. Assuming you have some basic theory under your belt, a major key progression is one that uses chords harmonized from the major scale; in the key of D, for example, the I, IV, and V chords are major: D–G–A. There are also three minor chords Em, F♯m, and Bm. (The vii chord, C♯°, doesn't occur very much in pop and rock music.) So if you see a progression that starts or ends with a major tonic, or I chord, odds are it's in a major key.

For the purposes of this lesson, we're going to work from the highly popular I–V–vi–IV progression in D, or D–A–Bm–G.

Major Pentatonic

Just as rock guitarists tend to go right to the minor pentatonic scale for minor key (or ambiguous) progressions, it makes sense that the major pentatonic would be a natural choice for major key progressions. The major pentatonic scale contains the 1–2–3–5–6 scale tones of the key center, or I chord. In the key of D, the scale is spelled D–E–F♯–A–B. Here are three essential fingerings for the D major pentatonic scale.

D MAJOR PENTATONIC SCALE PATTERNS

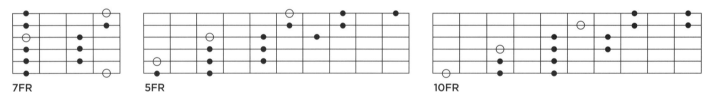

7FR   5FR   10FR

LICK 1

If you match the five notes from the D major pentatonic scale against the chord tones of the D–A–Bm–G progression, you'll find that at least two of the three chord tones for each chord appear in that scale, which means you can use the D major pentatonic scale over the whole progression, like this.

TRACK 20
0:00
CD 2

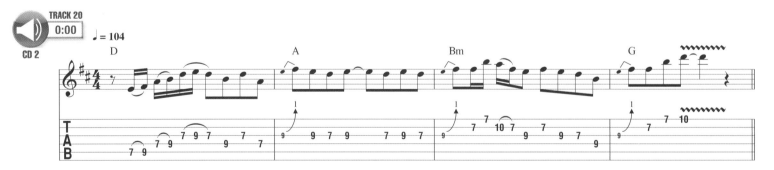

Still, you can't just go off willy-nilly on it; you've got to use your ear and your theory knowledge to make sure you're focusing on chord tones for each phrase. In the previous example, you see plenty of D, F♯, and A notes over the D chord, a tight focus on E (5th of A) over the A chord, plenty of B, D, and F♯ notes over Bm, and B and D notes over G in bar 4.

LICK 2

Of course, to further strengthen the odds that you're hitting chord tones throughout the progression, you can also play the changes; that is, change scales for every chord. Here are scale patterns for D major, A major, B minor, and G major pentatonic scales, which in turn are used to navigate the four-bar solo in the next example.

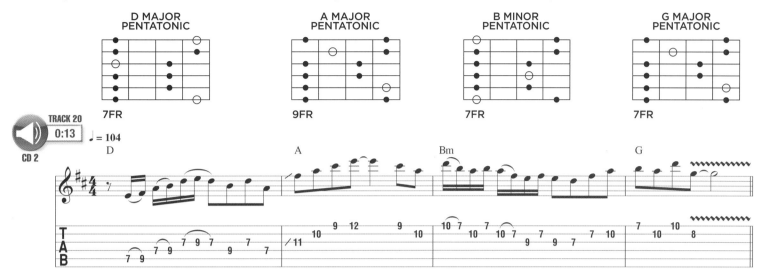

Again, make note of how chord tones were used over each chord in the progression.

Own It with Ionian

Finally, the most comprehensive way to approach a major key rock solo is to use the key center's complete major scale, or Ionian mode. In the key of D, this is: D–E–F♯–G–A–B–C♯, and it represents every possible diatonic chord tone. Here are three essential major scale patterns in D.

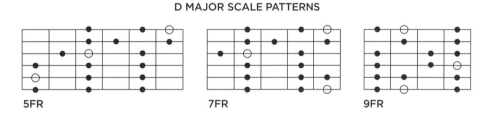

LICK 3

Even when you're armed with this mighty weapon, you need to pay attention to the chord changes. This example shows how playing an anticipatory chord tone on the final note of each bar helps usher along the changes.

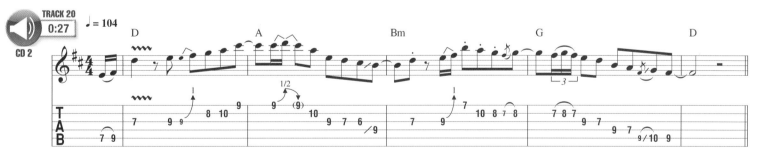

LICK 4

This final example presents a little more of a hard-rock flavor with a rapid-fire pickup beat and a tapped note in bar 2.

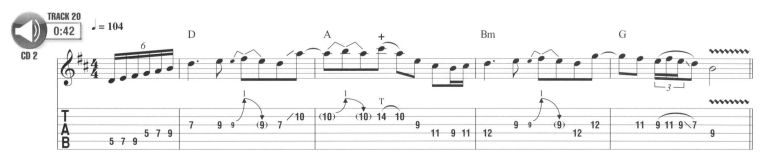

LESSON #72: INTRO TO THE MAJOR MODES

If there's one aspect of music theory that truly holds mystique among rock guitarists, it's the concept of the major modes. Part of it arises from their exotic Greek names, some from their frequent citation by guitar heroes, and a little simply because they're too often explained in a confusing manner. In this lesson, we will unlock the mystery of the major modes.

It's Just a Major Scale

When we say "major modes," it's actually shorthand referring to the modes of the major scale; in other words, the major modes simply represent different ways of playing a major scale. Yep, it's that simple. On to the next lesson, right? Well, not so fast. There actually is a little more than that happening, but at least it gives us a good start.

To begin, there are *seven* major modes—one for each note of the major scale. Their names, in scale order, are: Ionian, Dorian, Phrygian, Lydian, Mixolydian, Aeolian, and Locrian. The way this is most often taught is that a mode is just a major scale starting on a different scale tone. For example, if you begin a C major scale on C, or the root, you're playing the Ionian mode. If you then play a C major scale, but this time start on the second note, D, you're playing the D Dorian mode. Play a C major scale beginning on the 3rd, E, and you're playing E Phrygian, and so forth. In any case, you're simply playing the C major scale.

MODES OF THE C MAJOR SCALE IN ONE POSITION

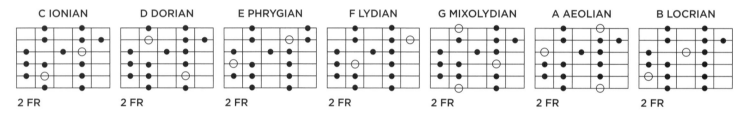

As you can see in the mini-diagrams above, all seven modes of C major contain the same notes; only the root note changes. Following is a fretboard-spanning series of C major mode scale patterns that rock guitarists find particularly useful—especially when soloing in a single key.

MODES OF THE C MAJOR SCALE ACROSS FRETBOARD

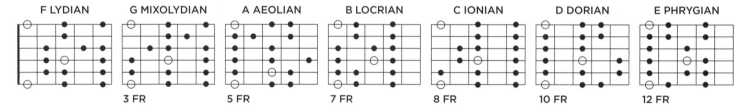

Parallel Modes

Too often, the major modes are taught as presented in the previous section, and rock guitarists walk away with a terrific fretboard navigation device, but they still don't comprehend the differences in *sound* and *vibe* that each mode represents. In this section, we'll dissect the modes in parallel fashion; rather than look at them as seven versions of a single major scale, we'll maintain the root and alter the spelling of each.

Sticking with the key of C, which has sharps or flats, you'll be readily able to discern the differences between each mode.

IONIAN

As I mentioned earlier, the Ionian mode is what we commonly call the "major scale." Using the number system, it contains the scale tones 1–2–3–4–5–6–7. It is most commonly used over major chords.

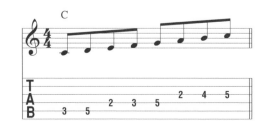

DORIAN (♭3, ♭7)

To create the Dorian mode, flat the 3rd and 7th scale tones: 1–2–♭3–4–5–6–♭7. Because of the flat 3rd, the Dorian mode is a minor scale. Thus, it is most often used over minor chords, particularly minor 7th chords (e.g., Cm7).

PHRYGIAN (♭2, ♭3, ♭6, ♭7)

The Phrygian mode contains four flatted notes and is spelled 1–♭2–♭3–4–5–♭6–♭7. The flat 3rd makes it a minor scale, and flat 2nd makes it a great choice for minor key soloing over chords a half-step apart—a popular harmony in modern metal.

LYDIAN (♯4)

The Lydian mode is a major scale with a raised, or sharp, 4th degree: 1–2–3–♯4–5–6–7. This mode is a great substitute for the major scale and tends to have an "uplifting" vibe to it. As a result, it's very popular in film scores.

MIXOLYDIAN (♭7)

The Mixolydian mode is a major scale with a flat 7th: 1–2–3–4–5–6–♭7. This one's a very popular scale in classic rock, due to its bluesy vibe. It's also useful over so-called Mixolydian chord progressions, where the normally diminished vii° chord is instead played as a major ♭VII chord, as in an A–E–G–D sequence, where G is the ♭VII.

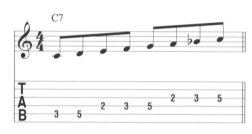

AEOLIAN (♭3, ♭6, ♭7)

Better known as the "natural minor scale," the Aeolian mode contains three flat scale degrees: 1–2–♭3–4–5–♭6–♭7. This is the most commonly used diatonic minor scale when soloing in a minor key.

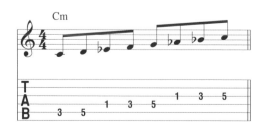

LOCRIAN (♭2, ♭3, ♭5, ♭6, ♭7)

This little-used (in rock) mode is essentially half-diminished in character, containing five flatted notes: 1–♭2–♭3–4–♭5–♭6–♭7. It might be used to create tension over the Bm chord in a progression like C–G–Bm–F, but be sure to resolve to strong chord tones when you reach the F chord.

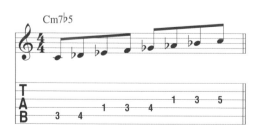

LESSON #73: THE DORIAN MODE

Soloing in minor keys is an essential element of rock guitar. As a result, most rock guitarists learn the minor pentatonic scale, the blues scale, and perhaps a couple of natural minor scale patterns early on. But sometimes there may be a better choice—a scale that better fits the underlying chord progression or one that gives your lines an element of intrigue. In this lesson, we'll explore the theory, popular patterns, and applications of one such scale: the Dorian mode.

Dorian Theory

The Dorian mode can be defined as the second of the major modes; that is, it's the major scale beginning on the second scale degree. But it's better to think of it instead as being a major scale with ♭3rd and ♭7th degrees: 1–2–♭3–4–5–6–♭7. Here's what it looks like in the key of C.

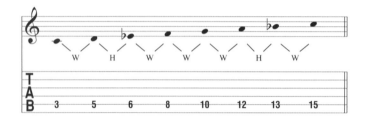

OK, let's hear what the Dorian mode sounds like. Here's the A Dorian mode set against an open-A drone.

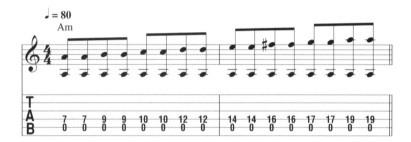

And here's how it sounds in the context of an uptempo rock riff.

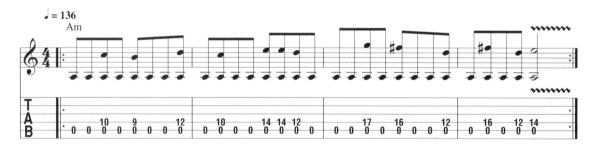

The only difference between the Aeolian mode, or natural minor scale, and the Dorian mode is the latter's possession of a natural 6th. Now try playing the same riff, but this time, play the F♯ notes as F naturals. Hear the difference? The Dorian version has a slightly brighter sound than the Aeolian one.

Dorian Patterns

Now that you've seen and heard how the Dorian mode sounds along a single string, let's take a look at some of the Dorian scale patterns that are most popular with rock guitarists.

DORIAN MODE

The first three patterns are all variations on the sixth-string root shape. For best results, you'll want to be able to combine the three, to use whichever fingerings best suit the phrase you're playing. The fourth one is a three-notes-per-string pattern popular among shred guitarists.

Dorian Lines

Depending on your ear and grasp of music theory, you may have recognized by now that the Dorian mode is a minor scale, due to the presence of the ♭3rd. As a result, you'll be using the Dorian mode over minor chords or minor key progressions.

So, when do you use the Dorian mode, rather than the natural minor scale typically employed in rock settings? One perfect opportunity is when you're faced with a i–IV progression, like Am–D. This minor key vamp has the same harmonic relationship as the ii–V in jazz, where the Dorian mode reigns supreme.

LICK 1

Carlos Santana famously used the Dorian mode over the i–IV progression of "Evil Ways." Here's an example in that style.

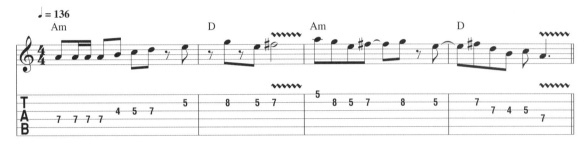

LICK 2

The Dorian mode is also an ideal choice when soloing over a static minor chord vamp; for example, if you need to solo over eight bars of Em, or especially Em7, the E Dorian mode makes an excellent choice.

LICK 3

Finally, here is a descending, legato shred line in A Dorian, played over an A5 chord. Many of the more interesting shred guitarists will mix up the modes over harmonically ambiguous vamps, giving their lines a much more attention-grabbing sound.

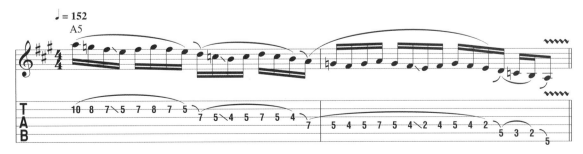

Rock guitarists—especially hard rock and metal types—simply love soloing in minor keys. Although the natural minor (Aeolian mode) and minor pentatonic scales can certainly fit the gig, in the world of heavy music there is sometimes a better choice, one that allows you to dive deep and really pull out something special. In this lesson, we'll explore the theory, finger patterns, and common uses of the modal equivalent of the prince of darkness—the Phrygian mode.

Phrygian Theory

The Phrygian mode can be defined as the third mode of the major scale; that is, it's the major scale beginning on the 3rd scale degree, but it's better to think of it instead as being a major scale with ♭2nd, ♭3rd, ♭6th, and ♭7th degrees: 1–♭2–♭3–4–5–♭6–♭7. Here's what it looks like in the key of C.

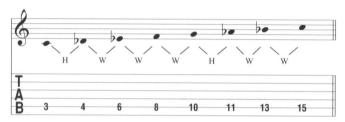

OK, let's hear what the Phrygian mode sounds like. Here's the A Phrygian mode set against an open-A drone.

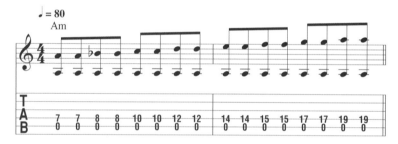

And here's how it sounds in the context of an uptempo rock riff.

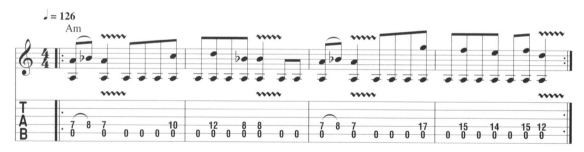

If that riff sounded a bit "metal" to you, it's because the Phrygian mode's ♭2nd—which also sets it apart from the Aeolian mode, or natural minor scale—has become a defining sound of the genre, put to a thorough thrashing by bands ranging from Metallica and Megadeth to Pantera and Children of Bodom.

Before we get on to some Phrygian phrasing, let's take a look at a few of the scale patterns favored by rock guitarists.

Phrygian Patterns

As the Phrygian mode and its rather "dark" sound is most associated with hard rock and heavy metal, we're going to present the three most commonly used fingerings by guitarists in those styles. The first is probably the most popular fingering, while the second pattern is simply an extended three-notes-per-string version ideal for shredders. The third pattern is also a three-notes-per-string fingering only with the root on the fifth string.

PHRYGIAN MODE PATTERNS

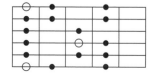
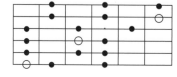
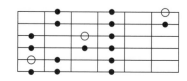

Phrygian Fun

PHRYGIAN RIFF

Perhaps the most obvious place to use the Phrygian mode is over a Phrygian progression. Rather than dissecting the harmonized Phrygian mode, let's just use power chords—since those are the harmonic currency of most hard rock and heavy metal. Using B as the root, the power chords you'll find in a Phrygian progression are: B5–C5–D5–E5–F♯5–G5–A5. From these chords, you can then craft your own Phrygian chord riffs, like this one.

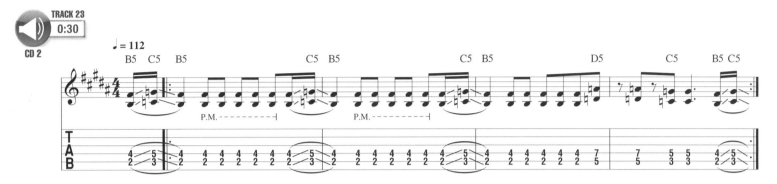

LICK 1

Now that you've got a progression, let's solo over it. This next example is crafted from the first Phrygian scale pattern shown earlier, in seventh position. Sustained unison bends hammer home the Phrygian tonality over the first three bars, before a descending Phrygian line adds heat to the proceedings.

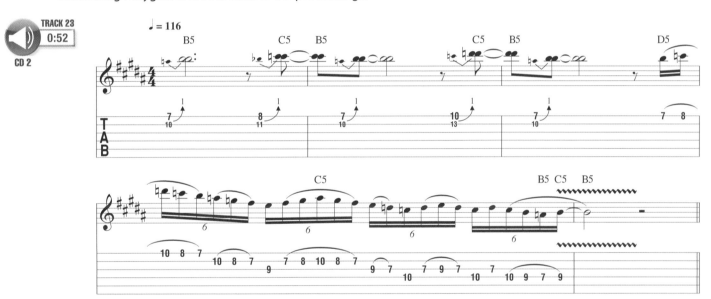

LICK 2

Finally, here's a progressive rock-style example, set as the end of a section or song, that uses the "key center" modal approach. With a key signature of E, you'd correctly see the B5 as a V chord, building tension prior to the final resolution to E5. However—and this is where your ear needs to override your eyes—the tonal center is *E minor* (or Aeolian), so that B5 actually calls for the B Phrygian mode, which is, after all, the E minor scale starting on the B note.

THE LYDIAN MODE

When soloing over a major key progression, if you think your only options are the major scale or the major pentatonic scale, you're not alone. But, just as the Dorian and Phrygian modes offer useful and exciting alternatives to the natural minor scale, there is also an exhilarating substitute for the common major scale. In this lesson, we'll explore this criminally neglected mode that can take your soloing to soaring new heights.

Lydian Theory

The Lydian mode is the fourth mode of the major scale and is itself a major mode. Its formula is 1–2–3–♯4–5–6–7.

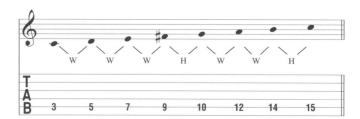

As you may have noticed, the only difference between the major scale and the Lydian mode is the Lydian's ♯4, but what a difference it makes. That little half step rise results in a series of three whole steps from the root, which in turn gives the mode added anticipation and mystery. It's for that reason the Lydian mode is a favorite amongst film composers!

Here's how the A Lydian mode sounds against an open A drone.

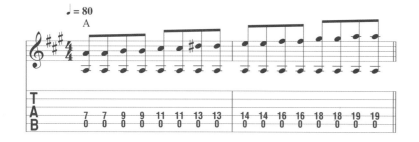

Now let's try it in the context of a modern rock-style riff.

Lydian Patterns

Following are three popular fretboard patterns for playing in the Lydian mode.

LYDIAN MODE PATTERNS

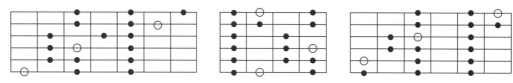

Lydian Lines

LICK 1

As mentioned earlier, that initial series of three whole steps in the Lydian mode supplies just the right dose of "drama" to otherwise stock major lines. In this first example, a slow progressive-leaning rock phrase in a Steve Vai style, the Lydian-defining #4th, A#, is dramatically sustained against an E chord in measure 1, before resolving to the major 3rd, G#.

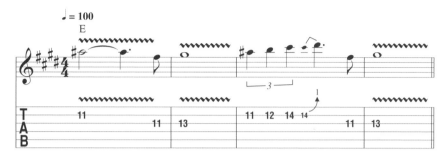

LICK 2

One of the shortcut "tricks" to using the Lydian mode is to play the minor pentatonic scale that falls a half step below the Lydian root. So, for example, if you're playing in E Lydian, you can craft a phrase from the D# minor pentatonic scale, like this one.

Be careful when using that strategy, though, as that minor pentatonic shape contains neither the Lydian root nor the 5th. As long as you use it sparingly and resolve to the root, as above, it can be a great tool.

LICK 3

Finally, the Lydian mode is the perfect fit for I–II chord progressions, like the Joe Satriani-inspired legato phrase shown here, over an E–F#/E progression.

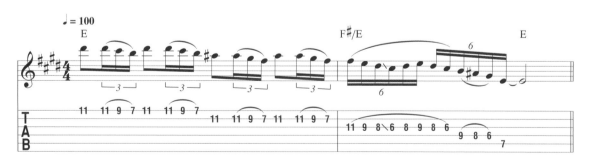

Some famous rock guitar examples of the Lydian mode in action include Joe Satriani's "Flying in a Blue Dream," Steve Vai's "The Riddle," David Gilmour's solo in Pink Floyd's "Time," and the main riff from Rush's "Freewill." Be sure to check these out to get a feel for how this fascinating mode works!

LESSON #76: THE MIXOLYDIAN MODE

If there is a mode just yearning to be used in a classic rock context, it's the Mixolydian mode. Exploited to great results by Led Zeppelin, the Allman Brothers Band, Boston, and Lynyrd Skynyrd, among many others, this mode—and the chord progressions based on it—is a must-know sound for all rock guitarists. In this lesson, we'll explore this bluesy scale in all its dominant glory.

Mixolydian Theory

The Mixolydian mode is the fifth mode of the major scale and is itself a major mode. Its formula is 1–2–3–4–5–6–♭7. The presence of the ♭7th—the only difference between Mixolydian and the major scale—further makes the Mixolydian mode a dominant scale, well suited for playing over the V chord in a progression, or over dominant seventh chords.

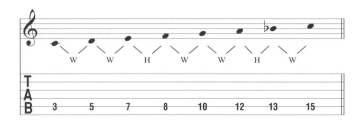

Here's how the A Mixolydian mode sounds against an open-A drone.

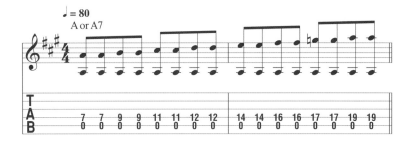

And here's a Led Zeppelin-inspired classic rock riff using the A Mixolydian mode, again with an open-A drone.

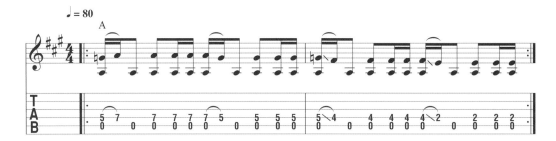

Mixolydian Patterns

Following are four popular fretboard patterns for playing in the Mixolydian mode—two with sixth-string roots and two rooted on the fifth string.

MIXOLYDIAN MODE PATTERNS

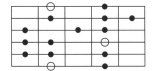 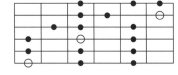  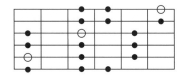

Mixolydian Progressions and Licks

Although the Mixolydian mode is effectively used in rock guitar soloing, it's even more pervasive in rhythm guitar parts and chord progressions. In normal diatonic harmony, there are seven triads associated with the major scale: I–ii–iii–IV–V–vi–vii. In a Mixolydian progression, that vii chord, which is a diminished triad, becomes the ♭VII, or a major triad. So, a G Mixolydian progression may contain various combinations of the following chords: G–Am–Bm–C–D–Em–F.

MIXOLYDIAN PROGRESSION

Here's an example of a Mixolydian progression. On initial examination of this progression, the presence of G, F, and C chords could be construed to mean it's a V–IV–I progression in the key of C, but since G is clearly the tonal center, that F chord must then be interpreted as a ♭VII chord, making the progression G Mixolydian. Famous examples of this harmonic construction include "Sweet Home Alabama," "Ramblin' Man," and the acoustic riff in "More Than a Feeling."

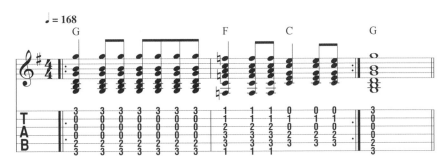

LICK 1

Using the Mixolydian progression from our previous example as the harmonic basis, here's a Mixolydian lick in the style of the Allman Brothers that fits over it.

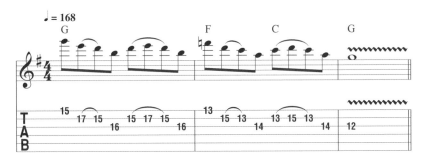

LICK 2

Because of its ♭7th degree, the Mixolydian mode is a great choice over blues-based progressions, particularly those using seventh chords or implied seventh chords (such as boogie rhythms). This next lick is a blues classic that shifts with the changes from A Mixolydian over the A7 chord to D Mixolydian over the D7 chord.

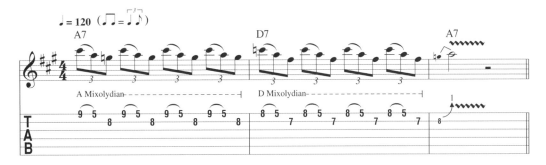

LESSON #77: MELODIC MOTIFS

You've all probably heard of "the hook" in terms of a great rock song. It's that special, distinctive, and generally pleasing phrase that grabs your ear and won't let go. Well, great rock guitar soloists—like master fishermen—know just how to hook their listeners using just the right aural bait. In this lesson, we'll explore melodic motifs—one of the best lures you can have in your soloing tackle box.

What's a Melodic Motif?

Essentially, a melodic motif is a short, musical pattern of notes found through a section of a solo. Although these patterns can be repeated verbatim, more often the melodic motif is revised and developed to form other musical phrases that share similar melodic contours. Rock guitarists from Angus Young to Ritchie Blackmore to Steve Vai have all used melodic motifs to great effect.

LICK 1

This first example, culled from the G Mixolydian mode, uses a very simple motif climbing the first four scale degrees over each chord before resolving to the major 3rd. When the progression goes back to G, in measure 3, the motif heard in measure 1 is repeated only an octave higher.

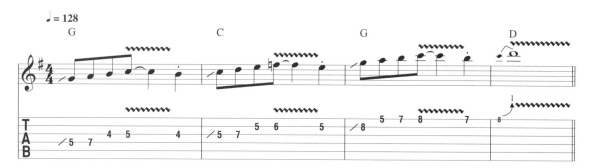

LICK 2

Here's a bluesy example using double-stop 6ths intervals.

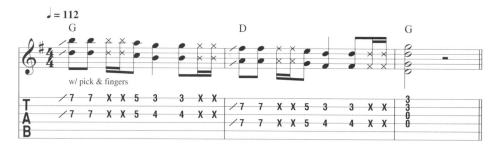

LICK 3

You can also use a melodic motif within the context of a single, short lick, like this E blues-scale rocker.

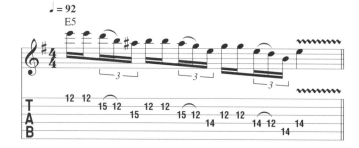

Rhythmic Variation

In those first three examples, you may have noticed that the rhythm of each repetition of the given melodic motif was identical. Though there's nothing wrong with that, melodic motifs can become even more effective with slight tweaks to the rhythm.

LICK 4

In this next example, the first two bars use identical rhythms for the motif, but in the third repeat, the motif is stretched over two bars.

LICK 5

In this next one, set over an Am–Em–G hard rock progression, the melodic contour of the primary motif (1–♭7–1–2–♭3) stays pretty much the same. However, the rhythm varies slightly, with the resolving note of each sequence receiving, in order, a quarter note, quarter note, 8th note, and dotted 8th.

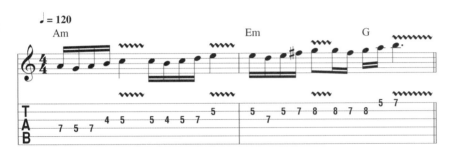

Intervallic Play

By definition, melodic motifs are based on a sequence of intervals, but what we're talking about in this section is using a set interval to create the motif.

LICK 6

In this next example, inspired by the '80s hard rock guitar sound, a sequence of stacked 3rds forms an ascending motif in bars 1–2, before a motif comprising 5ths takes the phrase back down the E minor scale.

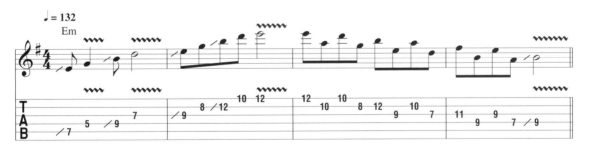

LICK 7

On the other side of the spectrum, you can also use chromaticism to great effect in creating melodic motifs. In the following Steve Morse-inspired and minor pentatonic-based phrase, the primary motif of beat 1 is repeated up a 4th on beat 2 and then up an octave on beat 4, with a transitional line on beat 3 also staying true to the quasi-chromatic spirit of the motif.

LESSON #78: RHYTHMIC MOTIFS

Motifs are a great way to create catchy "hooks" that grab the listener's attention. In addition to the idea of the melodic motif, there is also the equally formidable and important counterpart: the rhythmic motif. Let's learn about it!

What's a Rhythmic Motif?

Like the melodic motif, a rhythmic motif comprises a succession of notes that form a specific pattern that is repeated either verbatim or with variation. Of course, the difference is that the emphasis is placed squarely on the rhythm, while the melody is free to vary greatly.

RIFF 1

Just how powerful can these rhythmic motifs be? Consider the main riff to Jimi Hendrix's "Purple Haze," which uses a four-note motif comprising 8th notes. That rhythm is as integral to the timelessness of that riff as its counterpart melody. Here's a phrase using the exact same rhythmic motif.

RIFF 2

As you can see and hear, it's a very basic idea, but effective nonetheless in creating a rhythmic hook. Here's an example using three 8th notes and tied notes. Note the use of anticipation—hitting the sustained note on the "and" of beat 4—to add further interest.

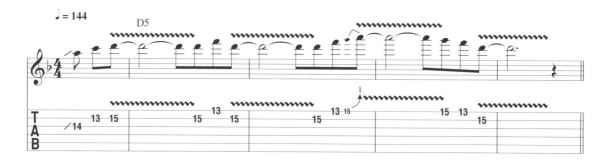

RIFF 3

Similarly, the following riff also uses a rhythmic motif comprising three 8th notes and starting on an upbeat; however, after restating the motif twice, we accelerate the repeats, giving only an 8th rest instead of the half-plus-an-8th in the first two bars.

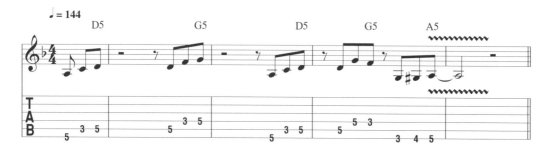

LICK 1

It's important to realize that you're not limited to short rhythmic ideas, even though they're the most commonly used types. In this next example, the six-bar solo in A minor comprises two three-bar rhythmic motifs.

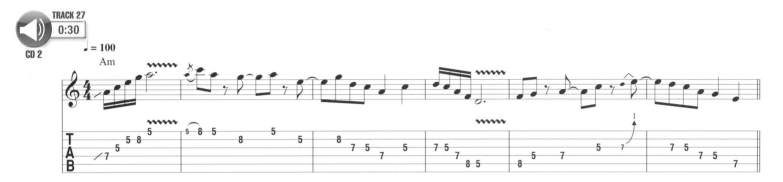

Combining Motifs

Not surprisingly, you'll occasionally hear phrases that use both rhythmic and melodic motifs in one line.

LICK 2

Here's a really basic idea using 16th-note triplets in a sequenced descent down the A minor pentatonic scale.

LICK 3

Here's a slippery phrase that descends the C Mixolydian mode using both a rhythmic and a melodic motif to make it memorable.

 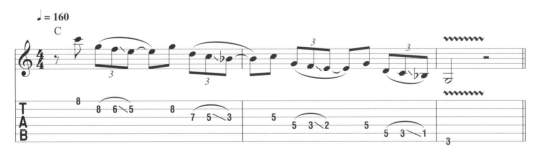

Some masterly examples of rhythmic motifs in the annals of rock guitar include David Gilmour's solo in "Money," Neal Schon's soulful lines in "Who's Crying Now," Billy Gibbons' "Gimme All Your Lovin'," and George Harrison's outro in "Come Together." Next time you're listening to your favorite guitarist, try to pick out examples of rhythmic motifs to further edify your soloing and riffing chops.

LESSON #79: DRONE RIFFS

From the sitars of India to the pipes of Scotland and even the monks (monastics, not Thelonious) of southwest Asia, the drone has a rich musical history. It is an engaging and versatile tool, which, in the able hands of guitarists ranging from Jimmy Page to Billy Corgan to Dave Matthews, has been at the root of many classic rock guitar riffs. In this lesson, we'll take a look at four methods for using these ringing, sustaining musical treasures.

Low Drones

A drone is quite simply a continuously sounded note or chord against which a melody is typically played. The drone can be either sustained or repeatedly attacked. Further, it can be voiced lower, higher, or even in between its counterpart melodic voice. Here, we'll begin with a lower-voiced drone.

Here's an E major scale beginning on the 5th (B) and played against a droning open low E string.

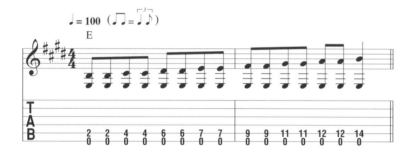

Technically speaking, a drone riff is arguably the most popular rock and blues device of all time—the classic boogie-woogie riff. Rather than using the typical shuffle rhythm, this next example is presented in a more roots rock-style driving 12/8 time, with accents on the downbeats and an ever-so-slight palm mute throughout.

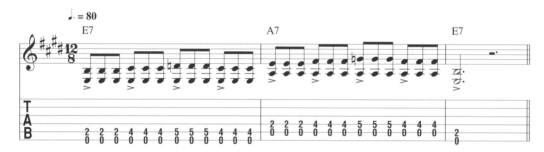

Examples of low drones in more hard rock contexts include Billy Corgan's brilliant octave riff against a droning low E in "1979," the droning D string in Collective Soul's "Shine," and the sinister sustained low E drone of Metallica's "Wherever I May Roam." This next example is in the style of the latter, to demonstrate the effectiveness of a prolonged, single, sustained drone.

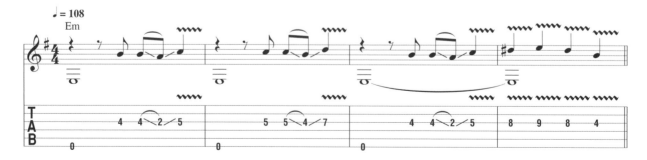

High Drones

Though it's often the case in rock guitar riffs, the drone note does not necessarily have to be played on a lower string. The *high* E string is a popular choice as well. Stevie Ray Vaughan (intro riff and solo in "Pride and Joy") and Angus Young (solo in "Back in Black") have made particularly good use of the high E as a soloing device.

This next riff is a modern alt-rocker in E minor featuring a repeatedly attacked high E string drone.

Middle Voice Drones

So far you've seen and heard the highs and lows of droning riffs, but sometimes, the drone note sits between a bass and melody voice. Classic examples of this approach in rock music include fingerstyle riffs like the Beatles' "Blackbird" and the Red Hot Chili Peppers' "Scar Tissue," as well as strummed rockers like Collective Soul's "The World I Know" and Dave Matthews Band's "Tripping Billies."

The following riff is in the style of those latter two titles. This drone approach is especially effective using an acoustic guitar for the riff.

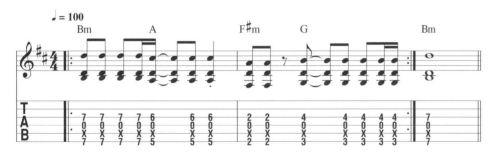

Chord Drones

In the intro we said a drone is a continuously sounded note or *chord*. So to wrap up this lesson on drone riffs, we'll take a look at a chord drone that has become very popular in mainstream rock. Similar to chord progressions from Matchbox Twenty and Oasis, this riff features a droning three-note G5 chord while the progression moves from G to Cadd9 to Em7, before resolving to a regular D triad in bar 4. But even then, we recall the G5 drone via the Dsus4 chord on the final two 16th-note strums to lead back to the tonic G.

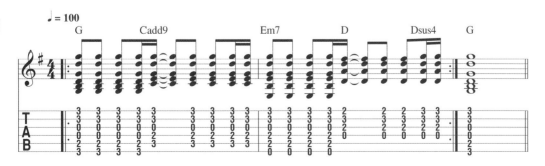

LESSON #80: TRIAD SUBSTITUTIONS

When taking on solos, fills, and riffs, rock guitarists almost always turn first to scales. But there's another easy and highly effective way to approach these melodic creations, and there's a good chance you're already familiar with the basic machinations: *Triads*. In this lesson, we'll show you how these little three-note shapes can make big rock sounds.

Shapes of Things

Generally speaking, when someone says "triad" while referring to guitar, they're often referring to basic major and minor chords, such as open chords or evwen barre chords. For the purposes of this lesson, we're talking about three-note shapes. Because a triad contains three notes, there are three possible arrangements, or inversions, for each chord.

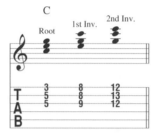

The root position shape has the chord root in the bass, with the 3rd and 5th stacked above it. The first inversion places the 3rd in the bass, while the root is moved up an octave. The second inversion sees the 5th in the bass, with the 3rd now moved up an octave. The same applies to minor triads.

For the purpose of better seeing the "fretboard roadmap," we've organized the chord frames below as they appear ascending the fretboard (string sets 3–1 and 4–2), rather than in order of inversion, but you should be familiar playing any inversion at the drop of a hat.

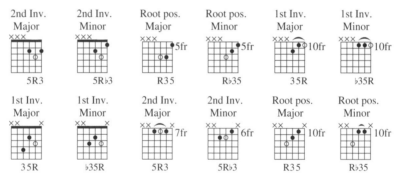

Before we move on to actually using triad substitutions in a soloing context, you'll need one small but essential harmony lesson. To use triad substitutions most effectively, you need a strong command of the harmonized scale for any given triad; that is, the seven triads that belong to each major or minor scale. For this lesson, we'll focus on the key of D major, and because it's so popular in rock guitar soloing and riffing, here's that harmonized scale using all second-inversion shapes.

TRACK 29
0:00

CD 2

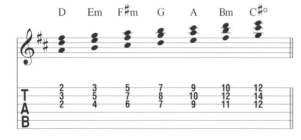

For best results in using triad substitutions, try harmonizing popular keys and scales using all three inversions in both major and minor tonalities.

Try Adding Triads

Now that you know where you can play any major or minor triad on the top four strings, let's put them to use. One reason why triad substitution is such an effective tool is that simply by using any two adjacent triads from a given key (e.g., D and Em, or Em and F♯m), you've got six of the root scale's seven tones. For example, D major contains the notes D–F♯–A, and Em comprises E–G–B. So, using just those two chords, you're missing only the major 7th, C♯.

LICK 1

This first phrase uses D, Em, F#m, and G triads over a static D chord. You can see that every note of the D major scale is present, but it sounds nothing like a typical scalar line.

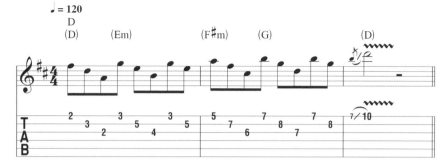

LICK 2

You can also use triad substitution to create modal lines. The next example is a V–I progression in D, so by alternating between A and G triads, we create a strong A Mixolydian sound, which resolves quite naturally to the tonic D. As for the structure of the phrase, we're simply playing every inversion, or partial inversion, of the A and G triads as we ascend the fretboard.

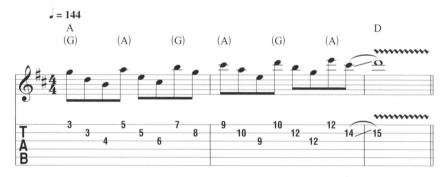

LICK 3

So far, we've used only strict chord shapes to ply these triad substitutions. You can also use two-string versions that more closely resemble scalar phrases. In the next example, we substitute I–IV–V (D–G–A) triads over a static D harmony in a playful ascending pattern. Though it looks tricky at first, note that the first four arpeggios use the exact same fingering pattern. The final two are also identical.

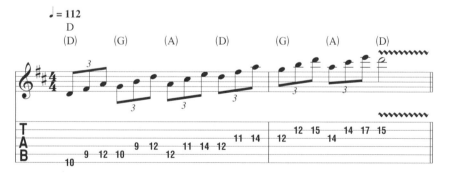

LICK 4

Finally, this last example uses triads, or arpeggios, that directly correspond with the underlying Bm–A–F#m–G progression. Note the "unusual" F#m triad in bar 4, where a whole-step bend is employed to reach the 5th (C#), before resolving to B, the 3rd of G.

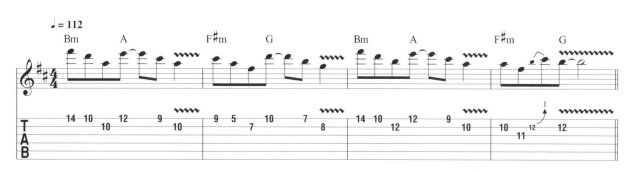

LESSON #81: EXOTIC SCALES

You're a rock guitarist, a soloing master in waiting. You've mastered the pentatonic scales, major and minor are old hat, and you're fluent in the modes of the major scale, and you're even comfortable borrowing from the harmonic minor scale from time to time. Ah, but have you tried out some Hungarian Gypsy minor lines, or buzzed through the Byzantine scale for Middle Eastern flavor, or fired up the Prometheus scale? If not, this lesson will introduce you to five exotic scales, their shapes, and some cool licks built from them. For each scale presented in this lesson, we'll show you its spelling in notation, in the key of C, along with two scale patterns (sixth- and fifth-string roots) and a lick, riff, or phrase using the scale.

Hebrew

The Hebrew scale (1–♭2–3–4–5–♭6–♭7) is the fifth mode of harmonic minor. You may already know it by its Western name of Phrygian dominant, or the slightly more exotic Spanish Phrygian. The Hebrew scale is popular among jazz guitarists, as it allows for easy improvisation over altered dominant chords, but it's also an exceptional tool for creating Middle Eastern sounds. For example, fusion guitarist Al Di Meola uses it to create a distinctly ethnic sound in his song "Egyptian Danza." Here is how the scale looks in notation, along with two scale patterns:

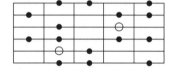
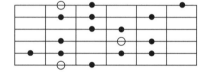

To hear it in action, let's pit the D Hebrew scale against an open D drone to create a Middle Eastern-style riff.

Hungarian Gypsy Minor

As its name implies, the Hungarian Gypsy minor scale (1–2–♭3–♯4–5–♭6–7) is popular among Gypsy jazz guitarists, and, with its ♭3rd and major 7th, is a terrific choice for soloing over minor-major seventh chords.

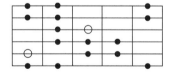
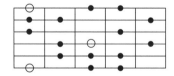

Despite its jazzy appeal, the Hungarian Gypsy minor scale is also quite useful in creating more ethnic sounds. The phrase below, which is how Uli Jon Roth might interpret a Hungarian folk song, focuses on the chromatic series of notes formed by the scale's ♯4, 5, and ♭6 degrees.

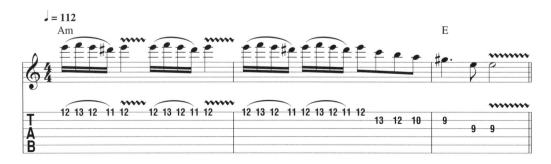

Byzantine

The Byzantine scale (1–♭2–3–4–5–♭6–7), also known as the Arabic or the double harmonic major scale, features two three-note series that use a half-step followed by an augmented 2nd. The scale is a musical palindrome, with the same scale intervals in both ascending and descending order. One of its most famous uses is heard in Dick Dale's surf-rocker "Misirlou," which is actually based on a Greek folk song with a Middle Eastern influence.

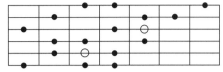
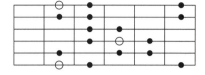

Like the Hungarian Gypsy minor scale, the Byzantine scale also features a chromatic three-note series, here consisting of the major 7th, root, and ♭2nd, and is highlighted in the riff below.

Enigmatic

The Enigmatic scale (1–♭2–3–♯5–♭6–7) is a six-note, or hexatonic, scale. Composer Giuseppe Verdi introduced this unique sound to Western music in the mid-19th century. Like all of the previous scales presented here, the Enigmatic features an augmented 2nd interval in its spelling. Because of its plethora of altered tones, this scale is rather effective over an altered dominant chord in a jazz or jazz-rock fusion context. For a heavy-rock context, try using it over a tritone power chord [e.g., F♯(♭5)].

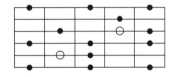
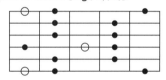

Here is a fusion-inflected lick you might hear from Mike Keneally or Guthrie Govan.

Prometheus

The Prometheus scale (1–2–3–♯5–♭7) is a five-note, or pentatonic, scale. Looking at its structure, you'll see that it's closely related to the whole tone scale, missing only what would be the 5th degree of that scale. As a result, the Prometheus scale is a terrific choice for playing over a static 7♯11 chord or over altered V chords in either major or minor keys.

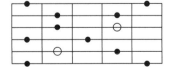
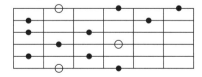

The lick below exploits the scale's tritones to kick off a trippy and slippery descent over a C7♯11.

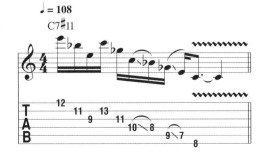

LESSON #82: SURF GUITAR

Surf's up, dude! From the early "rumbling" sounds of Link Wray to the exotic melodies of Dick Dale to the pitch perfect vocal harmonies of the Beach Boys, surf music is a cultural institution, as American as hot-rods, hot dogs, and hot days spent at the beach, watching those crazy young folk ride the waves and shoot the curls. In this lesson, we'll take a look at the essential elements of this great instrumental tradition.

Sound (of) Waves

Perhaps more than anything, surf guitar music is defined by its unique sound. Almost exclusively, Fender guitars and amps reigned supreme in the genre, with Stratocasters, Mustangs, and Jaguars being the primary planks, with Gretsch guitars also finding popularity in later years. Surf guitarists typically played through Fender tweed amps such as the Bassman or Princeton. But perhaps the main ingredient was reverb, whether a built-in spring version or a separate Fender reverb tank. Players of the day described the reverb-drenched sound as "wet," rather apropos to the surf style.

From Power Chords to Byzantine Melodies

Surf music came about in the late 1950s and early 1960s as part of the surf culture of southern California, serving as dance music for the youth of the day. The surf guitar style has its roots in the early instrumental rock guitar of artists like Link Wray and Duane Eddy. Though it doesn't exhibit the uptempo beat typical of surf music, Wray's 1958 breakthrough hit "Rumble" not only provided the tonal template, with its "wet" reverb and tremolo sound, but also introduced the power chord to rock 'n' roll guitar. Here's an example in that style.

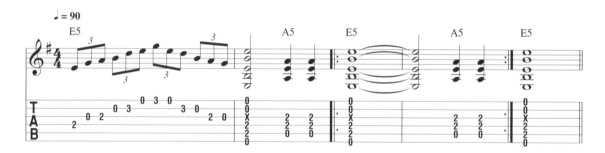

As simplistic as that sound and harmony is, surf guitar also dipped its toes into much more complex and exotic sounds, thanks to the legendary guitarist Dick Dale. With his classic recording "Misirlou," which was his take on an old Greek folk song with a strong Middle Eastern influence, Dale introduced the exotic-sounding Byzantine scale (or double harmonic major scale) to the genre. That exotic harmonic base, combined with rapid-fire tremolo picking also borrowed from Middle Eastern folk music, has since become a calling card of surf guitar.

Riff Tides and Melodies

One popular element of surf guitar is the straight 8th-driven and reverb-drenched riff played exclusively on the lowest two strings of the guitar. Dick Dale's "Misirlou" is a classic example, as are the Chantays' "Pipeline" and Duane Eddy's "Peter Gunn Theme." Here's an example in that tradition.

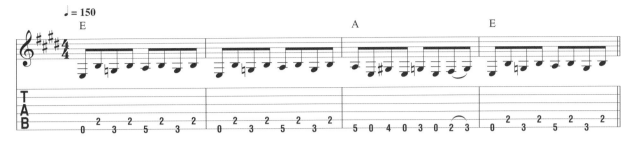

Of course, surf guitarists also played their melody lines in more traditional registers, too. And like the bass riffs of the genre, most surf melodies were played in a straight 8th-note groove. Perhaps the most famous surf melody is the Surfaris' timeless rocker "Wipeout." Here's a similar phrase.

Finally, surf guitarists, like any well-rounded guitarist, were well aware of the importance of chord tones and the effectiveness of dyads and triads in their phrasing. Both the Beach Boys' Carl Wilson and the Ventures' Bob Bogle were rather adept at this technique. Here is an example in the style of the Ventures' classic "Walk Don't Run." Note the use of the tremolo, or whammy, bar to create the wide vibrato in bars 1 and 3. This is another signature tool of surf guitar.

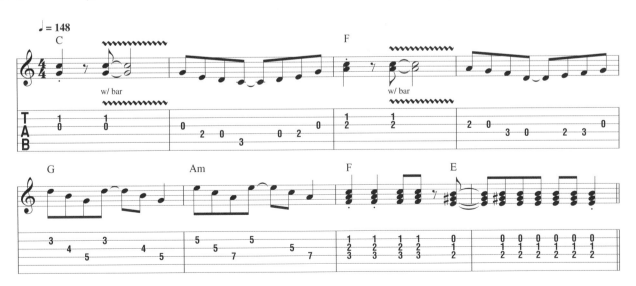

LESSON #83: SOUTHERN ROCK

Combining blues, country, and gospel music with the crunchy tones of the British rock bands of the late 1960s and early 1970s, the Allman Brothers Band, Lynyrd Skynyrd, the Outlaws, Molly Hatchet, Marshall Tucker Band, and even Texas boogie rockers ZZ Top established a uniquely American—and more specifically, Southern—rock sound that has stood the test of time. In this lesson, we'll examine a few of Southern rock guitar's signature sounds.

"Free Bird!"

A big part of Southern rock's sound is the prevalence of Mixolydian chord progressions. If you'll recall some basic harmony, the seventh chord of the harmonized major scale is a diminished chord; for example, B° is the vii chord in the key of C. But in a Mixolydian progression, that diminished vii chord is flatted a half step and becomes a major triad, so in the key of C, the new ♭VII chord is B♭ major.

Arguably the two greatest Southern rock anthems of all time—"Sweet Home Alabama" and "Free Bird"—both use this harmonic approach. Here's an example similar to another Southern rock classic, the Marshall Tucker Band's "Can't You See."

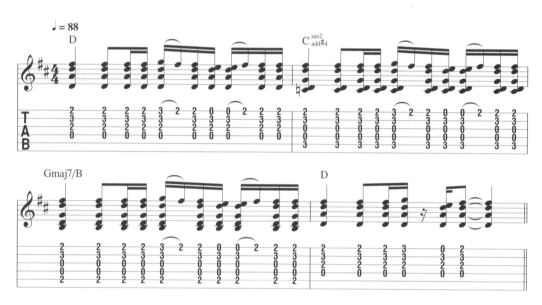

Another Mixolydian but modern Southern rock riff is .38 Special's "Hold on Loosely," which also features a highly economical way to change from the I to the V chord in a power-chord progression. In that riff, as well as in their smash hit "Caught Up in You," a simple one-fret downward shift of your index finger makes the chord change smooth as Kentucky's finest.

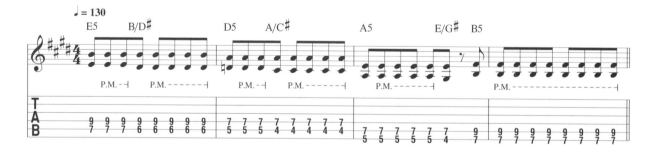

Major Mix o' Hexatonic

When it comes to Southern rock soloing, the major pentatonic scale (1–2–3–5–6) generally reigns supreme, with its minor counterpart getting the minor key duties. And with all the Mixolydian chord progressions, it should be no surprise that the Mixolydian mode (1–2–3–4–5–6–♭7) also sees its fair share of fret time. But there's another scale that is also popular, particularly in the legendary hands of Allman Brothers guitarist Dickey Betts—I call it the hexatonic major scale.

With a formula of 1–2–3–4–5–6, you can look at it as a major pentatonic scale with an added 4th or the Mixolydian mode sans the ♭7th. Whichever way you look at it, there's no denying that it's a fountain of melodic opportunity. Here's a Betts-style phrase using the hexatonic major scale in D.

Could You Repeat That? Again? And Again?

Another key element of Southern rock soloing is the prevalence of repeating licks. In fact, the outro solo to "Free Bird" alone is like a repeating lick dictionary. The four licks presented below, though essential, merely scratch the surface of the repeating lick arsenal of Southern rock guitarists. Note that the fourth lick, in D major pentatonic, repeats every three beats—a specialty of Dickey Betts.

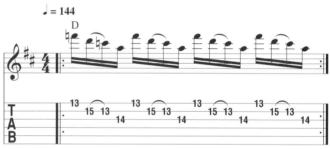

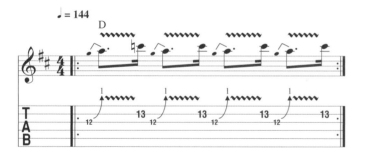

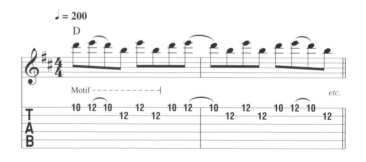

Slide

From Gary Rossington's mournful cries in "Free Bird" to the blistering "Statesboro Blues" of Duane Allman to Billy Gibbons' playful lines in "Tush," slide guitar has certainly made its mark on the Southern rock sound. Here's a fun example in the style of the Reverend Willy G., in standard tuning.

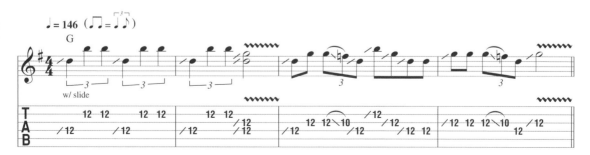

Take three chords, a tight and relentless rhythm section, a strong belief in antiestablishmentarianism, then turn it up loud, and you've got yourself a punk band! Well, it's not quite that easy, but more than any other rock style, the seminal punk rockers were minimalists—stripped-down and void of the perceived excesses of 1970s guitar rock. In this lesson, we'll lay bare that unpretentious ethos and find what lies behind the rage—at least in terms of the guitar.

Proto-Punk

There are many claims to the origination of punk music, especially from Stateside garage rockers like the Kingsmen and British mod rockers like the Kinks and the Who. But when you get down to brass tacks (or brass knuckles), it's tough to argue against Motor City. It was in Detroit, and its western suburb Ann Arbor, where in 1969 MC5 and the Stooges, respectively, released seminal debut punk albums.

This first example is a punk riff rocker in the style of Wayne Kramer's work in MC5's "Kick Out the Jams." In this tune, the band captured the fuzzed-out riff magic of the Rolling Stones, but plied it with the abandon and immediacy consistent with what would become punk rock, as opposed to the more laid-back R&B feel of the Stones.

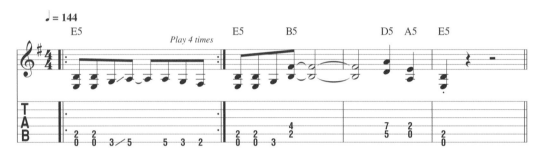

At the same time, the Stooges' Ron Asheton was crafting brutal and concise fuzz-drenched riffs in relentless 8th-note rhythms, like the dark and churning "I Wanna Be Your Dog." Here's a similar motif.

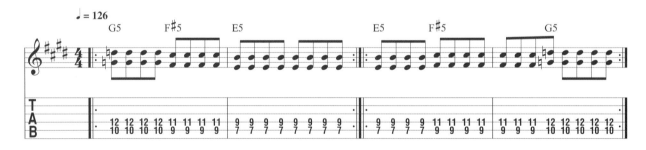

Some eight years later, performing as a solo artist, Stooges frontman Iggy Pop would record "Lust For Life," which while perhaps not seminal to the punk scene, featured a guitar riff that would become a sort of punk version of the Bo Diddley "Diddley beat" and later be reinterpreted by the New York Dolls on their 2006 song "Dance Like a Monkey" and even on Australian garage rockers Jet's smash single "Are You Gonna Be My Girl."

Note that the riff eschews the typical power-chord approach and instead favors full-on barre chords—another essential punk guitar move.

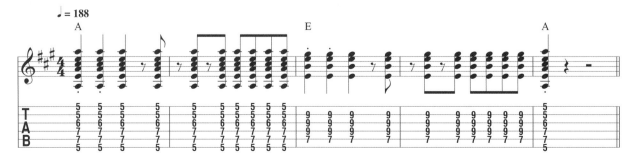

Hey! Ho! Let's Go!

While Detroit's punk scene was motoring along, the 1970s underground movement in New York City was also burgeoning. The New York Dolls were not only a member of the protopunk generation, but also brought the glam look (and sound) to bear on the genre, setting the bar for 1980s new wave/punk rockers, while Television's bassist/vocalist Richard Hell and Patti Smith championed the NYC punk look of ripped T-shirts and leather jackets.

But the most important group to emerge from the New York scene was a foursome out of Queens calling themselves the Ramones. With bassist Dee Dee Ramone's signature count-in of "1-2-3-4" kicking off every tune, this band of "brothers" practically defined the "loud, fast" punk ethos, finding more success with three chords than many more sophisticated artists of the era. This next example is in the style of the band's classic "Blitzkrieg Bop," which was the first song on the Ramones' 1976 self-titled debut, and in every way the perfect introduction to the group's aesthetic.

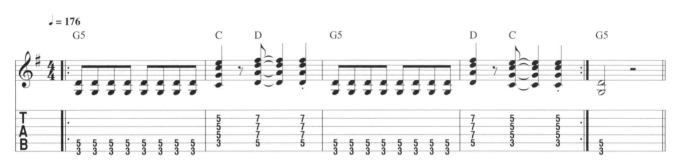

What About the Solos?

Although guitar solos do exist in punk music, they're typically sparse, simplistic, and more about noise and attitude than showing off your chops. Despite the disdain for the spotlight, some guitarists, like the New York Dolls' Johnny Thunders, fashioned some mighty tasty lines—often rooted in Chuck Berry-style riffs and licks. Here's an example in the style of Thunders, based on the harmony of the New York Dolls classic "Personality Crisis."

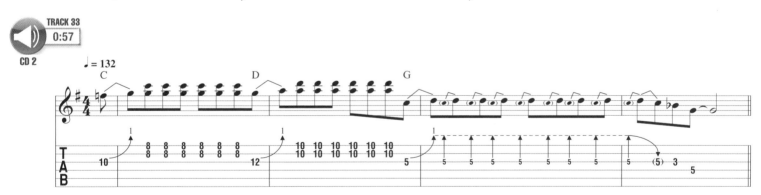

Following the mid-to-late 1970s, punk split into two distinct roads—the new wave style of the Talking Heads, Blondie, and the Cure, and the hardcore sounds of Black Flag, Dead Kennedys, and the Circle Jerks, among others. Then, in the late 1990s and early 2000s, the genre saw a revival in the form of the pop-punk sounds of Green Day, Blink-182, and Sum 41. Space limitations prevent a thorough dissection of the exciting guitar parts and sounds of all these bands, but if you're interested in punk, you need to check them out.

LESSON #85: POP ROCK GUITAR

Pop music, by definition, comprises many musical styles, ranging from rock 'n' roll, R&B, and soul to folk, country, and even hair metal. As a result, a two-page lesson on pop guitar is impossible. But if we narrow it down to pop rock, certain essential elements begin to come into focus. In this lesson, we'll take a look at some of the signature sounds and techniques of pop rock guitar from the 1980s till present.

Power Chords

The power chord is pretty much omnipresent in all styles of music, so it should be little surprise that it's had such an impact on pop rock guitar. From Rick Springfield and Bryan Adams of the 1980s to the Gin Blossoms and Wallflowers of the 1990s to Avril Lavigne and the Killers of the 2000s, the power chord has powered countless chart-topping hits. And when it's used in conjunction with a pop-friendly chord progression like the I–V–vi–IV example shown here, with well placed chord stabs and some slight palm-muting, you've got a recipe for reaching the Top 10.

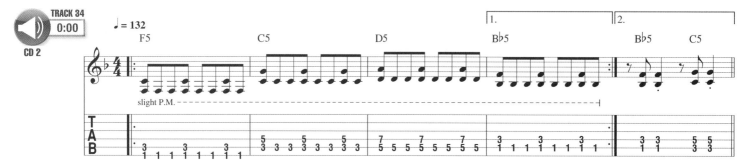

Pop Goes the Funky

Since the beginning of pop music, one of pop's biggest feeder streams has been R&B. Accordingly, many R&B and funk guitar styles have made their way into the pop rock arsenal. One group that proved particularly adept at weaving funk guitar rhythms and even R&B-influenced horn lines into a decidedly pop rock format was INXS. These Aussie rockers may best be described as the Down Under offspring of a Rolling Stones–James Brown bromance.

This funky guitar riff in the INXS style employs the eminently popular three-note chord voicings heard throughout the pop rock genre. Note the staccato attack—also quite relevant to the sound.

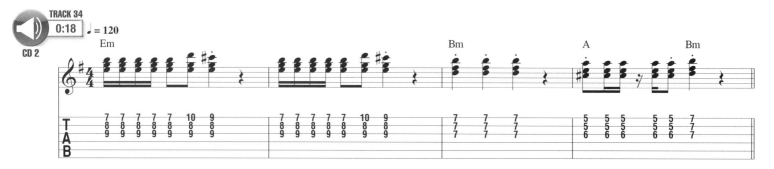

Modern-day pop icons Maroon 5 have also injected a strong R&B/funk influence into their pop grooves. Inspired by their smash hit "This Love," this next funky riff makes nifty use of syncopation and scratch rhythm—essential pop guitar tools.

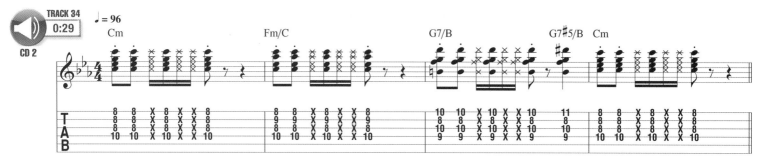

Yet another pop rock rhythm tool borrowed from the funk world is the staccato, single-note line. This minimalist groove machine can be heard in hit songs like "Der Kommissar," "Need You Tonight," "Rosanna," and countless others.

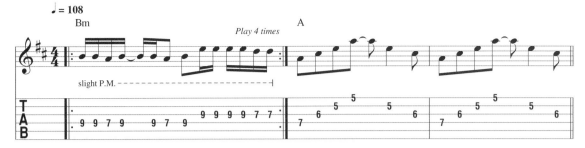

Jangly... Jangly... Jangly

The second half of our last example heralds the next pop rock guitar essential—a jangly, chorused and delay- or echo-drenched guitar tone filled with ringing arpeggios. Though it's a widely used approach, particularly in the world of British pop rock, its main progenitor is U2 guitarist the Edge. A master of textural guitar parts, the Edge used perfectly timed delay signals through a Vox AC-30 top-boost amp to craft one of the most unmistakable guitar sounds in pop rock history. One of his calling cards is his use of space in his parts. The following example, which uses delay repeats to subtly fill in the gaps, is reminiscent of his work on the band's monumental 1984 album *The Unforgettable Fire*.

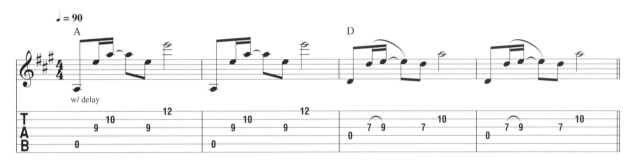

Soloing Strategies

Though not as sacred to the pop genre as they are to other forms, guitar solos nonetheless have their place, and they're often absolute gems. Since the late 1970s and early 1980s, it's a good bet that *nobody* has played more guitar solos on pop records than Toto guitarist and session man extraordinaire Steve Lukather. His list of credits is in the thousands, and because of his vast influence, Lukather's stamp is all over pop rock guitar soloing.

For the most part, pop rock solos are highly melodic affairs, frequently quoting the main vocal melody at some point. But even these soaring, melodic creations are interspersed with fret-burning lines. One of the all-time great pop guitar solos can be heard, courtesy of Lukather, in the James Ingram/Linda Ronstadt ballad "Somewhere Out There," from the film *An American Tale*. In that solo, Luke opens up with a blistering ascent that leads into a restatement of the song's main melody. Simple, yes, but highly effective. Here's a similar construction.

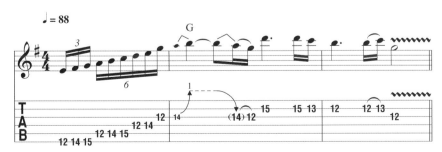

LESSON #86: HAIR METAL

OK, put aside the Aqua-Net and Spandex jokes and consider for a moment just how huge hair metal was from about 1984 until 1991. If you were running a guitar magazine during that time (as a few of my colleagues were), you couldn't go wrong! Lynch, DeMartini, Sambora, Steve Clark and Phil Collen, Reb Beach, C.C. DeVille… OK, so maybe you *could* go wrong, but even C.C. had his moments and was hugely important. In this lesson, we'll explore some of the riffing styles and techniques that helped make the 1980s arguably the greatest decade for guitar in history.

Spandex Pedal Pushers

One of the most frequently used rhythm tools in hair metal was the pedal tone. Given that E (both major and minor) was the most popular key of the era, followed closely by A, it comes as little surprise that the open E and A strings were the most frequently used pedal tones. (Note: there's somewhat of a "chicken or the egg" argument there, but either way, that's how it is.)

Our first example is a power chord riff in E minor set against an open E pedal tone. The chord progression itself is also one of the most popular of the hair metal era: vi–IV–V. Also note the A/C♯ chord in bar 4; this particular power chord-based voicing/ shape was also a favorite among hair metal guitarists.

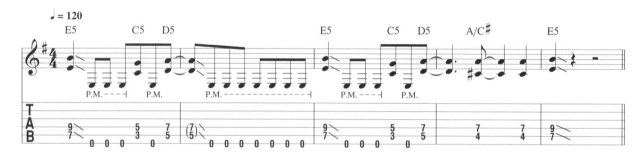

Keeping with the open low E pedal tone, we switch to the key of E major (Mixolydian, actually) for this next riff, which is a single-note boogie line with well-placed pinch harmonics—yet another signature hair metal riffing technique. Once you've played through it as written, also try it with a straight 16th feel; it works equally well either way.

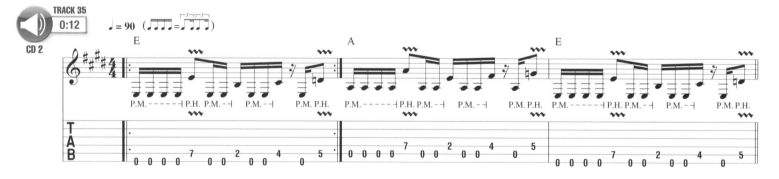

The final type of pedal riff we'll examine here is one that intersperses suspended chords among power chords and pedal tones, similar to the monster riffs of Ratt's "Lay It Down" or Winger's "Seventeen." In the next example, suspended 4ths and suspended 2nds are weaved into the rhythm across a I–♭VII–♭VI (E–D–C) progression, thus keeping your fret hand's pinky finger very, very busy.

Wide-Open Power

Even though AC/DC was far from being considered "hair metal," they had an undeniable impact on the genre. Bands such as Poison, Warrant, and Cinderella, among many others, crafted power-chord riffs with 8th-note syncopation echoing such classic rockers as "Back in Black," "T.N.T.," "Highway to Hell," and "You Shook Me All Night Long."

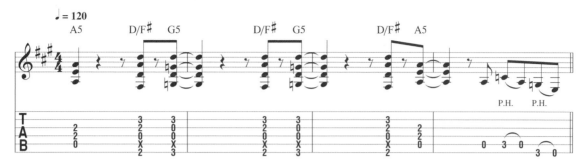

Bic-Waving Ballads

Of course, no discussion of hair metal riffs would be complete without visiting the "soft-loud" dynamic employed by virtually every hair metal band from Motley Crue, Ratt, and Dokken to Bon Jovi, Def Leppard, and Poison.

The next example, a minor key i–♭VI–♭VII progression (also called a vi–IV–V, in the relative major formula) inspired by Dokken is plied first in arpeggiated fashion either with an acoustic guitar or a clean-toned electric with a touch of chorus and reverb, before engaging full-on distortion for the power chord portion.

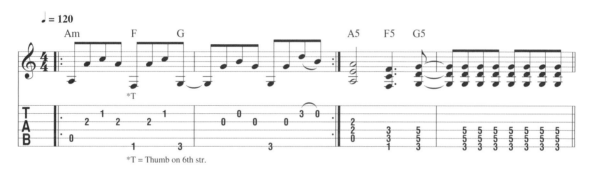

And finally, we have the power ballad. Few musical artists have ever perfected the art of the power ballad like the hair metal bands did. The favored key for these lighter-waving moments—from Poison's "Every Rose Has Its Thorn" to Skid Row's "I Remember You"—was G, typically featuring the ubiquitous G–Cadd9 chord change. The sample riff below features this theme.

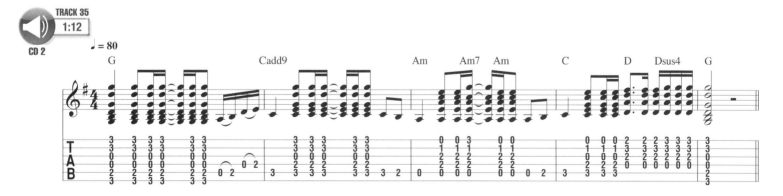

Now, to truly make that ballad complete, repeat this "soft" progression with a power chord-driven "loud" chorus, and you'll be on your way to hair metal heaven, which, as the song goes, really "isn't too far away."

LESSON #87: GRUNGE GUITAR

When "Smells Like Teen Spirit" hit MTV and radio with all the raw power of a tsunami, permanently altering the rock landscape in the process, record labels began scouring the Seattle, Washington, area for like-minded and like-sounding "grunge" (a term coined by singer/guitarist Mark Arm from Seattle rockers Mudhoney) bands. Soon, bands like Alice in Chains, Soundgarden, and Pearl Jam became the soundtrack to an entire generation of goateed coffee drinkers wearing flannel shirts and cargo shorts. In this lesson, we'll take a look at the riffing style that made Seattle famous.

Seattle's Finest

If 1980s rock was all about excess and a good time, grunge was about stripping the music down to raw power and angst. One of the first bands to crack the mainstream using that formula was a power trio out of Aberdeen, Washington, called Nirvana. While singer/guitarist Kurt Cobain became the face of "Generation X," the band's powerful riffs became a template for the grunge sound. Taking the soft-loud dynamic of rock music to a whole new level, Cobain once said that he "wanted to be totally Led Zeppelin in a way and then be totally extreme punk rock and then do real wimpy pop songs."

RIFF 1

Here, we offer a Cobain-style riff that moves between major chords a minor 3rd apart with a clean-toned electric, and then modulates up a whole step with a full-on distorted tone. Note the added "scratch strums" in the second half of the riff—a favorite move of Cobain.

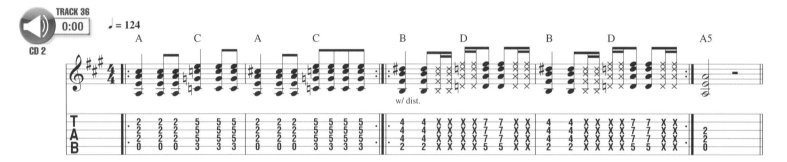

RIFF 2

Nirvana wasn't the only band to borrow from the early 1970s classic rock school of powerful riffs. Pearl Jam, led by the stellar guitar tandem of Stone Gossard and Mike McCready, crafted many dynamic riffs fueled by infectious grooves and frontman Eddie Vedder's electric presence. Two of the grunge guitar era's popular motifs are present in this Pearl Jam-style riff: Drop D tuning and suspended chords. Dial in a fat, mid-rangey distorted tone for this one.

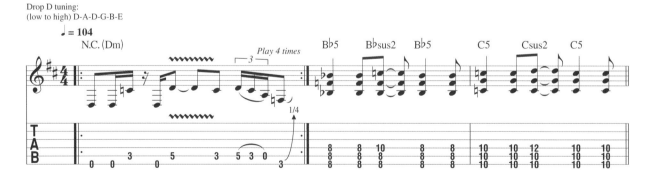

RIFF 3

While many consider grunge guitar to be rather simplistic, bands like Soundgarden and Alice in Chains famously created riffs that, while simple to play with regard to technique, were set in odd meter (7/4, 15/8, 7/8, etc.) to take the listener down an unexpected path. The following example, sort of a mash-up of what Soundgarden's Kim Thayil and Chris Cornell and Alice in Chains' Jerry Cantrell might concoct, sets a simple one-finger Drop D riff in 7/8 time before modulating to a 4/4 "bridge" section comprising chromatic chord movement, also popular to the grunge sound.

RIFF 4

This next example, played on either an acoustic or a clean-toned electric guitar, shows yet another level of harmonic complexity indicative of Cantrell's approach, where he uses open string drones in conjunction with a movable, partial barre-chord shape to create "Eastern"-style sounds.

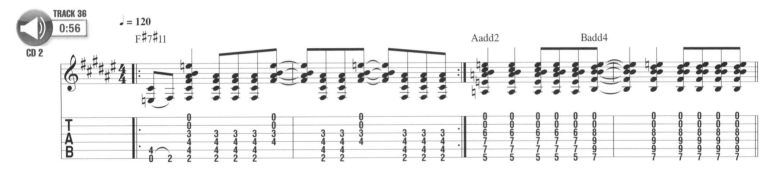

Grunge Finds SoCal

Though grunge's roots were clearly in Seattle and the Pacific Northwest, that was by no means the only region producing stellar artists. Way down "south" in San Diego, California, a quartet calling themselves Stone Temple Pilots—led by the brothers Dean and Robert DeLeo—would eventually become one of the most diverse and successful grunge bands of all time. One of guitarist Dean DeLeo's calling cards is his use of evocative and often unresolved dissonances. You could say he's using "jazz chords," but not in typical jazz harmony. Whereas jazz harmony typically resolves these dissonances, DeLeo instead treats each chord as unique and having specific purpose.

RIFF 5

In this example, open strings are used to create a B–B7/A–G♯m7♯5 chord sequence that "resolves" to a "Dancing Days"–inspired chord melody, similar to STP's "Trippin' on a Hole in a Paper Heart."

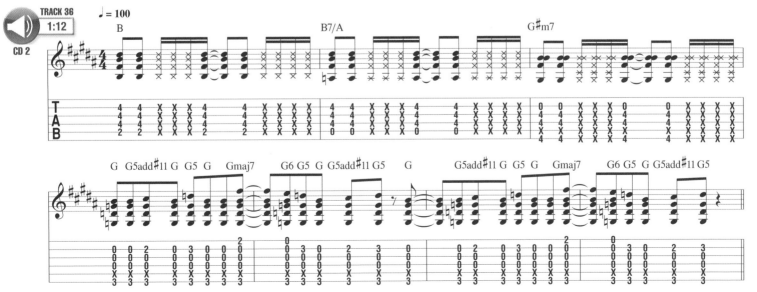

LESSON #88: PROGRESSIVE ROCK

Concept albums, 20-minute epics, frequent key and meter changes, Tolkiensian and philosophy-based lyrical themes, and you couldn't dance to it even if you had a Ph.D. from Fred Astaire Dance Studios. Hey, what's not to like? Although progressive rock has taken a lot of criticism over the years, there is no denying that the genre has produced some of the most interesting and complex guitar playing in rock history. In this lesson, we'll explore the key elements of progressive rock guitar, from riffs to solos and beyond.

The Genesis of Prog

Progressive rock, or prog rock, has its roots in the late 1960s and early 1970s, when bands like Genesis, Yes, Pink Floyd, King Crimson, and Rush were coming together. Informed as much by modern classical composers like Stravinsky and Bartök, jazz icons like John Coltrane, and Eastern music as they were by the rock ethos, these bands sought to explore diverse and complex sounds in an all-encompassing setting. The results of this blend form the definitive sounds of prog rock as listed in the intro, including frequent key and meter changes, complex rhythms, songs that don't adhere to the typical "verse-chorus" form, long songs often conceptually driven by a particular lyrical or musical theme, among others.

The prog rock genre arguably was born with the release of King Crimson's 1969 debut *In the Court of the Crimson King*. Led by guitarist Robert Fripp's "anything goes" approach, King Crimson would become prog's most influential force. This first example, similar to a portion of "21st Century Schizoid Man," offers insight into Fripp's motif-based, chromatic approach to soloing.

Perhaps no prog rock band was more influential in the area of "art rock" than early Genesis, which, led by singer Peter Gabriel, incorporated a strong theatrical element to their act. Despite the band's focus on image, they also produced some of the most elegant and complex progressive music of our time. In this example, modeled after "Watcher of the Skies," you see a highly syncopated rhythm in 6/4 time—the type of line that is often played in full unison (another essential prog element).

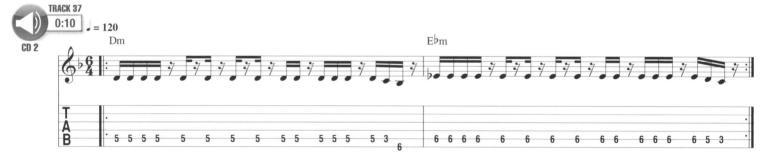

Few prog rock guitarists have done more to incorporate music of all types into their craft than Yes's Steve Howe, who managed to find space for jazz, bluegrass, ragtime, flamenco, classical, and yes, even some rock influence over the course of his 40-plus year career—sometimes even in the course of a single song! This example combines two of Howe's favorite devices: 6ths intervals careening up the neck followed by a rapid-fire, quasi-chromatic 16th-note ending.

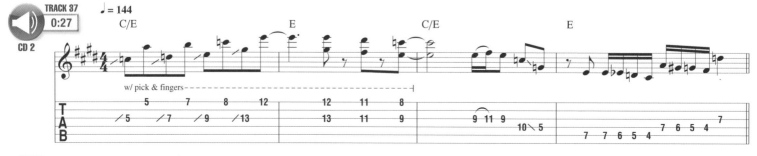

Change for the Meter?

Part of the fun of progressive rock music—at least if you're a music geek—is trying to figure out time signatures, especially when the meter changes from section to section or even measure to measure. Canadian prog legends Rush are among the most adept at this stratagem, which isn't surprising given that their drummer, Neil Peart, is pretty much the greatest stickman in rock history. The following riff, inspired by "Natural Science" from Rush's 1980 release *Permanent Waves*, alternates between 7/8 and 5/8.

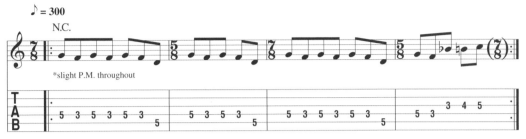

Another hallmark of progressive rock music is the use of suspended chords and complex chords using open-string drones. Rush guitarist Alex Lifeson has done more to advance this approach than anyone. Whether plied with a clean, ringing, chorused sound or slightly distorted with some delay, strummed or arpeggiated, Lifeson's huge chords form a major pillar of the Rush and greater prog sound.

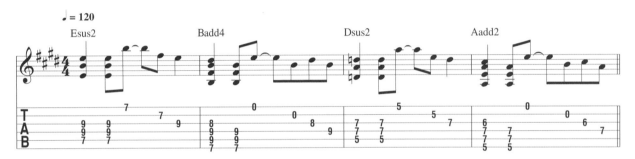

When Dream and Prog Unite

Aside from Rush, no prog rock band has had a more continuous and successful run than New York-based outfit Dream Theater. Already 25 years into their impressive career, this quintet led by founding guitarist John Petrucci has become the face of modern prog rock. Comprising five members with stellar, almost unimaginable chops, Dream Theater has advanced the cause of technical proficiency more than any band since Yes in the early 1970s.

Petrucci, a modern day guitar hero, brings an almost metronomic attack to everything he plays. Taking a cue from one of his heroes, Steve Howe, Petrucci has turned chromaticism into a signature element of his style. And whereas Howe liked to incorporate 6ths intervals into his solos, Petrucci has a penchant for 5ths. Both of those devices are explored here.

For further listening and exploration of modern prog rock guitar, check out bands ranging from Muse and Marillion to Tool and Opeth, and especially Porcupine Tree, which is led by Steven Wilson—one of the most gifted songwriters, guitarists, and producers of our time.

LESSON #89: MODERN METAL

As a society, we have this strange need to categorize things in our life, yet most people don't want to be categorized themselves. Nowhere is this truer than in the world of modern heavy metal. Heavy metal, death metal, nü metal, progressive metal, symphonic metal, metalcore, melodic metalcore, grindcore, folk metal, sludge metal, Christian metal, black metal, glam metal, power metal, industrial metal, thrash metal, speed metal, goth metal, groove metal… even Viking metal! In this lesson, we'll take a look at key elements and techniques of some of the more popular modern metal forms. Metal forever!

Modern Metal Made Nü

Modern metal arguably took root in the mid-to-late 1990s, when bands such as Korn, Papa Roach, Limp Bizkit, Disturbed, and Slipknot gained mass popularity as part of an alternative metal scene that was soon dubbed nü metal. Combining elements of rap, hip-hop, and even live DJs with a death metal sound and snarl, these acts found not only radio play and MTV airtime, but also helped turn Ozzfest into one of the most successful touring franchises of all time.

Of all those bands, Slipknot—the masked nonet from Iowa—has found the greatest staying power, thanks in large part to guitarists Mick Thomson and Jim Root, who have become modern metal guitar icons. Their thundering, floor-shaking riffs, like this highly syncopated Drop D assault inspired by "Duality," are tailor made for the band's percussive sound. Note also the triple picking (changing notes every three attacks) in bar 3, which yields an unpredictable hemiola effect, or "three-against-four" feel.

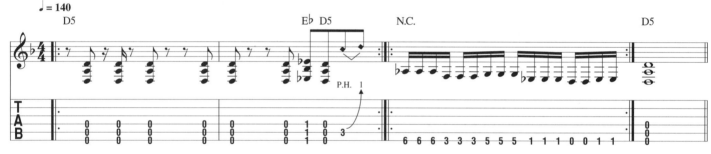

Two of the few nü metal guitarists to carry the guitar soloing torch, Thomson and Root also enjoy the occasional shred-inspired line, like this diminished string-skipping flurry.

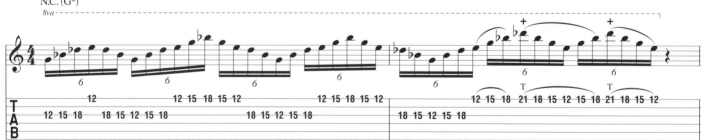

Death Rises Again

As nü metal's star began to burn out, more traditional heavy metal, albeit in a more modern style, began to fill the void. In particular, death metal, with its downtuned riffs and "cookie monster" vocals, brought street cred back to the metal brand. Led by guitarists Willie Adler and Mark Morton, the Virginia-based Lamb of God proved particularly adept at crafting riffs that were not only earth-shaking, but also captured a bit of groove. This next riff, modeled after "Laid to Rest" from the band's hallmark 2004 album *Ashes of the Wake*, is a great example of modern metal's essential single-note riffing approach, but set in a sweet 6/8 groove.

TRACK 38
0:23
CD 2

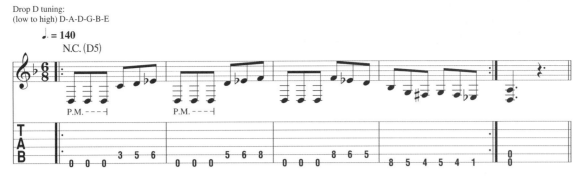

This next example, inspired by Killswitch Engage's "Rose of Sharyn," exemplifies the "melodic metalcore" approach, beginning in a unison riff and then switching to a pedaled riff harmonized in 3rds.

TRACK 38
0:33
CD 2

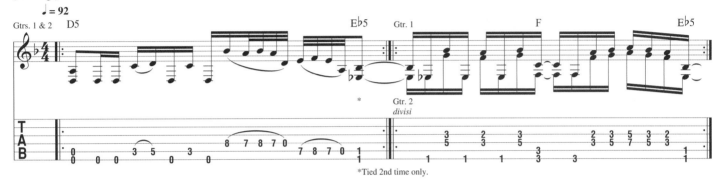

Metal Mainstream

As metal continued to rise in popularity, bands like Avenged Sevenfold and Five Finger Death Punch took to an even more "commercial" approach, eschewing the growling vocals for a more traditional yet gritty "singing" style. Furthermore, they often crafted technically proficient harmonized solos, like this blistering ascent harmonized in 3rds.

TRACK 38
0:49
CD 2

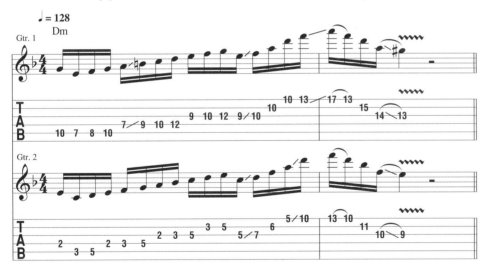

Prog-Metal

As metal bands turned to more technically challenging music, it's no surprise that many looked to progressive minded metal bands, like Dream Theater and the Mars Volta, to further up the ante. One of the more interesting bands of this style, Mastodon, took that prog influence to craft some of the most finger-twisting riffs in recent memory, but with a nod to metal's early, sludgy roots. This G Phrygian riff, inspired by Mastodon's "Ghost of Karelia," is set in a proggy 5/4 meter.

TRACK 38
0:55
CD 2

LESSON #90: JIMI HENDRIX

Jimi Hendrix is hands-down the most important and influential rock guitarist in history. His company in the pantheon of great art comprises the likes of Mozart, Picasso, Hemingway, and Coltrane. From his fiery abandon and otherworldly sonic explorations to his evergreen songwriting and tight grooves, Jimi's guitar spoke to the world like no one else's. In this lesson, we'll take a look at Jimi's unique and diverse playing style and learn some of the techniques that made him synonymous with rock guitar.

Electric Riffland

Although Hendrix is generally praised for his lead guitar prowess, he was also one of the finest rock rhythm guitarists of all time. From "Voodoo Child" and "Foxey Lady" to "Spanish Castle Magic" and of course, "Purple Haze," Jimi Hendrix created many of the finest riffs in rock guitar history, rivaled only by his peer Jimmy Page.

SINGLE-NOTE RIFFS

Let's start with a look at his single-note riffs. This first example, modeled after "Purple Haze," is constructed from the E minor pentatonic scale and features the bluesy quarter-step bend on the b3rd (G) in two octaves, an aggressive vibrato, and the classic Hendrix "bullet shot" slide on the final beat of measure 2. For a real Hendrix vibe, hit the strings hard.

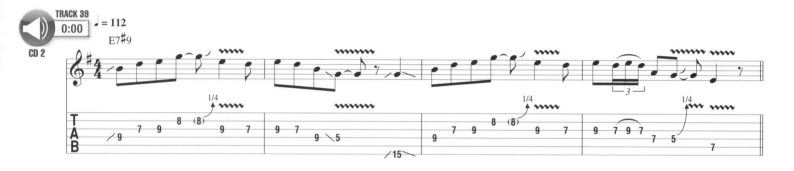

Hendrix was also a huge fan and master of R&B-style guitar, having backed artists like Little Richard, Ike and Tina Turner, and the Isley Brothers prior to his solo career. This next riff, built from the G major pentatonic scale, exudes a classic Motown flavor.

CHORDAL RIFFS

In addition to his scorching-hot single-note riffs, Hendrix was also a master of the chordal riff, using chord partials, dyads, and embellishments to generate harmonically rich phrases. One of the key techniques that Hendrix used in his rhythm playing was thumb fretting, where he curled his fret hand's thumb over the top of the neck to fret chord roots and other notes on the sixth string. This approach, as opposed to traditionally played barre chords, frees the pinky finger for chord embellishments on the higher strings. This is famously heard in "The Wind Cries Mary," but Hendrix pretty much always used thumb fretting for sixth-string rooted chords. Following is a chordal riff using the thumb fretting technique.

*T = Thumb on 6th str.

Note the R&B guitar-influenced lick at the end of bar 4 of that riff. Hendrix adopted this approach from his idol Curtis Mayfield and then took it to a whole new level. This next riff, which uses chord partials, is another staple of the Hendrix rhythm method.

Electric Sololand

Finally, we'll take a look at Hendrix's guitar soloing techniques and approach. For the most part, Hendrix based his solos in the same minor pentatonic and blues scale shapes as peers like Eric Clapton and Jimmy Page. What made Hendrix's lines stand out, though, was the *manner* in which he plied those lines—fierce attack, fiery abandon, and a "go for it" attitude on every note.

Still, there are a few key elements we can pull from his licks and solos to help hone your Hendrixian chops. As mentioned, Hendrix often mined the pentatonic landscape for his solos, but he often included the second scale degree for an added level of melodic complexity. Here's an example of this usage, inspired by his iconic solo in "All Along the Watchtower."

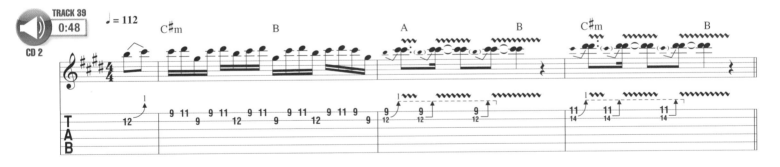

There may be no greater guitar solo in rock history than Hendrix's epic wailing in "Machine Gun," from the *Band of Gypsys* album. Conjuring the sound and fury of war, this three-and-a-half minute solo redefined what guitarists could do on the instrument. In this final example, we showcase a few of Jimi's key moves: a screaming, sustained, non-vibratoed note, whammy bar-shaking trills, and dramatic overbends with a gradual release.

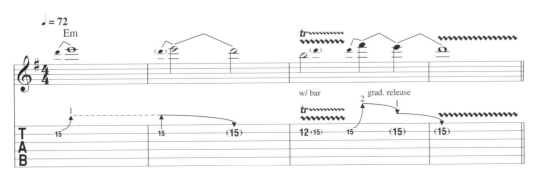

"Clapton is God." Those words, spray-painted by a fan on a wall of an Underground London station in Islington, have since become legend. Given that he's been the guitarist for several of the greatest classic rock groups of all time—Yardbirds, Cream, Blind Faith, Derek & the Dominos, and the Bluesbreakers, not to mention a stellar solo career—you can't help but wonder if somewhere in heaven there's graffiti stating "God is Clapton!" In this lesson, we'll explore some of the signature techniques and approaches of one of rock guitar's most iconic players.

Major-Minor Mix-up

Clapton may be (rightfully) considered a rock guitar god, but in his soul, he's a bluesman to the core. And much like his contemporaries Beck, Hendrix, and Page, Clapton skillfully mined the blues-based pentatonic scales, striking fretboard gold in the process. As you take a look at the first two licks here, you might think, "Hey, these are just stock blues licks in a rock context." And you'd be right; however, you must remember that the only reason they're "stock" licks is because Clapton and his pioneering peers made them so!

The first lick adheres strictly to the D minor pentatonic scale. It's one of E.C.'s "pet" licks heard throughout his catalog. Even more identifiable to Clapton's style, though, is the second lick. Similar in its basic construction to the first one, this version includes the bluesy minor 3rd-to-major 3rd (here, F–F♯) move that Clapton borrowed from his blues heroes. Its first instance (beat 1) is in hammer-on form, whereas the second instance is plied in typical Clapton fashion via a half-step bend with your fret hand's index finger. Watch your pitch on that bend; one of Clapton's calling cards is his impeccable pitch and intonation on bent notes.

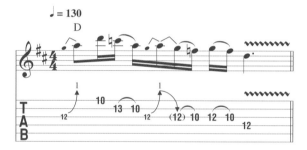

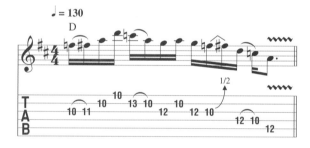

Although the inclusion of both the minor and major 3rd scale tones implies mixing of minor and major pentatonic scales and sounds, Clapton was often far more blatant in that regard. His monumental solo in "Crossroads," for example, often switches abruptly yet seamlessly between A major pentatonic and its minor cousin.

Again looking to "Crossroads," we find more Claptonian phrasing devices. In bar 1 of the next example, unison bends are offset by repeated stabs on the 17th-fret E note, a move borrowed from Clapton favorite Freddie King. A rollicking round of double-stop 3rds pull-offs and bends follows, with staggered, swing-style major 3rds to further muddy the minor-major waters capping off the phrase.

Sweet Woman Tone

Throughout his career, Eric Clapton has played with a variety of amazing guitar tones, but none is more famous than the so-called "woman tone" achieved with his 1964 Gibson SG ("The Fool"), with the tone knob of the neck pickup rolled all the way back, and heard on Cream classics such as "I Feel Free" and "Sunshine of Your Love."

Here's an example inspired by Clapton's vocal-like lines in "I Feel Free." Note the inclusion of the 6th (C♯) and 9th (F♯), which lend added melodicism to the phrase. Clapton's vibrato, which—along with B.B. King's—is one of the most beautiful and identifiable in the annals of rock guitar, gives the phrase added lift. Slowhand creates this wonderful sound using his elbow as a fulcrum, allowing his fret hand to "float" while shaking the note. It's not an easy technique to cop, nor necessarily should you cop it, but having a steady and in-tune vibrato is essential to phrases like this one.

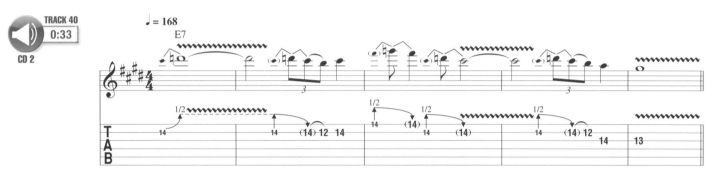

The next example shows Clapton's masterly command of pitch while bending notes. Hitting that "blue" note between a half- and whole-step bend takes practice, but is well worth the effort.

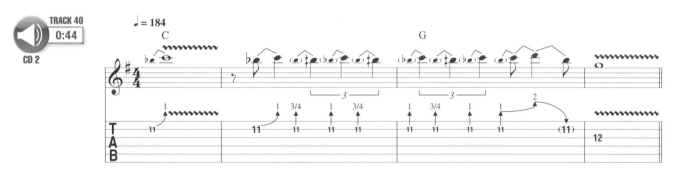

D Minor: God's Key

The great guitarists seemed to prefer certain keys: Jimi Hendrix owned E, Jimmy Page gets an A for his efforts, and Jeff Beck, well, he just plays in the key of music. But the key of D (major, minor, Mixolydian—makes no difference) lived in the hands of God himself, Eric Clapton. "Tales of Brave Ulysses," "Sunshine of Your Love," "White Room," "Badge," and "Layla" are all in D, in one form or another. It's not just that Clapton loved soloing in tenth position; he was also hooked on the chord progressions. Variations of the riff below are heard in "Tales of Brave Ulysses," "White Room," and "Badge."

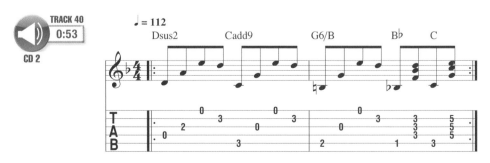

LESSON #92: JEFF BECK

Although he never achieved the commercial success of his fellow British Big Three guitar heroes, Eric Clapton and Jimmy Page, guitarist Jeff Beck has had as much if not more influence on rock and blues guitar playing and technical innovation as any guitarist ever has. And to top it off, nearly 50 years after his debut, Beck is as much a force in rock guitar as he's ever been. Case in point: at the 25th Anniversary Rock and Roll Hall of Fame concert in New York City, in 2011—arguably one of the greatest gatherings of rock 'n' roll talent ever assembled in one place—it was Jeff Beck's amazing performances that had people talking for weeks afterward. In this lesson, we'll show you some of the wild and unpredictable licks and techniques that have made this renowned master a rock guitar icon for the ages.

El Becko Blues

Over the course of his impressive career, Beck has taken on rock, fusion, funk, and even electronic music and, of late, rockabilly. But, like his peers Clapton and Page, Beck is at heart a bluesman, steeped heavily in the sounds of Otis Rush, Buddy Guy, and B.B. King. But even when he plays the blues, Beck injects his own idiosyncrasies; for example, in what would be in the hands of most players a stock descending blues run, Beck injects 3rd and 4th intervals and a smashing dose of trilled notes—a signature Beck device— to give a line like this a special twist.

Proto-Shred

Rapid-fire pull-offs, divebombs, screaming harmonics… you'd think we were describing a Joe Satriani tune, right? Long before Satch or Eddie Van Halen or Randy Rhoads, Jeff Beck was stretching the boundaries of what not only *could* be done on the guitar, but also what *should* be done on the guitar.

In his 1967 eponymously titled classic "Beck's Bolero," which was actually written by Jimmy Page, Beck lets loose with a flurry of triplet-based pull-offs to the open E string. It's an approach that would later be echoed by the aforementioned trio of shred icons as well as metal heroes like Metallica's Kirk Hammett. Here's a similar line.

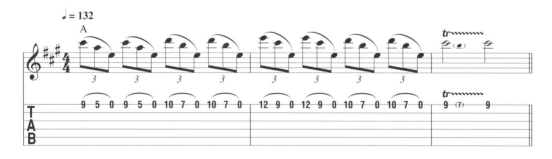

Even to this day, after players like Satriani, Van Halen, and Steve Vai have taken the whammy bar to its greatest extremes, Beck's use of that little bar is simply legendary. From violent vibrato and divebombs to melodic manipulation as subtle as a falling leaf, Beck's bar control and accompanying sense of pitch are unmatched. Following are examples of the two extremes.

In the first, we visit Beck's wild side, using pull-offs from the 15th-fret to the open G string in concert with whammy dives and scoops to create melodic havoc. In the second example, we use natural harmonics and subtle bar manipulation to create a Beck-style melody.

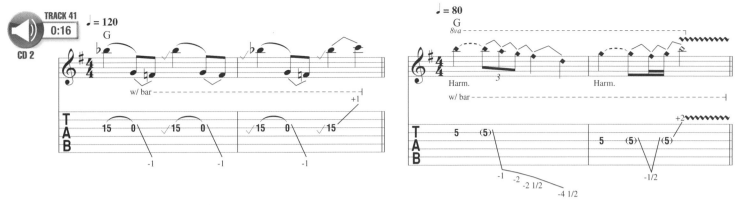

Rhythmic Anarchy

Beck's lines are often not only melodically adventurous, but also rhythmically off kilter. One of his favorite moves is to take something as innocuous as an octave shape and play it in such a manner as to keep the listener a little off balance. In the next example, the root, G, is established on the downbeat and is then immediately followed by a rhythmically displaced 3/8 hemiola, or three-against-four feel, starting on the "and" of beat 1.

Bend It Like Becko

Beck's approach to string bending, like most aspects of his playing, is best described as elegantly random. For starters, unlike most blues-rock guitarists, Beck is utterly unafraid to employ bends on the lowest three strings. Here's an example of how Beck might treat a descent down the A Dorian mode.

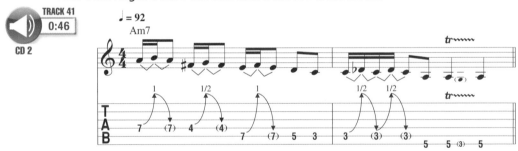

Even when using bends in typical blues-rock style, such as unison bends or in the context of a minor pentatonic run, Beck's approach is anything *but* typical. Here's a four-bar phrase that encapsulates his approach. Take those opening triplet salvos slowly.

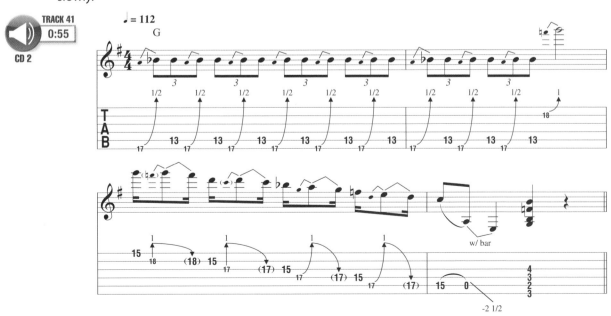

LESSON #93: DUANE ALLMAN

One of the three greatest guitarists in rock history to leave this world much too early, Duane Allman possessed a musical maturity and completeness at the age of 24 that few artists achieve over a lifetime. The first rock guitarist to master slide guitar technique, Allman's jazz- and blues-fueled explorations set the bar not only for the burgeoning Southern rock sound, but also for improvisational rock music in all decades since. In this lesson, we'll take a look at Allman's monumental slide style as well as his traditionally fretted approach.

Heavy Frettin'

Though he's best known for his unmatched slide guitar technique, Duane Allman was just as likely to tear the house down when playing "traditionally fretted" lines. In fact, his and fellow Allman Brothers axeman Dickey Betts' solo on "Blue Sky" is generally held up as one of the all-time great guitar solos in rock history.

Allman typically favored pentatonic sounds when playing in fretted style. But even then, his lines rarely sounded like those of his heroes Eric Clapton or Jimi Hendrix. Here's an example—inspired by "Whipping Post"—of how Allman might ascend an A minor pentatonic scale. Note the 6/8 time signature and the resulting triplet feel of the phrase.

Although he played in a traditionally fretted manner before mastering slide technique, his fretted lines still often drew inspiration from the slide realm, using overbends and legato slides for position shifts to produce a smooth legato sound.

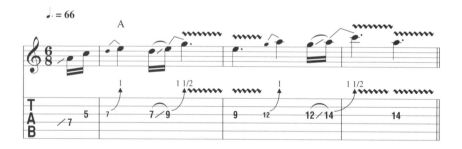

Sick Slide Technique

Gregg Allman reportedly used to tell the story about how in 1968 Duane was laid up for a few weeks with a nasty cold, for which he was given a cold and flu medicine called Coricidin. Gregg brought him a copy of Taj Mahal's self-titled album, to help perk his brother up. When Gregg saw Duane a few days later, he was playing slide guitar using the empty glass Coricidin bottle. From that point forward, it became Duane's trademark tool.

With influences ranging from Albert King to Chet Atkins to Jimi Hendrix to John Coltrane, it's not surprising that Allman's unique sound comprised such an improvisational-based fusion of styles. Yet, at the same time, Allman played with such melodic force, hugging the chord tones, that his lines rarely came off as too outside.

On the Allman Brothers' stellar jam, "One Way Out," Allman doubles Dickey Betts' bluesy motif, pounding the chord tones of a dominant seventh chord with a particular focus on the ♭7th. The next example works in similar fashion and also depicts a signature Duane Allman—and by extension, blues-rock slide guitar in general—move: 1–♭7–5 (in the key of E: E–D–B). As you work through this, muting is of utmost importance, as you don't want the fourth and fifth strings ringing together. Note: the following examples are in the slide-friendly Open E tuning (E–B–E–G♯–B–E).

Allman also had a penchant for sliding double and triple stops to and from chromatic neighbor tones. Here, we employ the technique in jazzy fashion, similar to how a horn section might cradle the chord tones of an E major triad. For that final G♯/E dyad, you'll need to angle your slide diagonally across the top two strings—it's tricky, but you'll get it.

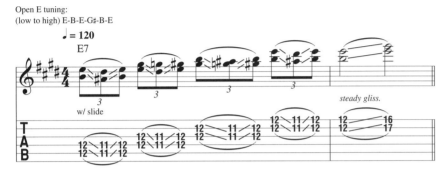

This bluesy phrase, inspired by "Statesboro Blues," features interplay between the ♭7th and major 7th, as well as a wide-interval jump from A to G (♭7th)—another signature Duane device.

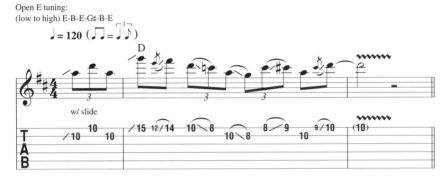

"Ear-ie" Skills

According to an old military academy bunkmate of Allman's, he'd come home and find Duane playing along to a B.B. King album, barefoot, using his toe to stop and hold the record while he learned a lick, then letting the record go until he found the next one—for hours at a time. It's said that he could absorb a lick and then reconstitute it in his own style in just minutes. That, my friends, is an incredible ear.

For proof of just how good Allman's ear was, and as a result his pitch and intonation, look no further than the main solo in Derek & the Dominos' "Layla." Therein lie two sections in which Allman plays on the "imaginary" fretboard above the 22nd fret of his cherished Les Pauls. Once you enter this sort of uncharted territory, it's *all* ears. Here's a similar example that travels all the way up to the high D note at the theoretical 34th fret—an *octave above* the 22nd fret!

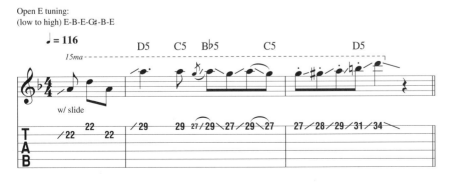

Classic rock guitar's shaman of soulful sounds, Carlos Santana brought his Latin roots to bear on the instrument, combining it with rock, blues, and fusion to create one of the most identifiable guitar styles—and tones—in rock history. From his smooth, soaring melodies to his fiery pentatonic licks, Santana brings passion to the art of rock guitar like few others. In this lesson, we'll explore some of the essential elements that compose his singular sound.

Samba y Montuno

Carlos Santana was born in Mexico, began playing violin at age five and guitar at age eight, and later moved to the San Francisco area during his middle school years. But even as he began to explore American blues, jazz, and rock music, his Latin roots ran deep, and as a result, he naturally fused these styles together when he began his own performing career.

One listen to Santana classics like "Oye Como Va," "Evil Ways," or "Soul Sacrifice" will immediately expose the preponderance of Latin rhythms, particularly Samba-based ones, in his music. Also typical of Santana's rhythm, or compositional approach, is the i–IV progression.

In this first example, the first two bars offer a more "rock" version of the rhythm employed in "Oye Como Va" and other tunes, whereas the final bar moves to a cut-time rhythm feel similar to that heard in portions of "Soul Sacrifice."

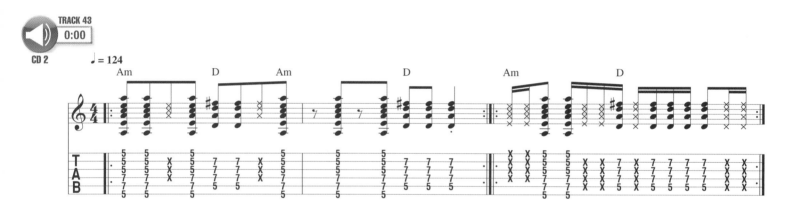

Santana also occasionally employs another classic Latin device, the montuno, a rhythmic device that comes full circle every eight beats (two bars). This one features a descending chromatic bass line against a static E/C dyad. The montuno is followed by another classic Santana i–IV rhythm.

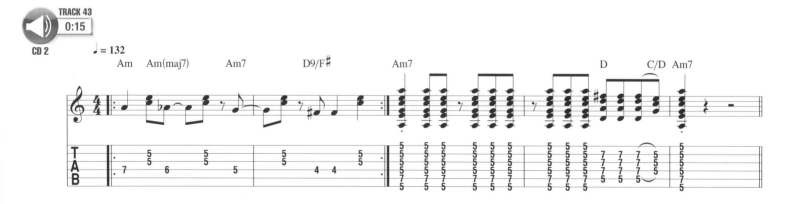

The "Minor-Penta-Dorian" Mode

Like most classic rock guitarists of his era, Carlos Santana bases most of his licks and solos in the minor pentatonic scale (1–♭3–4–5–♭7); however, perhaps more than most of his contemporaries, Santana very effectively mixed natural minor (1–2–♭3–4–5–♭6–♭7) and Dorian (1–2–♭3–4–5–6–♭7) sounds into his lines, always seeming to place that one "different" note in just the right place.

The next example is an eight-bar mini-solo in classic Santana style. For the most part, it's rooted in the A minor pentatonic scale (A–C–D–E–G), but with savvy (and very precise) injections of the major 6th (F♯, with a grace-note hammer-on from F) over the D chord (F♯ is the major 3rd of D). You also get one of Santana's pet rhythmic treatments with the syncopated pull-offs in bars 5 and 7.

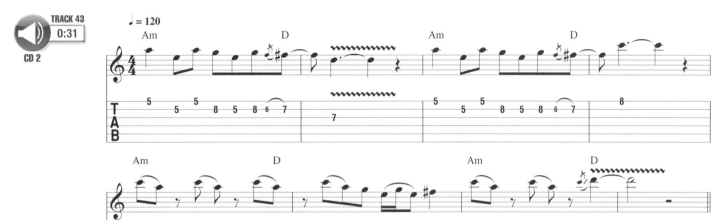

Aided by his creamy, smooth guitar tone, Santana's solos just seem to sing. Part of that effect is generated via the guitarist's mastery of string bending and legato techniques to create vocal-like phrases. This next example, inspired by his take on Peter Green's "Black Magic Woman" features crying pre-bends in the first half and a fairly stock pentatonic lick in the second that quickly turns Dorian with the crafty resolution to the 9th (E) just in time for the Am7 change (E is the 5th of Am7).

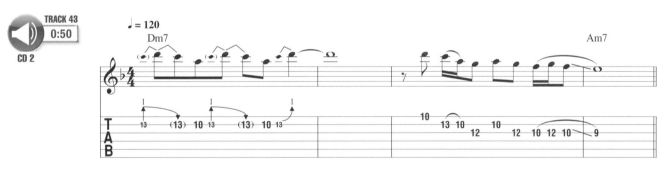

Finally, for all the talk of "passion" and "soulfulness" in Santana's playing, you can't forget that the man can outright rip when the mood strikes. This final example depicts another signature Santana move—rapid-fire pull-offs in a sextuplet rhythm. These legato fireworks are followed by a down 'n' dirty minor pentatonic lick of which there are plenty in the shaman's arsenal.

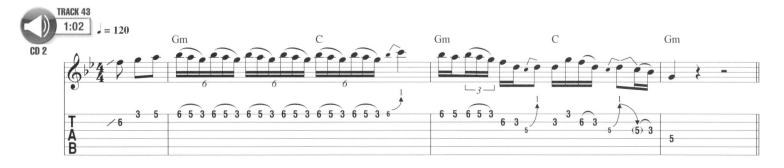

LESSON #95: JIMMY PAGE

Even though Jimmy Page is one of the most revered guitarists in rock history, there is a contingent of (mostly guitar-playing) fans who cast aside his lead playing as merely sloppy luck. But those folks would be mistaken. Sure, his technique may be a bit on the "loose" side, but you've got to remember that in those burgeoning years of hard rock, only Jimi Hendrix and Jeff Beck could match Pagey's intensity and fiery abandon. In this lesson, we'll examine the blues-rooted soloing devices that placed the Led Zeppelin guitarist upon the Mt. Rushmore of guitar idols.

Hammer of the Blues Gods

Although all of the early guitar heroes took the lion's share of their soloing cues from the blues, none exploited it as plainly as Jimmy Page. Carrying the torches of Otis Rush, Willie Dixon, Buddy Guy, and Elmore James, among others, Page set the rock guitar world on fire with his all-out fretboard assault. Though he may occasionally crash and burn, there always seems to be a redeeming spark of magic just around the bend.

If there's one blues phrase that has completely permeated the rock guitar repertoire, it's the opening salvo in our first example. You can hear this, or a permutation of it, in "Good Times Bad Times," "Dazed and Confused," "Whole Lotta Love," "Communication Breakdown," and "The Lemon Song," just to name a few. Though it's often employed in triplet rhythm, it's presented in 16th notes here thus causing the accents to fall on shifting parts of the bar.

The second half of the example depicts another of Pagey's favorite tools—the repeating lick. This particular lick is most famously heard at the end of his solo in "Stairway to Heaven."

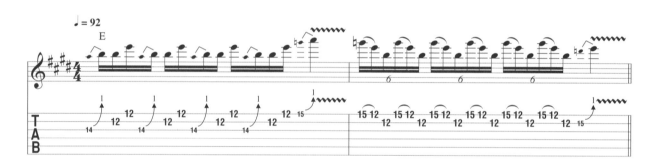

Sticking with repeating licks, this next example follows suit while incorporating another favorite Page lick into the first bar, which, with its inclusion of the 9th (B) and 6th (F♯), invokes a Dorian tonality. To cap off the lick, we stick with Dorian, but then resolve the lick to a major tonality via that half-step bend to C♯. This mixing of minor and major pentatonics in a single pattern is another signature Page-ism.

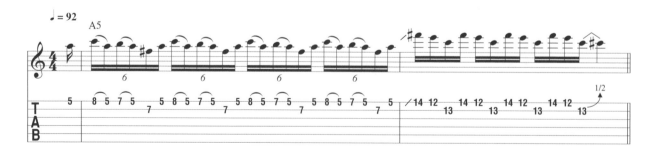

Scale Sequences

Page frequently peppered his lines with scale sequences, such as in the next example. Here, a groups-of-three sequence cascades down the E minor pentatonic scale similar to the phrase that kicks off his outro solo in "Good Times Bad Times."

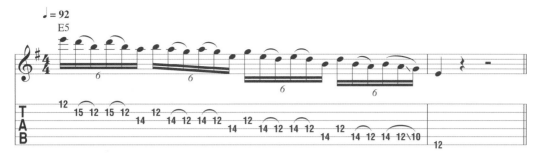

As heard in "Heartbreaker" and "Whole Lotta Love," among others, Page also shows a penchant for pulling off to open strings. In this example, we set this technique within the context of a descending sequence of pull-offs.

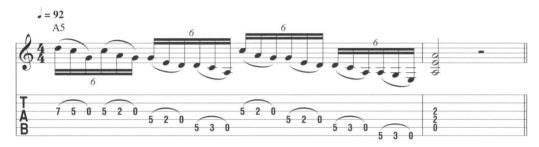

Over the Bends and Far Away

As you may recall, when Page executes those pull-offs to the open G string in "Heartbreaker," he reaches behind the nut of his Telecaster and bends the fretted C up two whole steps. Similarly, the traditionally fretted "over-bend" is another of Page's calling cards, found in "The Lemon Song" and "Whole Lotta Love," as are oblique ("You Shook Me") and unison ("Stairway to Heaven") bends.

This next example starts with an oblique bend in bar 1, followed by a challenging series of bends that climb one, two, and finally two-and-a-half steps. To pull this one off, first eat your Wheaties, then place your ring finger at the 15th fret and use your middle and index fingers to help push the string up while squeezing the top of the neck with your thumb to create extra force. You might want to keep an extra B string around, too, in case it breaks.

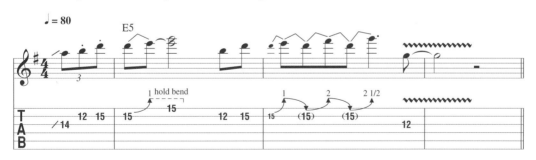

Our last lick contains a couple of more traditional string bends, but also a signature Page move heard in both "You Shook Me" and "Whole Lotta Love"—the opening bend from the 5th (B) to the 6th (C♯) followed by a chromatic 5–♭5–4 (B–B♭–A) run down the E hybrid blues scale. Hammer of the Gods, indeed!

We've all heard the phrase "play with feel," and some may even wonder what exactly that means. Well, look no further than Pink Floyd guitarist David Gilmour, whose heartfelt and atmospheric fretboard excursions have been tingling spines for over 40 years. In this lesson, we'll explore the rhythmic and melodic devices that have made his emotive lines required listening for any serious guitarist.

Breathe...

David Gilmour's solos are often described with words like "majestic," "soaring," or "poignant." So how does a guitarist using primarily the same minor pentatonic scale as everyone else on the planet garner such praise?

Of course, there are several factors at work here: graceful bends, sustained notes with heaps of vibrato, and a laser focus on chord tones immediately come to mind. But one of the key ways in which Gilmour produces this affect is via his generous use of space—he lets his lines *breathe*. It's a theme that you'll see in each of the three soloing examples presented here. Be sure to keep this method in mind as you craft your own phrases and solos—sometimes silence speaks volumes.

LICK 1

Our first example is inspired by Gilmour's timeless solo in "Comfortably Numb," which has made several lists as one of the five greatest rock solos of all time. This line features a couple of Gilmour's trademarks: the slow, vibratoed bend at the end of measure 1 and the bend- and legato-fueled arpeggio-based, slippery descent down the D major scale. These elements combine to give the phrase a melodic vocal-like feel. Be careful not to over-bend those half-step moves.

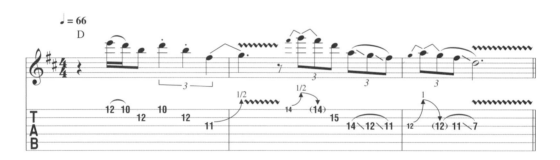

LICK 2

This second soloing example borrows from the classic track "Money." Despite the long, sustained notes, the double stops and pinch harmonic—two more favorite Gilmour devices—offer the sparse phrase some grit. For all his subtlety, Gilmour could also really dig in and attack the strings aggressively, which is exactly what's called for here.

LICK 3

The last lead phrase takes cues from both "Another Brick in the Wall (Part 2)" and "Comfortably Numb." The first of the two main stars here is the trademark Gilmour multiple bend, where he bends a note to pitch, sustains it, and then bends to an even higher pitch before releasing the note. The multiple bend in bar two requires some oomph, as it rises up two whole steps! Fret the original C note with your third finger, using your second finger to reinforce the bend. The second device is the classic blues-scale descent in bar 4. Gilmour plays variations of this line at least three times in the outro solo to "Comfortably Numb," a more rhythmic version in "Brick," and in countless other tracks.

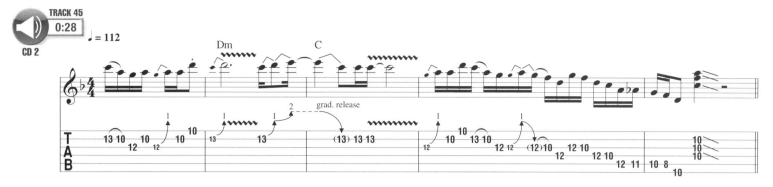

...In the Air

While Gilmour's majestic phrases get most of the glory, his rhythm guitar and compositional approaches are equally glorious. Using drones, complex chord voicings, and a mix of effected electric, 6- and 12-string acoustic, and nylon-string acoustic guitars, Gilmour's ethereal canvases are often as gorgeous as his solos.

RIFF 1

Whether using steel-string acoustics or chorused, clean-toned electrics, Gilmour loves to paint his rhythm parts with ringing open strings—often drones—to craft wonderfully complex sounds. In this first example, inspired by "Breathe," the Em(add9)–A7–Cmaj7–B7add4 progression is further enhanced by the droning high E string. Let all the notes ring throughout, and note the upstroke on the Em(add9) chord on beat 2 of bar 1—another Gilmour favorite.

RIFF 2

For all of Pink Floyd's grandiosity, Gilmour could be just as effective with a plain, old nylon-string acoustic guitar. In this next example, similar to "Goodbye Blue Sky," a D Mixolydian riff pedaled against a droning D string comprises the first two bars, whereas bars 3–4 feature droning F♯ and G notes for a cool minor-2nd dissonance (classic Gilmour—see also the acoustic riff in "Hey You" for a similar sound), against a moving bass line (see also "Is There Anybody Out There?").

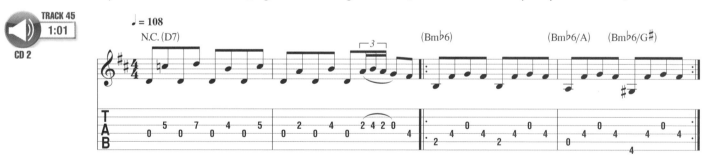

RIFF 3

Our final example, styled after "Run Like Hell," revisits the open-D drone, this time set against three-note triad voicings on the top three strings—yet another great Gilmour-ism.

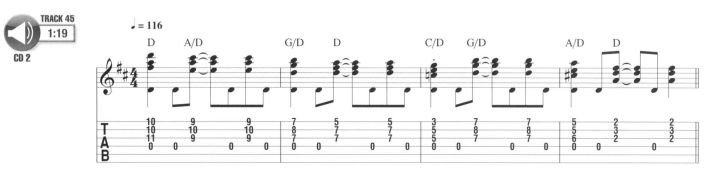

LESSON #97: ANGUS YOUNG

The owner of one of rock guitar's sweetest vibrato techniques as well as a hilarious personality, Angus Young's place in rock history is most certainly in the pantheon of greats. Combining a deft blues touch that guides his note-perfect rock phrasing with a killer guitar tone that is true simplicity, Young set the blues-rock guitar standard for generations to come. In this lesson, we'll take a look at the no-nonsense techniques like string bending, vibrato, and minor pentatonic mastery that have made this wee-bitty AC/DC guitarist a rock 'n' roll giant.

Let There Be Rock

Ever since Jim Marshall put together that first JTM-45 in the back of his shop outside of London and then gave it to the Who's Pete Townshend, "Marshall" has been synonymous with the sound of rock guitar. And *no one* has furthered that notion more than Angus Young. For nearly 40 years, Young's simplistic tone print of "Gibson SG to guitar cable to Marshall amp" has produced one of the biggest, baddest, and most recognizable guitar tones in rock history. So as you endeavor to cop Young's blue-collar style, keep it simple: eschew the high gain and effects processing, and just plug 'n' play.

You could say Angus Young's guitar soloing approach is like a musical jelly called "Blues 'n' Berry," drawing equally from bluesmen and rockers alike. From Chuck Berry and Elmore James comes not only the spark to create instantly recognizable riffs, but also a bit of Young's incomparable showmanship; from Albert King those stinging blues licks and stunning vibrato; and from Jimi Hendrix the challenge to go beyond the blues box, and, of course, some more showmanship.

LICK 1

This first example, which draws from Young's solo in "Highway to Hell," shows Berry's influence with the opening salvo. Then, the deft addition of the F♯ on the double-stop bend brings the gritty hybrid blues sounds of Hendrix, followed by a wholesale yet seamless shift to the parallel *major* pentatonic scale to wrap the lick up.

LICK 2

This second lick depicts Young's mastery of the "Albert King box" of the minor pentatonic scale. Here you get bluesy quarter-step bends on the 3rd (C) resolving to the root (A)—a trademark Young move straight from the blues—and to end the lick a series of oblique bends, another move heard throughout the AC/DC catalog. Where called for, strive to nail Young's peerless vibrato. Master it by listening to a lot of AC/DC and do your best to mimic the sound!

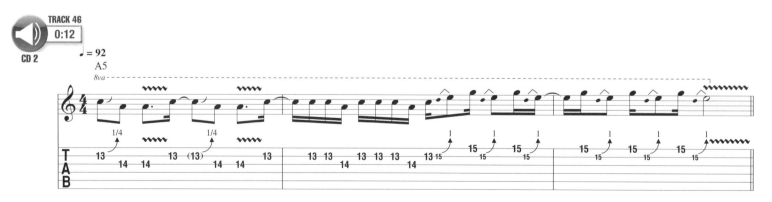

LICK 3

String bending plays a major role in Young's soloing act. The following phrase starts with three measures of unison bends ("T.N.T.," "For Those About to Rock"), before a classic minor pentatonic lick caps it off.

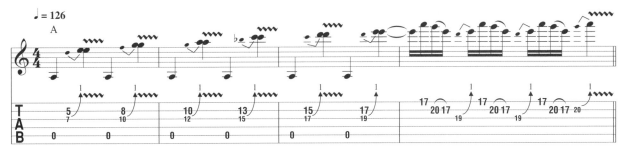

LICK 4

No one will ever mistake Angus Young for Eddie Van Halen or Joe Satriani, but even schoolboys like to have some guitar hero-style legato fun from time to time. So, every once in a while, Young will electrify the audience with some fiery, triplet-fueled pull-offs to open strings. You can either pick the first note of each triplet, as written, or perform the entire phrase legato, as Young sometimes opts to do—while holding his pick hand straight up over his head flashing the rock 'n' roll goat horns symbol, of course.

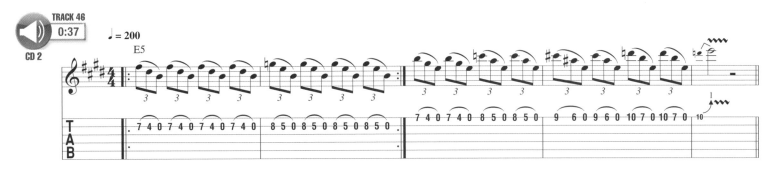

High Voltage Rhythm

No rock band in history has gotten more mileage from open-position power chords and sparse rhythms than AC/DC. Never has a guitarist done so much with so little as Angus and brother Malcolm in crafting such timeless riffs as "Back in Black," "Highway to Hell," and "T.N.T."

RIFF 1

The next example is in the style of "Back in Black," including a crisp minor pentatonic fill on the repeat. Note the treatment of the B5 chord in bar 2. That pull-off to the open A while still fretting the F♯ is a signature Young chording device. Similarly, Angus and Malcolm will sometimes instead pull off from the 5th to the 4th.

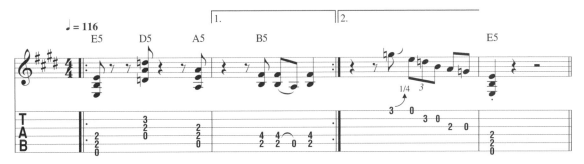

RIFF 2

They don't do it often, but when they do, Angus and Malcolm can craft some pretty nifty single-note riffs, like the interlude in "Back in Black," which informs the first half of the next example. You'll note the second bar is identical to the first, only an octave higher. The droning high E string makes the line reminiscent of the opening drone statement of the outro solo in "Back in Black."

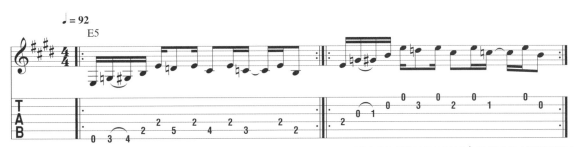

LESSON #98: EDDIE VAN HALEN

Not even ten years after Jimi Hendrix turned the guitar playing world on its ear, a young Dutch kid in Los Angeles was mounting his very own revolution. And just as Jimi forever changed the way the guitar was played and the way it sounded, Eddie Van Halen achieved the same thing, only taking it up a notch in the process. In this lesson, we'll explore a few of the key aspects of Eddie's lead and rhythm guitar techniques.

Tap Into Something Special

Eddie Van Halen's mix of blues licks, legato, and harmonics made him one of the most revered lead guitarists of all time. But if there is one technique with which he is synonymous, it's tapping. In the early days of Van Halen's career, Eddie would actually play with his back to the audience to keep his technique secret. Since that time, however, countless guitarists have added tapping to their own arsenals. Still, nothing tops the original.

LICK 1

Eddie's most often-used tapping approach, as heard in "Hot for Teacher" and, of course, "Eruption," is to outline triad arpeggios, like this.

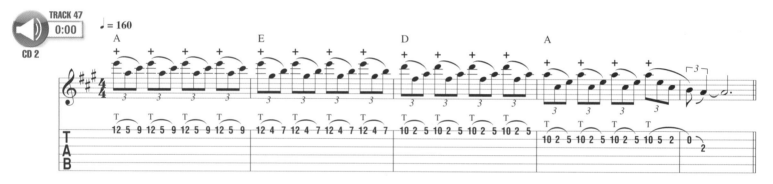

LICK 2

Another of Eddie Van Halen's signature techniques is the inclusion of open strings in both tapped and traditionally picked passages. The scorching tapping intro to "Hot for Teacher" is one example of tapped lines that include pull-offs to open strings. Another is found in "Spanish Fly," on which Eddie shreds on an acoustic guitar. Here's a sample phrase in which notes are pulled off to the open D string.

Before we move on, did you notice the quintuplet rhythm in which those tapping sequences were set? This is a favorite rhythmic device of Van Halen, heard in songs including "Eruption," "Hot for Teacher," "Spanish Fly," and "Jump," among others. A quintuplet contains five evenly spaced notes per beat. Counting the subdivisions can be tricky, so you might want to find a word or phrase that has five syllables and use that—perhaps "Ed-die-Van-Ha-len."

LICK 3

Our final tapping example shows Ed's signature bend-and-tap technique, as heard in "Panama," "You Really Got Me," and every spotlight guitar solo he's ever played live. First, bend the D a whole step up to E, then tap on the indicated frets (12 and then 10), where the tapped notes will sound a whole step higher than the fretted note, due to the bend. In the second bar, you'll find a series of tapped harmonics. Here, maintain the A note at the 7th fret while tapping a finger down *directly onto the metal fret wire* of the fret indicated in parentheses, to sound the harmonics.

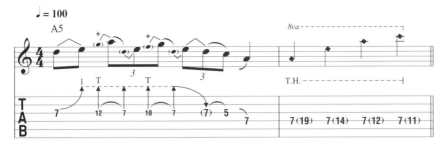

The EVH Scale

The Eddie Van Halen scale, or "EVH scale," is a symmetrical, three-notes-per-string pattern that he uses for both major and minor keys, and is unique to this living legend. Heard in such classics as "Jump," "Ice Cream Man," "I'm the One," "On Fire," and "Spanish Fly," among others, the scale contains both minor and major 3rds and 7ths, making it tonally ambiguous. It's most often used for speedy passages and should always resolve to a strong chord tone.

LICK 4

The EVH scale is shown below, and the accompanying example depicts another EVH technique—alternating legato and picked sequences. This might feel awkward at first, but it comes fairly easy with steady practice.

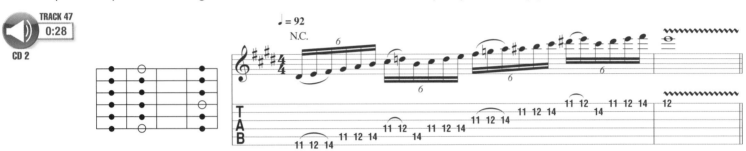

He's Got Rhythm

Like Hendrix before him, Eddie Van Halen is as accomplished a rhythm guitarist as he is a soloist. In fact, we'd go so far as to say that Jimi and Eddie are the two greatest rhythm guitarists in rock history. There's far too much to cover here, but we'll touch on a few keystones.

RIFF 1

One of Eddie's hallmarks is that he rarely made power chords the primary element of his riffs. Instead, he'd use more harmonically rich triads and suspended chords, frequently voiced on strings 2–4 and played against either his own pedal tones or those of the bass. You can hear this approach in "Runnin' With the Devil," "Dance the Night Away," "Unchained," and "Panama," the latter two of which inform our next example.

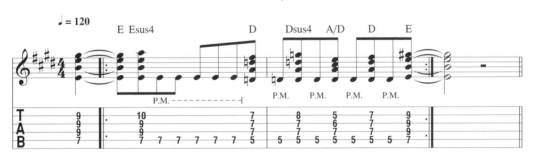

RIFF 2

Just as he eschewed the simplicity of power chords, Eddie likewise often used dyads rather than single notes in his riffs. Here's an example inspired by "Feel Your Love Tonight."

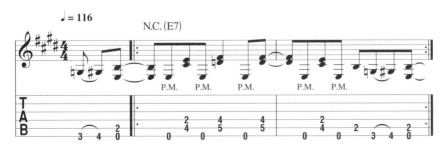

LESSON #99: RANDY RHOADS

Randy Rhoads created quite possibly the smallest yet most influential body of work in the history of heavy metal guitar. Combining classical elements with bold, powerful riffs and solos, he revitalized the genre and paved the way for the shred movement that soon followed. In this lesson, we'll examine the essential elements of his unique style, from pedal point riffs and arpeggios to repeating licks and sequences.

Rhoads Scholar

Randy Rhoads was a classically trained guitarist, and as a result, he brought several elements of the classical music realm to bear on heavy metal, such as his use of trills, ornamentation, and pedal point in composition. We're going to start our discussion with a look at the latter.

RIFF 1

A pedal tone is essentially a note—typically a bass note—that is repeatedly played against an underlying melody or set of chord changes. In a single-note metal riff, both the pedal tone and the counter melody are typically palm-muted to some extent. "Crazy Train" and "Diary of a Madman" are both great examples of this type of pedal point riff. Here's a similar phrase.

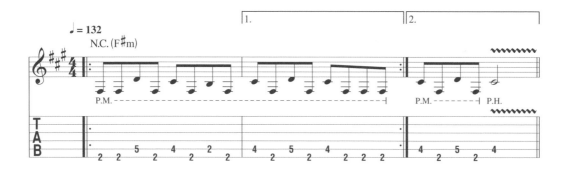

Note the pinch harmonic on the second repeat. Rhoads just loved to inject fills into his rhythm parts, and the pinch harmonic is one of the simplest and most efficient yet "metal" means of doing so.

RIFF 2

A pedal tone can also be used against chord stabs—a very popular metal riff construction heard in the verse riff of "Crazy Train" and the main riff of "I Don't Know," the latter of which informs this next riff. Again, note the fill used on the repeat. This one simply outlines the notes of an Am chord with pull-offs to open strings—another classic Rhoads move.

RIFF 3

Perhaps due to his classical training, Rhoads was a master of dynamics. He'd often arpeggiate chords with a clean tone—in a bridge or interlude, for example—as a form of contrast to the bombast of his high-gain riffs. He'd normally stick to chord tones, adding ornamentation here and there for extra color, as in the following example.

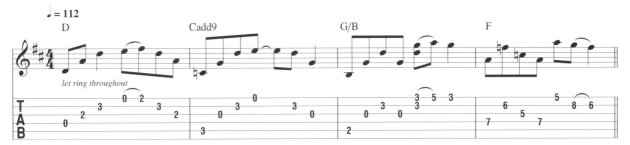

Off-Rhoading

When it came to soloing, Rhoads ranks among the all-time heavy metal greats. Technically challenging yet always memorable, his solos were often as melodic as they were virtuosic.

LICK 1

One of the reasons Rhoads is considered a pioneer of shred guitar was his blistering legato technique. His tremendous ability to travel the neck via legato-fueled three-notes-per-string patterns can be heard in the solos to "Crazy Train," "Suicide Solution," and "Mr. Crowley," among others. The first bar of our next example contains a legato ascent up the A minor scale, leading to another of Rhoads' favorite soloing devices—scale sequences. Here, the A natural minor ascent is answered with a descending minor pentatonic sequence.

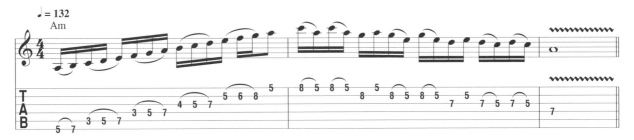

LICK 2

Another of Rhoads' signature sounds was his mixture of the natural minor and blues scales. He loved the blues scale and milked that flatted 5th for all its worth. This next example is a typical Rhoads lick using the hybrid form of the minor and blues scales.

LICK 3

Another classic Rhoads move is to take a short lick or arpeggio pattern and move it chromatically up or down the fretboard. You can hear this in some of the fills in "Crazy Train" and in the solos of "I Don't Know" and "Suicide Solution." Here's an example using a mixture of minor and major arpeggios.

Black Sabbath may have invented heavy metal, and bands like Judas Priest and Iron Maiden took it to a whole new level, but Bay Area thrashers Metallica redefined the genre, playing it faster and heavier than ever before while at the same time finding commercial success. In this lesson, we'll take a look at the pummeling rhythms and screaming leads of metal's most valuable players, James Hetfield and Kirk Hammett.

Faster, Master

James Hetfield pretty much wrote the book on heavy metal rhythm guitar playing. With such killer riffs as "Master of Puppets," "Seek and Destroy," and "One" under his belt, he's earned every ounce of metal cred garnered over the past 30 years.

At the heart of it all stands the almighty power chord. Hetfield prefers the simple root–5th version, with no added octave. Play those through a high-gain amp with the midrange EQ controls turned way down for the classic thrash "scooped" sound, and you're good to go.

RIFF 1

This first example is an uptempo power-chord riff in E, with the evil tritone B♭5—a staple of heavy metal and a favorite of Hetfield's—making its presence felt. Part of Hetfield's power comes from his ability to downpick every chord at ridiculously fast tempos. Try it here, but work up to it slowly and make sure you're not tensing up too much.

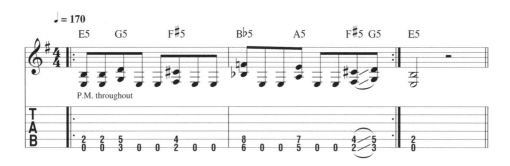

RIFF 2

This next riff combines single notes with power chords (and again, with the ♭5th, B♭) in the style of "The Shortest Straw" as well as "Master of Puppets," "Enter Sandman," and "Wherever I May Roam," among others.

RIFF 3

Of course, even thrash-meisters understand the power of the "soft-loud" dynamic, and Hetfield is no exception. The Metallica catalog is filled with examples of clean, arpeggiated intros that later give way to pummeling fists of power-chord fury—"Fade to Black," "One," "Enter Sandman," "Wherever I May Roam," and many more. Next up is a typical clean-toned Hetfield intro.

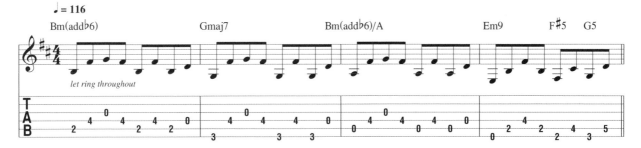

RIFF 4

Serving as the perfect "bridge" to our Kirk Hammett soloing section coming up next, here's an example of how Hetfield might arrange a bridge or interlude using unison power chords and then a harmony line with Hammett, harmonized in 3rds, just the way James likes it.

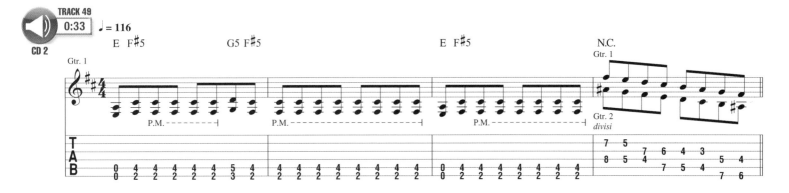

Hammerin' Hammett

You could say that Kirk Hammett essentially borrowed a slew of Lynyrd Skynryd licks and played them twice as fast with his gain setting on "11." But you'd also have to mention that in the process he created the definitive thrash metal lead guitar style.

LICK 1

One of Hammett's early pet soloing devices was the use of sequences, heard famously in songs like "Seek and Destroy," "For Whom the Bell Tolls," and "Fade to Black," which informs this example.

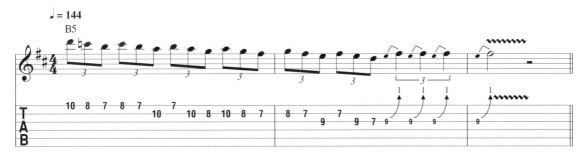

LICK 2

As alluded to earlier, Hammett's hallmark soloing tool is the repeating lick—be it a stock blues lick, rapid-fire pull-offs, or even double-stop bends. Once he gets his hands around a phrase he likes, Hammett milks it for its worth. Here's a sample phrase similar to lines heard in "Fade to Black," "Master of Puppets," and "One."

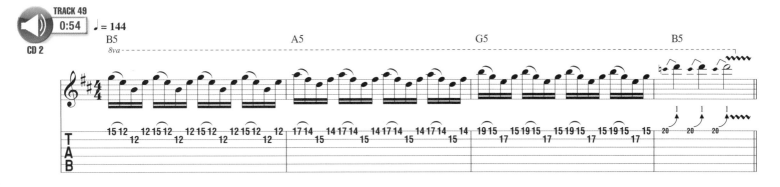

GUITAR RECORDED VERSIONS®

Guitar Recorded Versions® are note-for-note transcriptions of guitar music taken directly off recordings
This series, one of the most popular in print today, features some of the greatest
guitar players and groups from blues and rock to country and jazz.

Guitar Recorded Versions are transcribed by the best transcribers in the business
Every book contains notes and tablature. Visit www.halleonard.com for our complete selection.

AUTHENTIC TRANSCRIPTIONS WITH NOTES AND TABLATURE

00690898	John 5 – The Devil Knows My Name	$22.95
00690959	John 5 – Requiem	$22.95
00690814	John 5 – Songs for Sanity	$19.95
00690751	John 5 – Vertigo	$19.95
00694912	Eric Johnson – Ah Via Musicom	$19.95
00690660	Best of Eric Johnson	$22.99
00690845	Eric Johnson – Bloom	$19.95
00691076	Eric Johnson – Up Close	$22.99
00690169	Eric Johnson – Venus Isle	$22.95
00690846	Jack Johnson and Friends – Sing-A-Longs and Lullabies for the Film Curious George	$19.95
00690271	Robert Johnson – The New Transcriptions	$24.95
00699131	Best of Janis Joplin	$19.95
00690427	Best of Judas Priest	$22.99
00690651	Juanes – Exitos de Juanes	$19.95
00690277	Best of Kansas	$19.95
00690911	Best of Phil Keaggy	$24.99
00690727	Toby Keith Guitar Collection	$19.99
00690888	The Killers – Sam's Town	$19.95
00690504	Very Best of Albert King	$19.95
00690444	B.B. King & Eric Clapton – Riding with the King	$22.99
00690134	Freddie King Collection	$19.95
00691062	Kings of Leon – Come Around Sundown	$22.99
00690975	Kings of Leon – Only by the Night	$22.99
00690339	Best of the Kinks	$19.95
00690157	Kiss – Alive!	$19.95
00690356	Kiss – Alive II	$22.99
00694903	Best of Kiss for Guitar	$24.95
00690355	Kiss – Destroyer	$16.95
14026320	Mark Knopfler – Get Lucky	$22.99
00690164	Mark Knopfler Guitar – Vol. 1	$19.95
00690163	Mark Knopfler/Chet Atkins – Neck and Neck	$19.95
00690780	Korn – Greatest Hits, Volume 1	$22.95
00690836	Korn – See You on the Other Side	$19.95
00690377	Kris Kristofferson Collection	$19.95
00690861	Kutless – Hearts of the Innocent	$19.95
00690834	Lamb of God – Ashes of the Wake	$19.95
00690875	Lamb of God – Sacrament	$19.95
00690977	Ray LaMontagne – Gossip in the Grain	$19.99
00690890	Ray LaMontagne – Till the Sun Turns Black	$19.95
00690823	Ray LaMontagne – Trouble	$19.95
00691057	Ray LaMontagne and the Pariah Dogs – God Willin' & The Creek Don't Rise	$22.99
00690658	Johnny Lang – Long Time Coming	$19.95
00690679	John Lennon – Guitar Collection	$19.95
00690781	Linkin Park – Hybrid Theory	$22.95
00690782	Linkin Park – Meteora	$22.95
00690922	Linkin Park – Minutes to Midnight	$19.95
00690783	Best of Live	$19.95
00699623	The Best of Chuck Loeb	$19.95
00690743	Los Lonely Boys	$19.95
00690720	Lostprophets – Start Something	$19.95
00690525	Best of George Lynch	$24.99
00690955	Lynyrd Skynyrd – All-Time Greatest Hits	$19.99
00694954	New Best of Lynyrd Skynyrd	$19.95
00690577	Yngwie Malmsteen – Anthology	$24.95
00694845	Yngwie Malmsteen – Fire and Ice	$19.95
00694757	Yngwie Malmsteen – Trilogy	$19.95
00690754	Marilyn Manson – Lest We Forget	$19.95
00694956	Bob Marley – Legend	$19.95
00690548	Very Best of Bob Marley & The Wailers – One Love	$22.99
00694945	Bob Marley – Songs of Freedom	$24.95
00690914	Maroon 5 – It Won't Be Soon Before Long	$19.95
00690657	Maroon 5 – Songs About Jane	$19.95
00690748	Maroon 5 – 1.22.03 Acoustic	$19.95
00690989	Mastodon – Crack the Skye	$22.99
00691176	Mastodon – The Hunter	$22.99
00690442	Matchbox 20 – Mad Season	$19.95
00690616	Matchbox Twenty – More Than You Think You Are	$19.95
00690239	Matchbox 20 – Yourself or Someone like You	$19.95
00691034	Andy McKee – Joyland	$19.99
00690382	Sarah McLachlan – Mirrorball	$19.95
00120080	The Don McLean Songbook	$19.95
00694952	Megadeth – Countdown to Extinction	$22.95
00690244	Megadeth – Cryptic Writings	$19.95
00694951	Megadeth – Rust in Peace	$22.95
00690011	Megadeth – Youthanasia	$19.95
00690505	John Mellencamp Guitar Collection	$19.95
00690562	Pat Metheny – Bright Size Life	$19.95
00691073	Pat Metheny with Christian McBride & Antonion Sanchez – Day Trip/Tokyo Day Trip Live	$22.99
00690646	Pat Metheny – One Quiet Night	$19.95
00690559	Pat Metheny – Question & Answer	$19.95
00690040	Steve Miller Band Greatest Hits	$19.95
00690769	Modest Mouse – Good News for People Who Love Bad News	$19.95
00102591	Wes Montgomery Guitar Anthology	$24.99
00694802	Gary Moore – Still Got the Blues	$22.99
00691005	Best of Motion City Soundtrack	$19.99
00690787	Mudvayne – L.D. 50	$22.95
00691070	Mumford & Sons – Sigh No More	$22.99
00690996	My Morning Jacket Collection	$19.99
00690984	Matt Nathanson – Some Mad Hope	$22.99
00690611	Nirvana	$22.95
00694895	Nirvana – Bleach	$19.95
00690189	Nirvana – From the Muddy Banks of the Wishkah	$19.95
00694913	Nirvana – In Utero	$19.95
00694883	Nirvana – Nevermind	$19.95
00690026	Nirvana – Unplugged in New York	$19.95
00120112	No Doubt – Tragic Kingdom	$22.95
00690226	Oasis – The Other Side of Oasis	$19.95
00307163	Oasis – Time Flies... 1994-2009	$19.99
00690358	The Offspring – Americana	$19.95
00690203	The Offspring – Smash	$18.95
00690818	The Best of Opeth	$22.95
00691052	Roy Orbison – Black & White Night	$22.99
00694847	Best of Ozzy Osbourne	$22.95
00690399	Ozzy Osbourne – The Ozzman Cometh	$22.99
00690129	Ozzy Osbourne – Ozzmosis	$22.95
00690933	Best of Brad Paisley	$22.95
00690995	Brad Paisley – Play: The Guitar Album	$24.99
00690866	Panic! At the Disco – A Fever You Can't Sweat Out	$19.95
00690939	Christopher Parkening – Solo Pieces	$19.99
00690594	Best of Les Paul	$19.95
00694855	Pearl Jam – Ten	$22.99
00690439	A Perfect Circle – Mer De Noms	$19.95
00690661	A Perfect Circle – Thirteenth Step	$19.95
00690725	Best of Carl Perkins	$19.99
00690499	Tom Petty – Definitive Guitar Collection	$19.95
00690868	Tom Petty – Highway Companion	$19.95
00690176	Phish – Billy Breathes	$22.95
00691249	Phish – Junta	$22.99
00690428	Pink Floyd – Dark Side of the Moon	$19.95
00690789	Best of Poison	$19.95
00693864	Best of The Police	$19.95
00690299	Best of Elvis: The King of Rock 'n' Roll	$19.95
00692535	Elvis Presley	$19.95
00690925	The Very Best of Prince	$22.99
00690003	Classic Queen	$24.95
00694975	Queen – Greatest Hits	$24.95
00690670	Very Best of Queensryche	$19.95
00690878	The Raconteurs – Broken Boy Soldiers	$19.95
00694910	Rage Against the Machine	$19.95
00690179	Rancid – And Out Come the Wolves	$22.95
00690426	Best of Ratt	$19.95
00690055	Red Hot Chili Peppers – Blood Sugar Sex Magik	$19.95
00690584	Red Hot Chili Peppers – By the Way	$19.95
00690379	Red Hot Chili Peppers – Californication	$19.95
00690673	Red Hot Chili Peppers – Greatest Hits	$19.95
00690090	Red Hot Chili Peppers – One Hot Minute	$22.95
00691166	Red Hot Chili Peppers – I'm with You	$22.99
00690852	Red Hot Chili Peppers – Stadium Arcadium	$24.95
00690893	The Red Jumpsuit Apparatus – Don't You Fake It	$19.95
00690511	Django Reinhardt – The Definitive Collection	$19.95
00690779	Relient K – MMHMM	$19.95
00690643	Relient K – Two Lefts Don't Make a Right ... But Three Do	$19.95
00690260	Jimmie Rodgers Guitar Collection	$19.95
14041901	Rodrigo Y Gabriela and C.U.B.A. – Area 52	$24.99
00690014	Rolling Stones – Exile on Main Street	$24.95
00690631	Rolling Stones – Guitar Anthology	$27.95
00690685	David Lee Roth – Eat 'Em and Smile	$19.95
00690031	Santana's Greatest Hits	$19.95
00690796	Very Best of Michael Schenker	$19.95
00690566	Best of Scorpions	$22.95
00690604	Bob Seger – Guitar Anthology	$19.95
00690659	Bob Seger and the Silver Bullet Band – Greatest Hits, Volume 2	$17.95
00691012	Shadows Fall – Retribution	$22.99
00690896	Shadows Fall – Threads of Life	$19.95
00690803	Best of Kenny Wayne Shepherd Band	$19.95
00690750	Kenny Wayne Shepherd – The Place You're In	$19.95
00690857	Shinedown – Us and Them	$19.95
00690196	Silverchair – Freak Show	$19.95
00690130	Silverchair – Frogstomp	$19.95
00690872	Slayer – Christ Illusion	$19.95
00690813	Slayer – Guitar Collection	$19.95
00690419	Slipknot	$19.95
00690973	Slipknot – All Hope Is Gone	$22.99
00690733	Slipknot – Volume 3 (The Subliminal Verses)	$22.99
00690330	Social Distortion – Live at the Roxy	$19.95
00120004	Best of Steely Dan	$24.95
00694921	Best of Steppenwolf	$22.95
00690655	Best of Mike Stern	$19.95

RECORDED VERSIONS GUITAR®

AUTHENTIC TRANSCRIPTIONS WITH NOTES AND TABLATURE

00690949	Rod Stewart Guitar Anthology	$19.99
00690021	Sting – Fields of Gold	$19.95
00690689	Story of the Year – Page Avenue	$19.95
00690520	Styx Guitar Collection	$19.95
00120081	Sublime	$19.95
00690992	Sublime – Robbin' the Hood	$19.99
00690519	SUM 41 – All Killer No Filler	$19.95
00691072	Best of Supertramp	$22.99
00690994	Taylor Swift	$22.99
00690993	Taylor Swift – Fearless	$22.99
00691063	Taylor Swift – Speak Now	$22.99
00690767	Switchfoot – The Beautiful Letdown	$19.95
00690830	System of a Down – Hypnotize	$19.95
00690531	System of a Down – Toxicity	$19.95
00694824	Best of James Taylor	$16.95
00694887	Best of Thin Lizzy	$19.95
00690871	Three Days Grace – One-X	$19.95
00690891	30 Seconds to Mars – A Beautiful Lie	$19.95
00690030	Toad the Wet Sprocket	$19.95
00690233	The Merle Travis Collection	$19.99
00690683	Robin Trower – Bridge of Sighs	$19.95
00699191	U2 – Best of: 1980-1990	$19.95
00690732	U2 – Best of: 1990-2000	$19.95
00690894	U2 – 18 Singles	$19.95
00690775	U2 – How to Dismantle an Atomic Bomb	$22.95
00690997	U2 – No Line on the Horizon	$19.99
00690039	Steve Vai – Alien Love Secrets	$24.95
00690172	Steve Vai – Fire Garden	$24.95
00660137	Steve Vai – Passion & Warfare	$24.95
00690881	Steve Vai – Real Illusions: Reflections	$24.95
00694904	Steve Vai – Sex and Religion	$24.95
00690392	Steve Vai – The Ultra Zone	$19.95
00690024	Stevie Ray Vaughan – Couldn't Stand the Weather	$19.95
00690370	Stevie Ray Vaughan and Double Trouble – The Real Deal: Greatest Hits Volume 2	$22.95
00690116	Stevie Ray Vaughan – Guitar Collection	$24.95
00660136	Stevie Ray Vaughan – In Step	$19.95
00694879	Stevie Ray Vaughan – In the Beginning	$19.95
00660058	Stevie Ray Vaughan – Lightnin' Blues '83-'87	$24.95
00690036	Stevie Ray Vaughan – Live Alive	$24.95
00694835	Stevie Ray Vaughan – The Sky Is Crying	$22.95
00690025	Stevie Ray Vaughan – Soul to Soul	$19.95
00690015	Stevie Ray Vaughan – Texas Flood	$19.95
00690772	Velvet Revolver – Contraband	$22.95
00690132	The T-Bone Walker Collection	$19.95
00694789	Muddy Waters – Deep Blues	$24.95
00690071	Weezer (The Blue Album)	$19.95
00690516	Weezer (The Green Album)	$19.95
00690286	Weezer – Pinkerton	$19.95
00691046	Weezer – Rarities Edition	$22.99
00690447	Best of the Who	$24.95
00694970	The Who – Definitive Guitar Collection: A-E	$24.95
00694971	The Who – Definitive Guitar Collection F-Li	$24.95
00694972	The Who – Definitive Guitar Collection: Lo-R	$24.95
00690672	Best of Dar Williams	$19.95
00691017	Wolfmother – Cosmic Egg	$22.99
00690319	Stevie Wonder – Some of the Best	$17.95
00690596	Best of the Yardbirds	$19.95
00690844	Yellowcard – Lights and Sounds	$19.95
00690916	The Best of Dwight Yoakam	$19.95
00690904	Neil Young – Harvest	$29.99
00690905	Neil Young – Rust Never Sleeps	$19.99
00690443	Frank Zappa – Hot Rats	$19.95
00690624	Frank Zappa and the Mothers of Invention – One Size Fits All	$22.99
00690623	Frank Zappa – Over-Nite Sensation	$22.99
00690589	ZZ Top – Guitar Anthology	$24.95
00690960	ZZ Top Guitar Classics	$19.99

HAL•LEONARD® CORPORATION
7777 W. BLUEMOUND RD. P.O. BOX 13819 MILWAUKEE, WI 53213

Complete songlists and more at **www.halleonard.com**

Prices, contents, and availability subject to change without notice.

1112

INCLUDES TAB

This series will help you play your favorite songs quickly and easily. Just follow the tab and listen to the CD to hear how the guitar should sound, and then play along using the separate backing tracks. Mac or PC users can also slow down the tempo without changing pitch by using the CD in their computer. The melody and lyrics are included in the book so that you can sing or simply follow along.

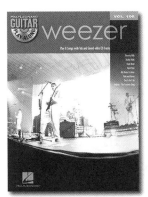

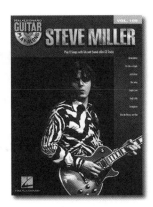

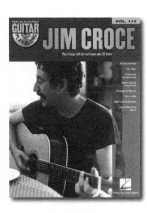

76. COUNTRY HITS
00699884.....................$14.95

77. BLUEGRASS
00699910.....................$14.99

78. NIRVANA
00700132.....................$16.99

79. NEIL YOUNG
00700133.....................$24.99

80. ACOUSTIC ANTHOLOGY
00700175.....................$19.95

81. ROCK ANTHOLOGY
00700176.....................$22.99

82. EASY ROCK SONGS
00700177.....................$12.99

83. THREE CHORD SONGS
00700178.....................$16.99

84. STEELY DAN
00700200.....................$16.99

85. THE POLICE
00700269.....................$16.99

86. BOSTON
00700465.....................$16.99

87. ACOUSTIC WOMEN
00700763.....................$14.99

88. GRUNGE
00700467.....................$16.99

90. CLASSICAL POP
00700469.....................$14.99

91. BLUES INSTRUMENTALS
00700505.....................$14.99

92. EARLY ROCK INSTRUMENTALS
00700506.....................$14.99

93. ROCK INSTRUMENTALS
00700507.....................$16.99

95. BLUES CLASSICS
00700509.....................$14.99

96. THIRD DAY
00700560.....................$14.95

97. ROCK BAND
00700703.....................$14.99

98. ROCK BAND
00700704.....................$14.95

99. ZZ TOP
00700762.....................$16.99

100. B.B. KING
00700466.....................$16.99

101. SONGS FOR BEGINNERS
00701917.....................$14.99

102. CLASSIC PUNK
00700769.....................$14.99

103. SWITCHFOOT
00700773.....................$16.99

104. DUANE ALLMAN
00700846.....................$16.99

106. WEEZER
00700958.....................$14.99

107. CREAM
00701069.....................$16.99

108. THE WHO
00701053.....................$16.99

109. STEVE MILLER
00701054.....................$14.99

111. JOHN MELLENCAMP
00701056.....................$14.99

112. QUEEN
00701052.....................$16.99

113. JIM CROCE
00701058.....................$15.99

114. BON JOVI
00701060.....................$14.99

115. JOHNNY CASH
00701070.....................$16.99

116. THE VENTURES
00701124.....................$14.99

118. ERIC JOHNSON
00701353.....................$14.99

119. AC/DC CLASSICS
00701356.....................$17.99

120. PROGRESSIVE ROCK
00701457.....................$14.99

121. U2
00701508.....................$16.99

123. LENNON & MCCARTNEY ACOUSTIC
00701614.....................$16.99

124. MODERN WORSHIP
00701629.....................$14.99

125. JEFF BECK
00701687.....................$16.99

126. BOB MARLEY
00701701.....................$16.99

127. 1970s ROCK
00701739.....................$14.99

128. 1960s ROCK
00701740.....................$14.99

129. MEGADETH
00701741.....................$16.99

131. 1990s ROCK
00701743.....................$14.99

132. COUNTRY ROCK
00701757.....................$15.99

133. TAYLOR SWIFT
00701894.....................$16.99

134. AVENGED SEVENFOLD
00701906.....................$16.99

136. GUITAR THEMES
00701922.....................$14.99

138. BLUEGRASS CLASSICS
00701967.....................$14.99

139. GARY MOORE
00702370.....................$16.99

140. MORE STEVIE RAY VAUGHAN
00702396.....................$17.99

141. ACOUSTIC HITS
00702401.....................$16.99

142. KINGS OF LEON
00702418.....................$16.99

144. DJANGO REINHARDT
00702531.....................$16.99

145. DEF LEPPARD
00702532.....................$16.99

147. SIMON & GARFUNKEL
14041591.....................$16.99

149. AC/DC HITS
14041593.....................$17.99

150. ZAKK WYLDE
02501717.....................$16.99

153. RED HOT CHILI PEPPERS
00702990.....................$19.99

157. FLEETWOOD MAC
00101382.....................$16.99

158. ULTIMATE CHRISTMAS
00101889.....................$14.99

161. THE EAGLES – ACOUSTIC
00102659.....................$16.99

162. THE EAGLES HITS
00102667.....................$17.99

166. MODERN BLUES
00700764.....................$16.99

7777 W. BLUEMOUND RD. P.O. BOX 13819 MILWAUKEE, WI 53213

For complete songlists, visit Hal Leonard online at
www.halleonard.com

Prices, contents, and availability subject to change without notice.

Get Better at Guitar

...with these Great Guitar Instruction Books from Hal Leonard!

101 GUITAR TIPS
INCLUDES TAB

STUFF ALL THE PROS KNOW AND USE

by Adam St. James

This book contains invaluable guidance on everything from scales and music theory to truss rod adjustments, proper recording studio set-ups, and much more. The book also features snippets of advice from some of the most celebrated guitarists and producers in the music business, including B.B. King, Steve Vai, Joe Satriani, Warren Haynes, Laurence Juber, Pete Anderson, Tom Dowd and others, culled from the author's hundreds of interviews.
00695737 Book/CD Pack.........................$16.95

AMAZING PHRASING
INCLUDES TAB

50 WAYS TO IMPROVE YOUR IMPROVISATIONAL SKILLS

by Tom Kolb

This book/CD pack explores all the main components necessary for crafting well-balanced rhythmic and melodic phrases. It also explains how these phrases are put together to form cohesive solos. Many styles are covered – rock, blues, jazz, fusion, country, Latin, funk and more – and all of the concepts are backed up with musical examples. The companion CD contains 89 demos for listening, and most tracks feature full-band backing.
00695583 Book/CD Pack.........................$19.95

BLUES YOU CAN USE
INCLUDES TAB

by John Ganapes

A comprehensive source designed to help guitarists develop both lead and rhythm playing. Covers: Texas, Delta, R&B, early rock and roll, gospel, blues/rock and more. Includes: 21 complete solos • chord progressions and riffs • turnarounds • moveable scales and more. CD features leads and full band backing.
00695007 Book/CD Pack.........................$19.99

FRETBOARD MASTERY
INCLUDES TAB

by Troy Stetina

Untangle the mysterious regions of the guitar fretboard and unlock your potential. *Fretboard Mastery* familiarizes you with all the shapes you need to know by applying them in real musical examples, thereby reinforcing and reaffirming your newfound knowledge. The result is a much higher level of comprehension and retention.
00695331 Book/CD Pack.........................$19.95

FRETBOARD ROADMAPS – 2ND EDITION

ESSENTIAL GUITAR PATTERNS THAT ALL THE PROS KNOW AND USE

by Fred Sokolow

The updated edition of this bestseller features more songs, updated lessons, and a full audio CD! Learn to play lead and rhythm anywhere on the fretboard, in any key; play a variety of lead guitar styles; play chords and progressions anywhere on the fretboard; expand your chord vocabulary; and learn to think musically – the way the pros do.
00695941 Book/CD Pack.........................$14.95

GUITAR AEROBICS
INCLUDES TAB

A 52-WEEK, ONE-LICK-PER-DAY WORKOUT PROGRAM FOR DEVELOPING, IMPROVING & MAINTAINING GUITAR TECHNIQUE

by Troy Nelson

From the former editor of *Guitar One* magazine, here is a daily dose of vitamins to keep your chops fine tuned! Musical styles include rock, blues, jazz, metal, country, and funk. Techniques taught include alternate picking, arpeggios, sweep picking, string skipping, legato, string bending, and rhythm guitar. These exercises will increase speed, and improve dexterity and pick- and fret-hand accuracy. The accompanying CD includes all 365 workout licks plus play-along grooves in every style at eight different metronome settings.
00695946 Book/CD Pack.........................$19.99

GUITAR CLUES
INCLUDES TAB

OPERATION PENTATONIC

by Greg Koch

Join renowned guitar master Greg Koch as he clues you in to a wide variety of fun and valuable pentatonic scale applications. Whether you're new to improvising or have been doing it for a while, this book/CD pack will provide loads of delicious licks and tricks that you can use right away, from volume swells and chicken pickin' to intervallic and chordal ideas. The CD includes 65 demo and play-along tracks.
00695827 Book/CD Pack.........................$19.95

INTRODUCTION TO GUITAR TONE & EFFECTS

by David M. Brewster

This book/CD pack teaches the basics of guitar tones and effects, with audio examples on CD. Readers will learn about: overdrive, distortion and fuzz • using equalizers • modulation effects • reverb and delay • multi-effect processors • and more.
00695766 Book/CD Pack.........................$14.95

PICTURE CHORD ENCYCLOPEDIA

This comprehensive guitar chord resource for all playing styles and levels features five voicings of 44 chord qualities for all twelve keys – 2,640 chords in all! For each, there is a clearly illustrated chord frame, as well as *an actual photo* of the chord being played! Includes info on basic fingering principles, open chords and barre chords, partial chords and broken-set forms, and more.
00695224.........................$19.95

SCALE CHORD RELATIONSHIPS
INCLUDES TAB

by Michael Mueller & Jeff Schroedl

This book teaches players how to determine which scales to play with which chords, so guitarists will never have to fear chord changes again! This book/CD pack explains how to: recognize keys • analyze chord progressions • use the modes • play over nondiatonic harmony • use harmonic and melodic minor scales • use symmetrical scales such as chromatic, whole-tone and diminished scales • incorporate exotic scales such as Hungarian major and Gypsy minor • and much more!
00695563 Book/CD Pack.........................$14.95

SPEED MECHANICS FOR LEAD GUITAR
INCLUDES TAB

Take your playing to the stratosphere with the most advanced lead book by this proven heavy metal author. *Speed Mechanics* is the ultimate technique book for developing the kind of speed and precision in today's explosive playing styles. Learn the fastest ways to achieve speed and control, secrets to make your practice time really count, and how to open your ears and make your musical ideas more solid and tangible. Packed with over 200 vicious exercises including Troy's scorching version of "Flight of the Bumblebee." Music and examples demonstrated on CD. 89-minute audio.
00699323 Book/CD Pack.........................$19.95

TOTAL ROCK GUITAR
INCLUDES TAB

A COMPLETE GUIDE TO LEARNING ROCK GUITAR

by Troy Stetina

This unique and comprehensive source for learning rock guitar is designed to develop both lead and rhythm playing. It covers: getting a tone that rocks • open chords, power chords and barre chords • riffs, scales and licks • string bending, strumming, palm muting, harmonics and alternate picking • all rock styles • and much more. The examples are in standard notation with chord grids and tab, and the CD includes full-band backing for all 22 songs.
00695246 Book/CD Pack.........................$19.99